Hatter M

THE

LOOKING GLASS WARS

In memory of my father,
Frank Beddor, Jr. (1924 - 2007).

Thanks a million!

Hatter M

THE LOOKING GLASS WARS

Written by Frank Beddor & Liz Cavalier
Art by Ben Templesmith

AUTOMATIC
PICTURES
PUBLISHING

Hatter M: The Looking Glass Wars®

Volume 1: Issues 1–4

Writers
Frank Beddor
Liz Cavalier

Art
Ben Templesmith

Letterer
Jason Hanley

Editor
C.J. Wrobel

Cartographic Chronicler & Historian
Greg Cook

Reconnaissance & Analysis
Nate Barlow

Logo Designed by
Christina Craemer

Interiors Designed by
Vera Milosavich

www.lookingglasswars.com

The Looking Glass Wars® is a trademark of Automatic Pictures, Inc.
Cover, Design Pages, and Compilation Copyright © 2008 Automatic Pictures, Inc.
All rights reserved.

First published in hardback 2007.

Excerpt from *Seeing Redd: The Looking Glass Wars, Book Two* used with permission of
Penguin Books for Young Readers. All rights reserved.

ISBN 978-0-9818737-0-1

This is not the story
of a Mad Hatter

Thank You

Scholars, Antiquarians,
Reasoners, Logicians, Rationalists,
and Knights Errant

Contents

The Quest

The Rest

Dare to cross the threshold from the known to the unknown and join us inside the Hatter M Institute for Paranormal Travel.

"There are things known and there are things unknown, and in between

Introduction

Greetings fellow searchers and welcome to *The Looking Glass Wars: Hatter M Geo-Graphic Novel #1* detailing and mapping the adventures of Royal Bodyguard Hatter Madigan, expert bladesman, and ranking High Cut of the Wonderland Millinery.

Who are we?

The Hatter M Institute for Paranormal Travel is a devout assemblage of radical historians, cartographers and geographic theorists pledged to uncovering and documenting the full spectrum journey of Hatter Madigan as he traversed our world from 1859–1872 searching for Princess Alyss of Wonderland.

Tattered, annotated maps and coded journals discovered in a Victorian era trunk first profiled a truly extreme traveler in search of something profound, but the ultimate questions remained, who was this man and what did he search for? With the recent revelations of the controversial exposé The Looking Glass Wars, the mystery of how Hatter and Alyss had come to be in our world was illuminated. Despite the shrill and fanatical efforts of a militant faction of the Lewis Carroll Society to suppress it, the truth behind the fiction of Alice in Wonderland was finally told and a highly guarded literary lie EXPOSED! Alice Liddell did not fall down a rabbit hole. Princess Alyss was lost in our world. In short, Lewis Carroll changed everything!

Located in the once resplendent 1930's deco area of Los Angeles, California known as the 'Miracle Mile', the Hatter M Institute through the medium of comics and ably assisted by the other worldly talent of artist Ben Templesmith, is committed to disseminating the stranger than fiction adventures of this heroic royal bodyguard as he searched for his lost princess. As you turn the pages uncovering the long buried history, take heart in the knowledge that truth is always waiting to be revealed to those who are willing to search.

Thank you for joining us in following the glow.

The Hatter M Institute for
Paranormal Travel

are the doors of perception." –ALDOUS HUXLEY

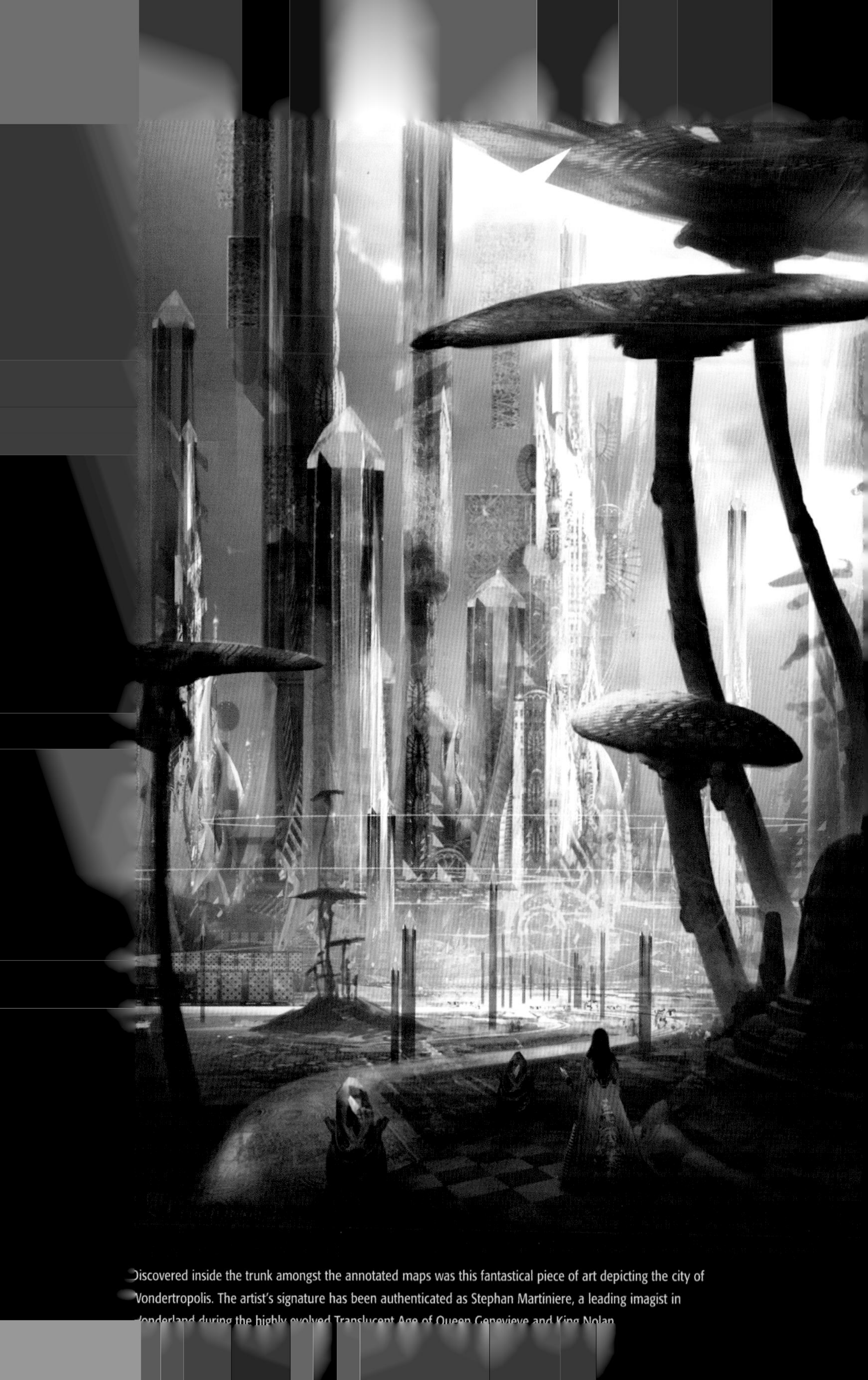

Discovered inside the trunk amongst the annotated maps was this fantastical piece of art depicting the city of Wondertropolis. The artist's signature has been authenticated as Stephan Martiniere, a leading imagist in Wonderland during the highly evolved Translucent Age of Queen Genevieve and King Nolan.

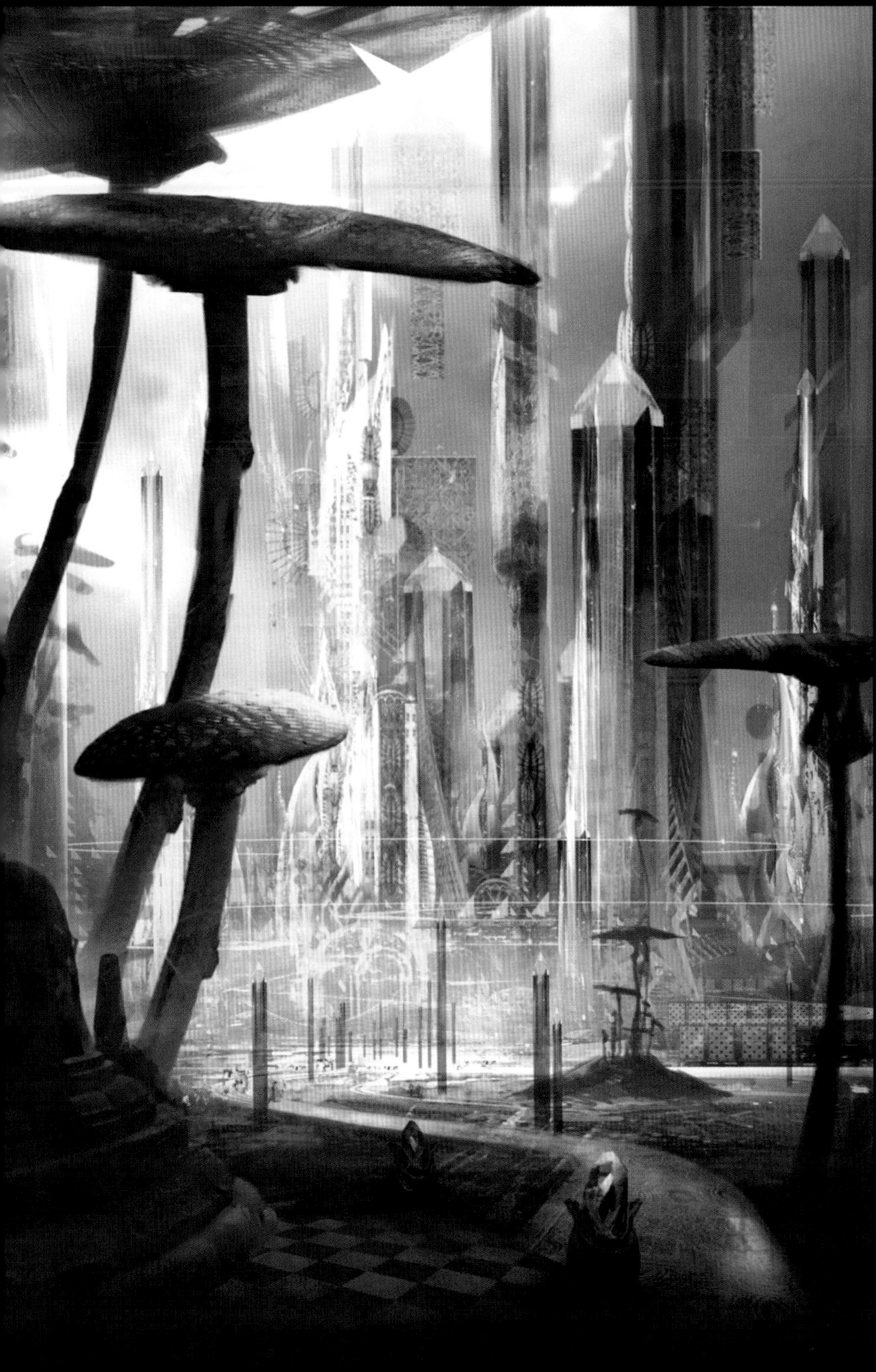

Let this journal be the record of my failure. Of my disgrace. Of my search.

As Royal Bodyguard for Queen Genevieve I was forced to deny my every impulse to defend her and flee with her daughter, Princess Alyss, while knowing my Queen would die at the hand of her vile hag sister. Genevieve's final order was for me to leave Wonderland and take her daughter somewhere safe. Keep her safe, she cried, promise me, you will keep her safe. At this, I have failed, for the child is lost. LOST, as I too am lost in this strange world where Imagination is fleeting and its proponents seemingly few.

Almost immediately I encountered violence and enemies of my search. The aggressors were plodding and awkward, their simplistic attacks should have been instantly countered. But my reflexes have slowed in this dull vibratory atmosphere. I fear I am not entirely myself. If I am to regain my speed and coordination…if I am to find Alyss…I must train. It seems some here prefer the single shot armaments which are crude and linear. Against those I will be at full advantage with my blades, but it will take practice and focus if I am to regain my Millinery mark of 72 cuts in 7 seconds.

It will take everything I have to find Alyss and keep her safe.

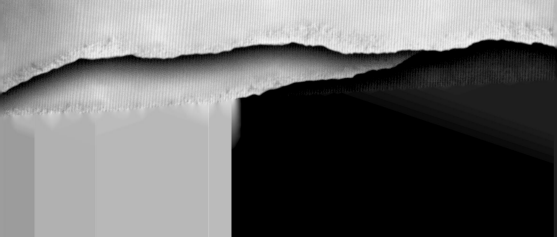

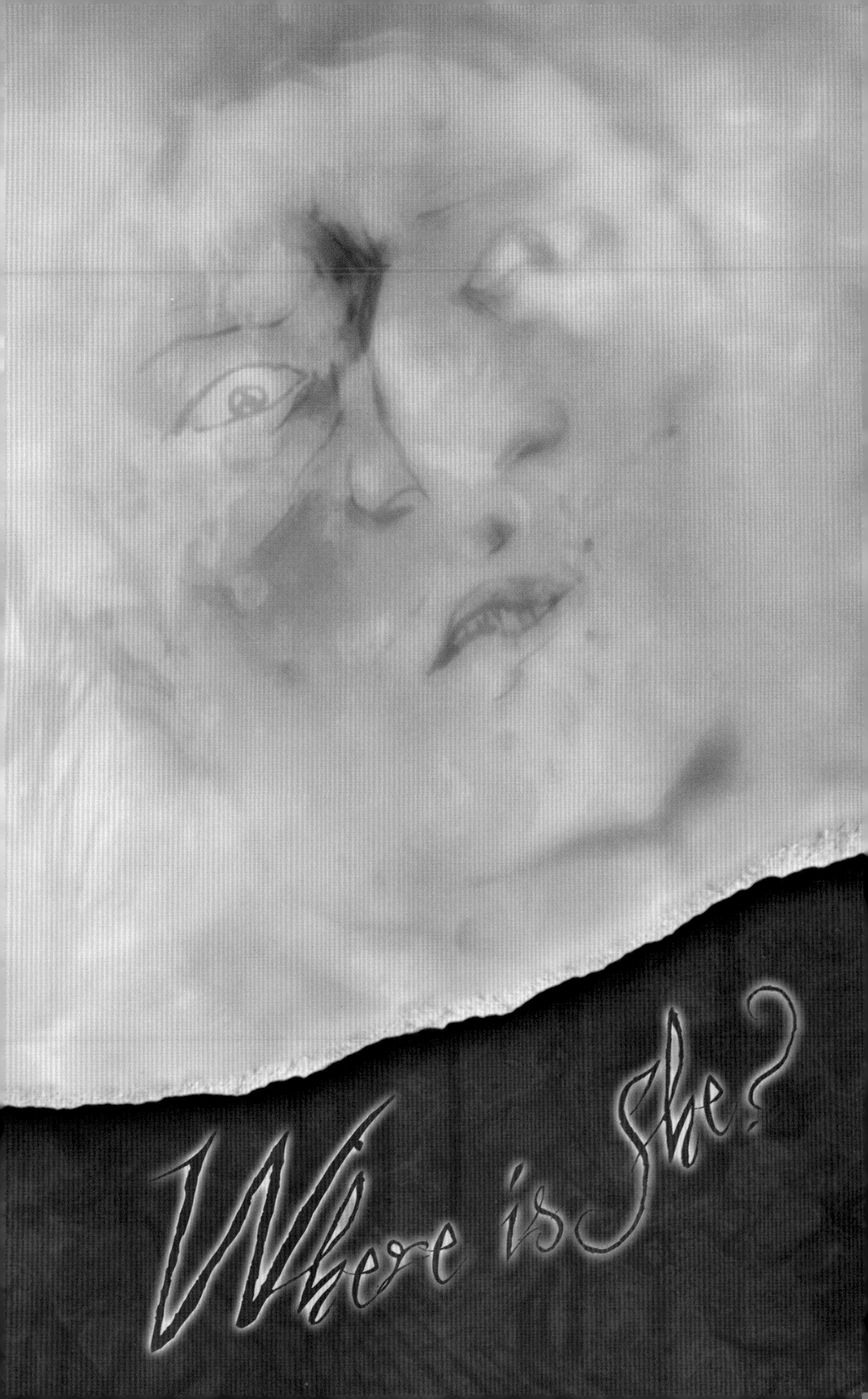
Where is She?

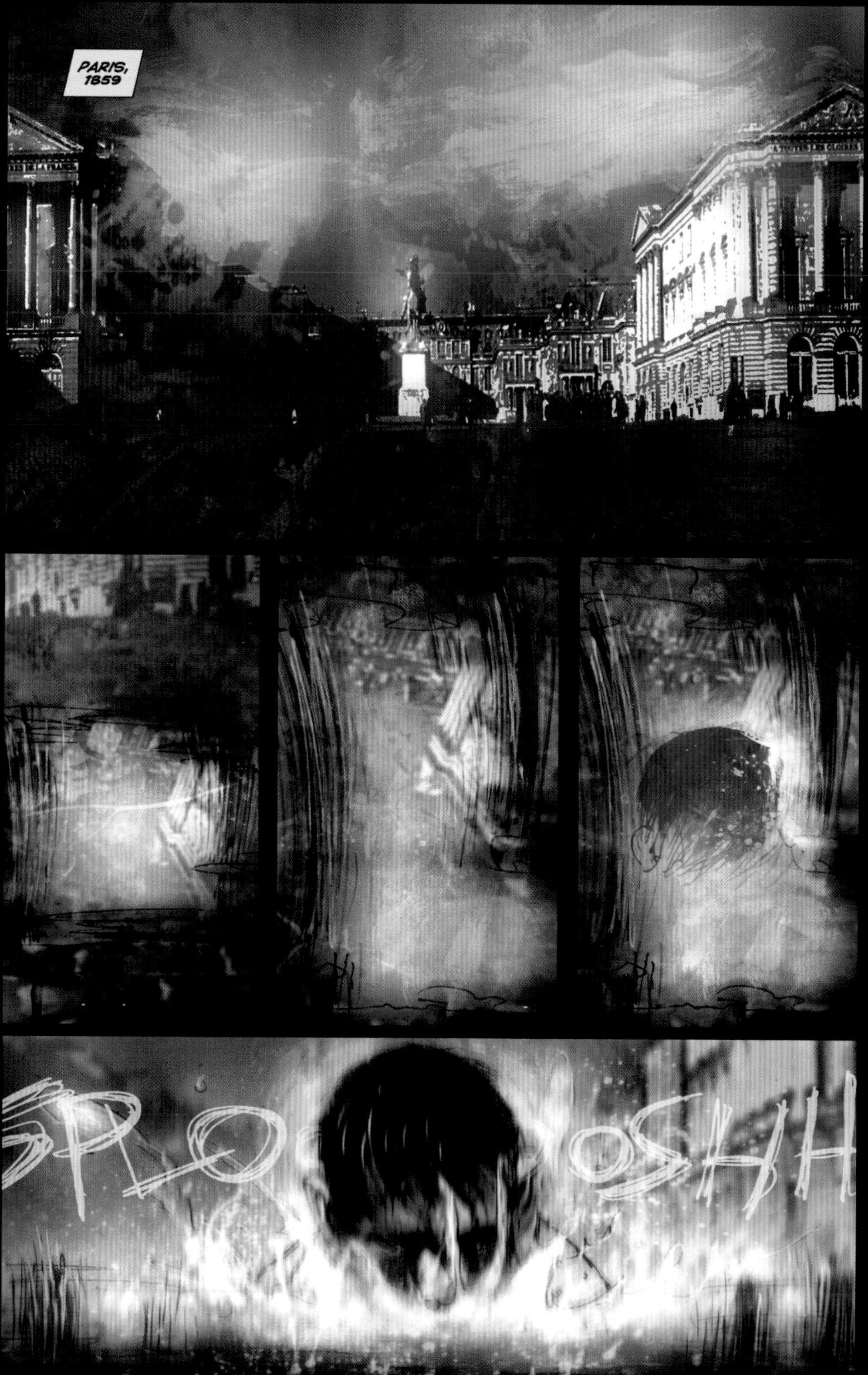
PARIS, 1859
SPLO OSH

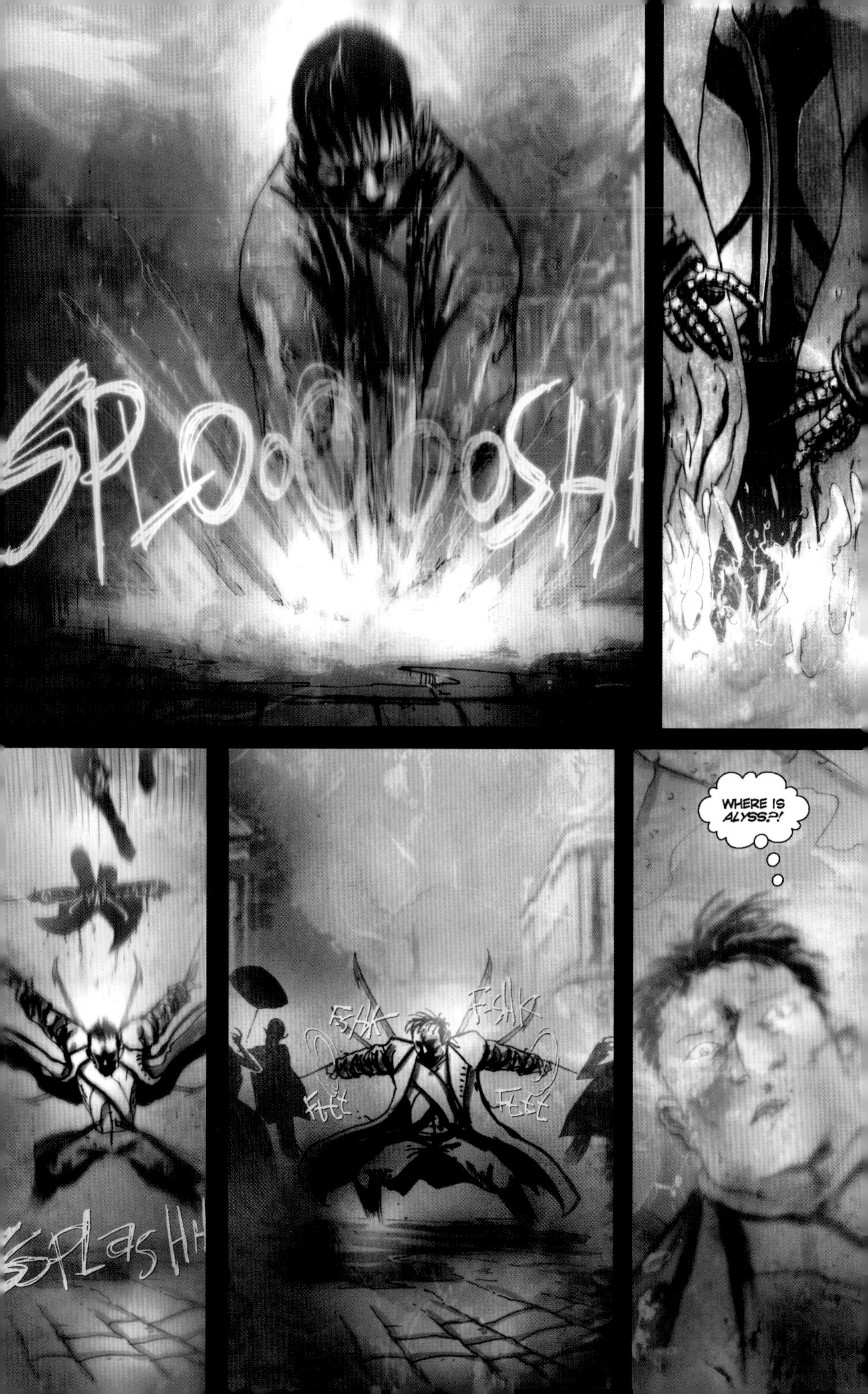
SPLOOOOOSHH
SPLASHH
FSHK
FSHK
FEET
FEET
WHERE IS ALYSS?!

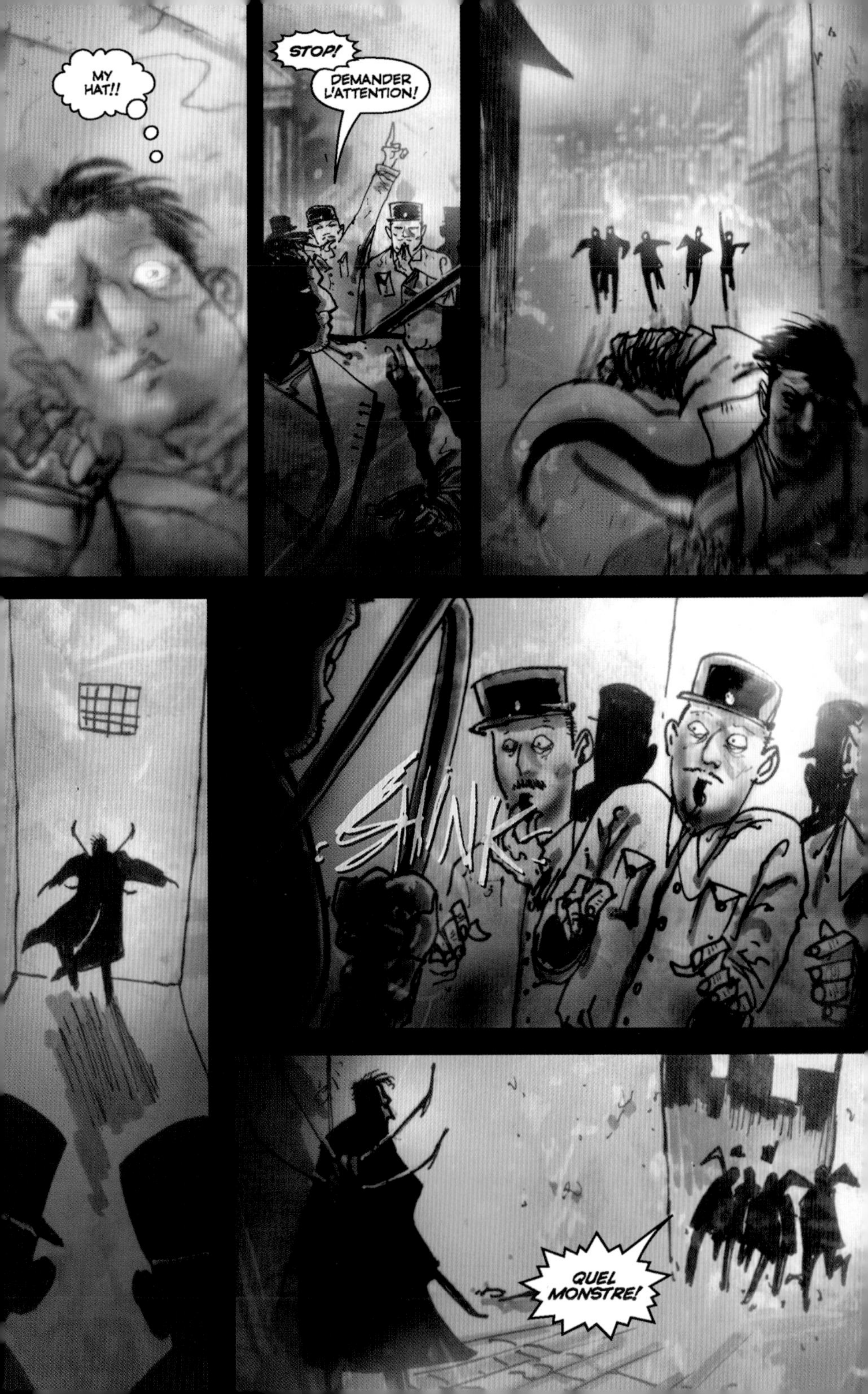
MY HAT!!
STOP!
DEMANDER L'ATTENTION!
SHINK
QUEL MONSTRE!

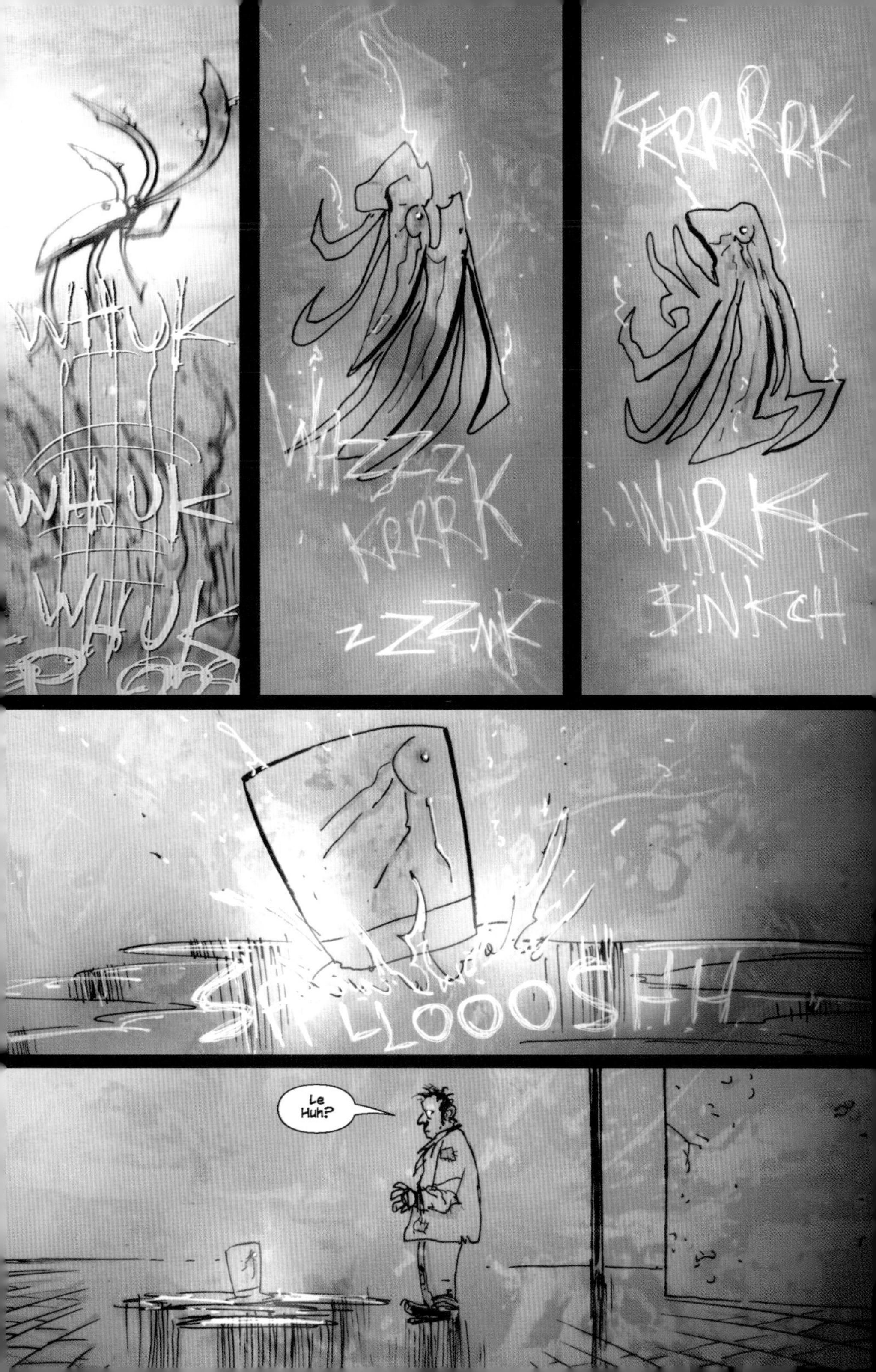
WHUK
WHUK
WHUK
WHZZZK
KRRRK
ZZZNK
KRRRRRK
WHRK
BINKCH
SPLLOOOSHH
Le Huh?

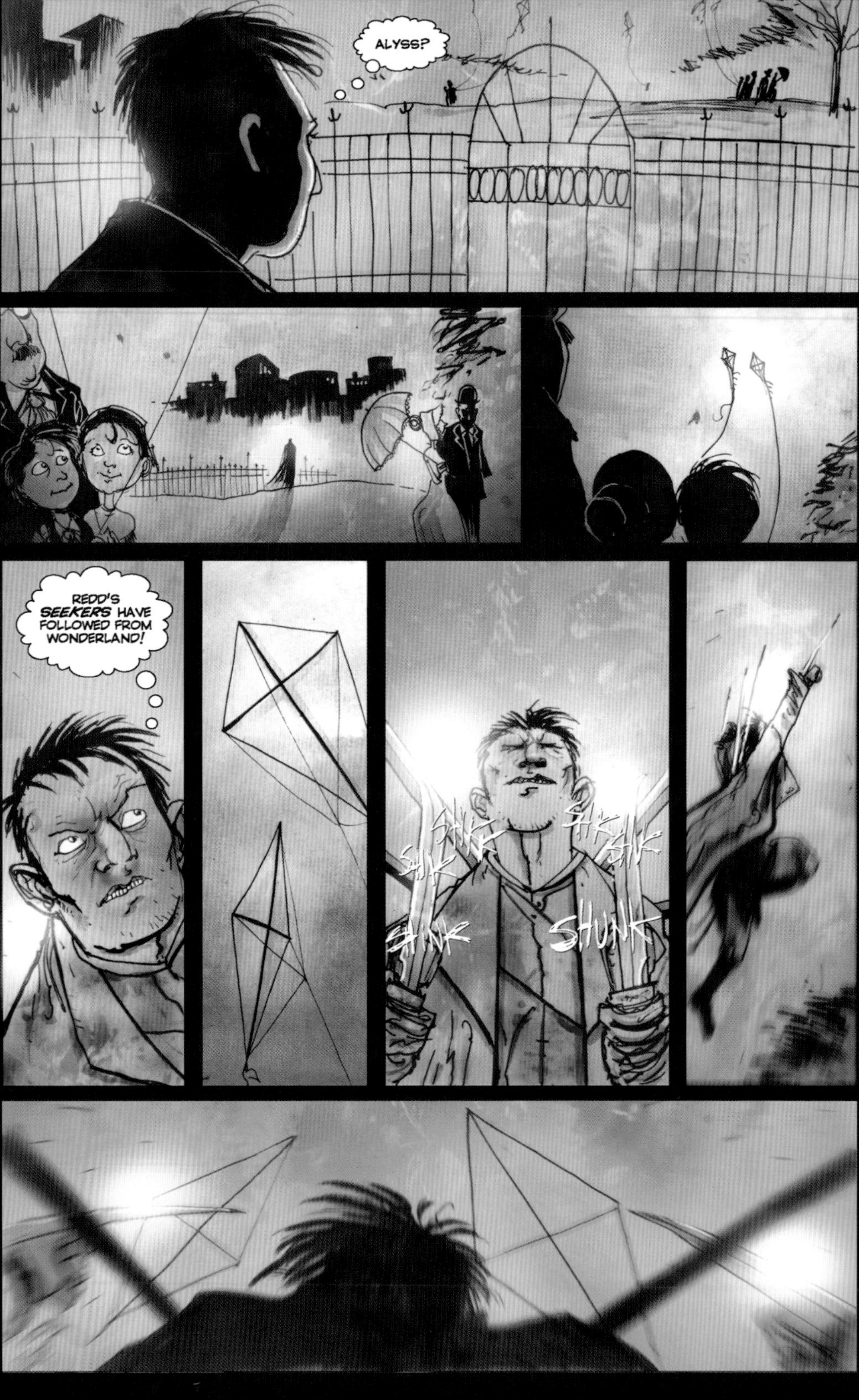
ALYSS?
REDD'S SEEKERS HAVE FOLLOWED FROM WONDERLAND!
SHIK SHIK SHIK SHIK
SHINK
SHUNK

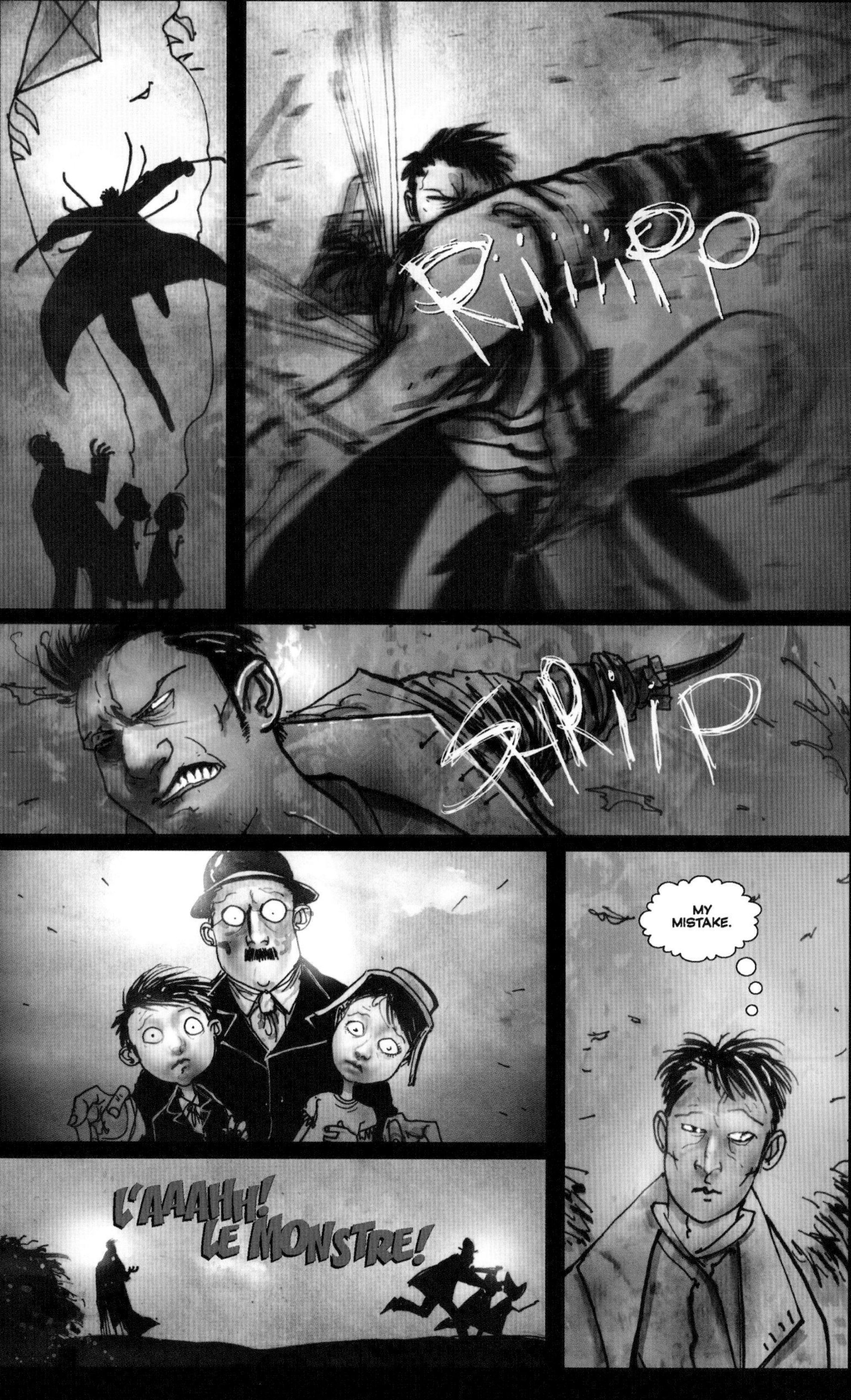
RIIIIPPP
SHRIIP
MY MISTAKE.
L'AAAHH! LE MONSTRE!

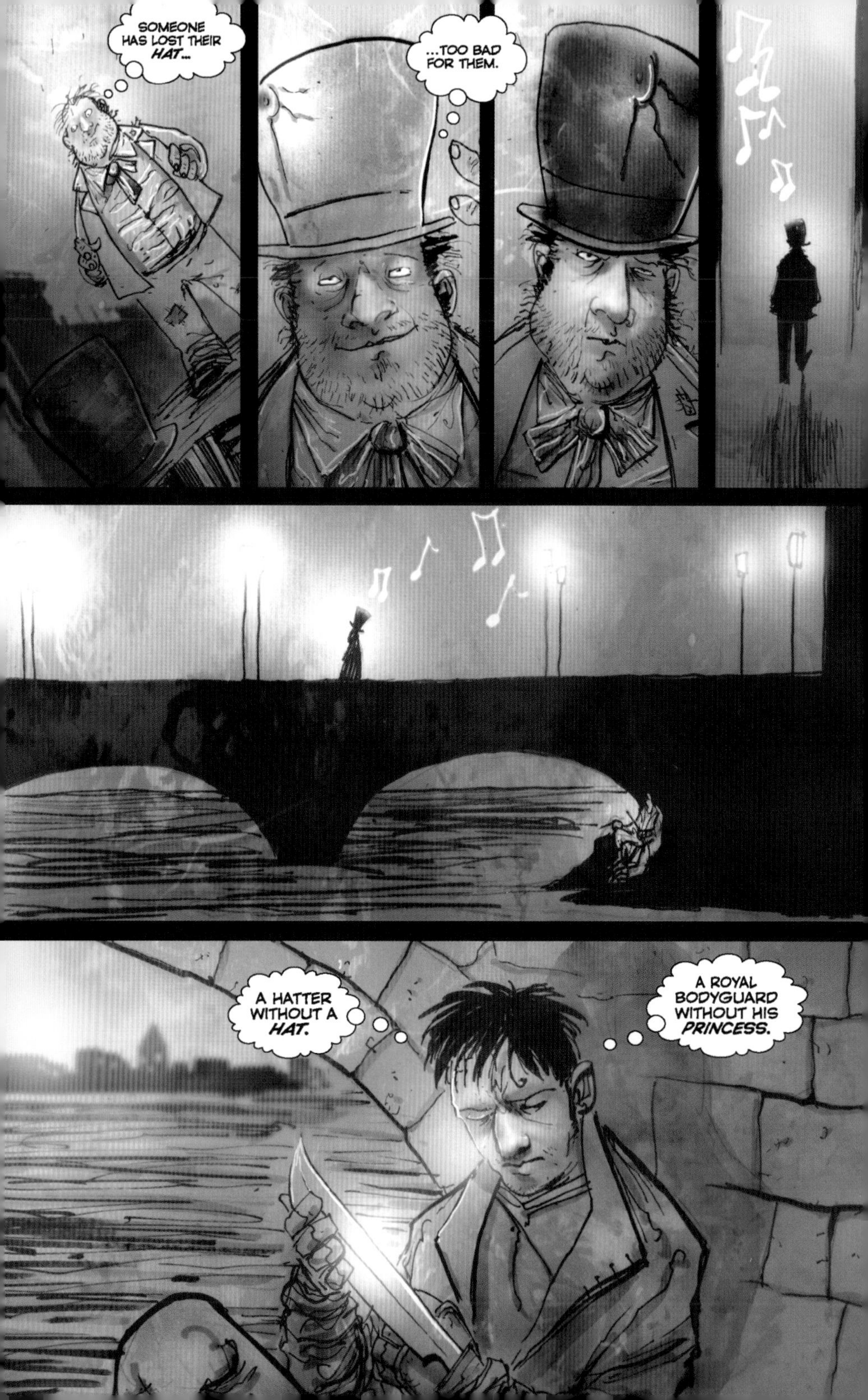
SOMEONE HAS LOST THEIR *HAT*...
...TOO BAD FOR THEM.
A HATTER WITHOUT A *HAT*.
A ROYAL BODYGUARD WITHOUT HIS *PRINCESS*.

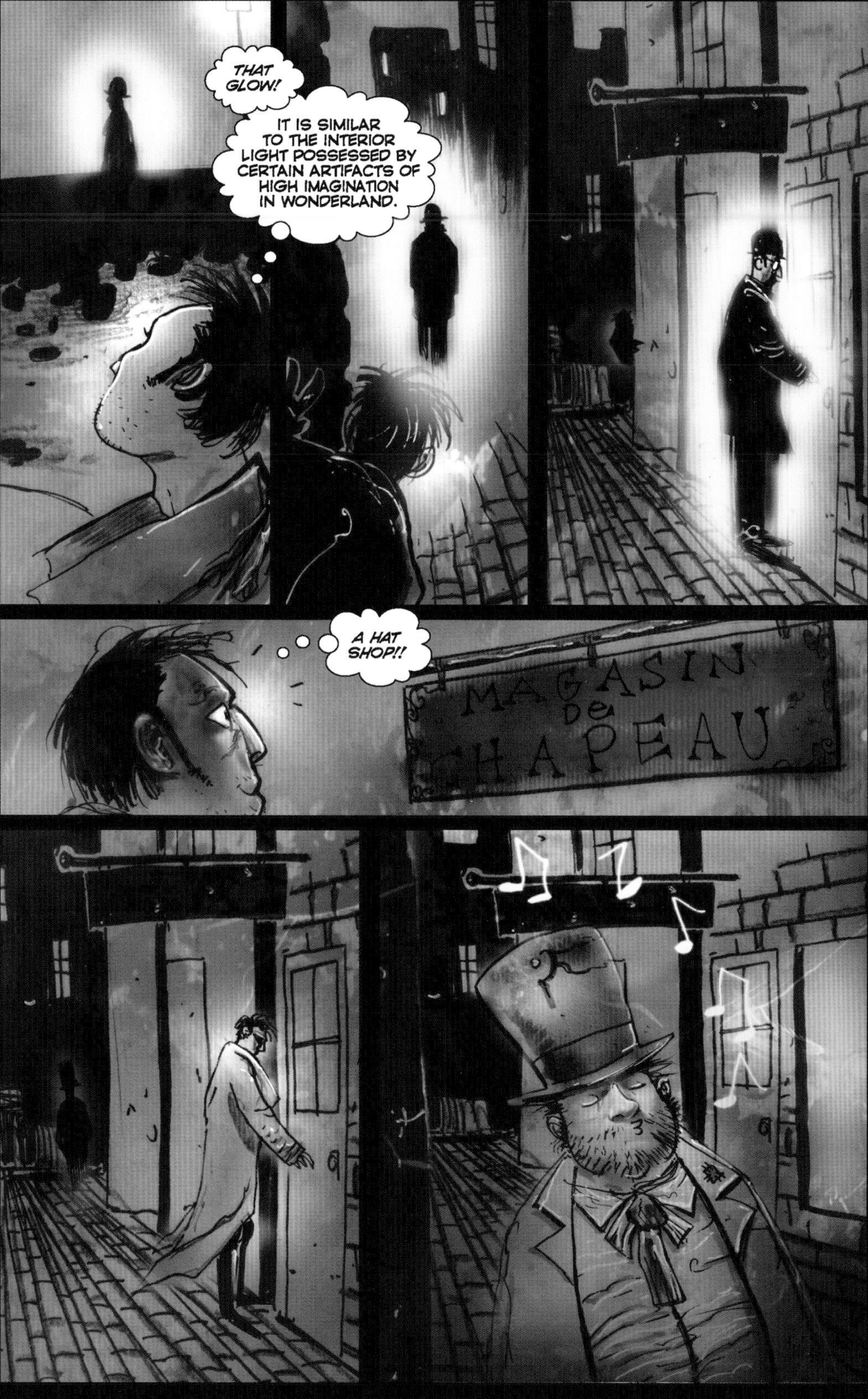
THAT GLOW!
IT IS SIMILAR TO THE INTERIOR LIGHT POSSESSED BY CERTAIN ARTIFACTS OF HIGH IMAGINATION IN WONDERLAND.
A HAT SHOP!!
MAGASIN de CHAPEAU

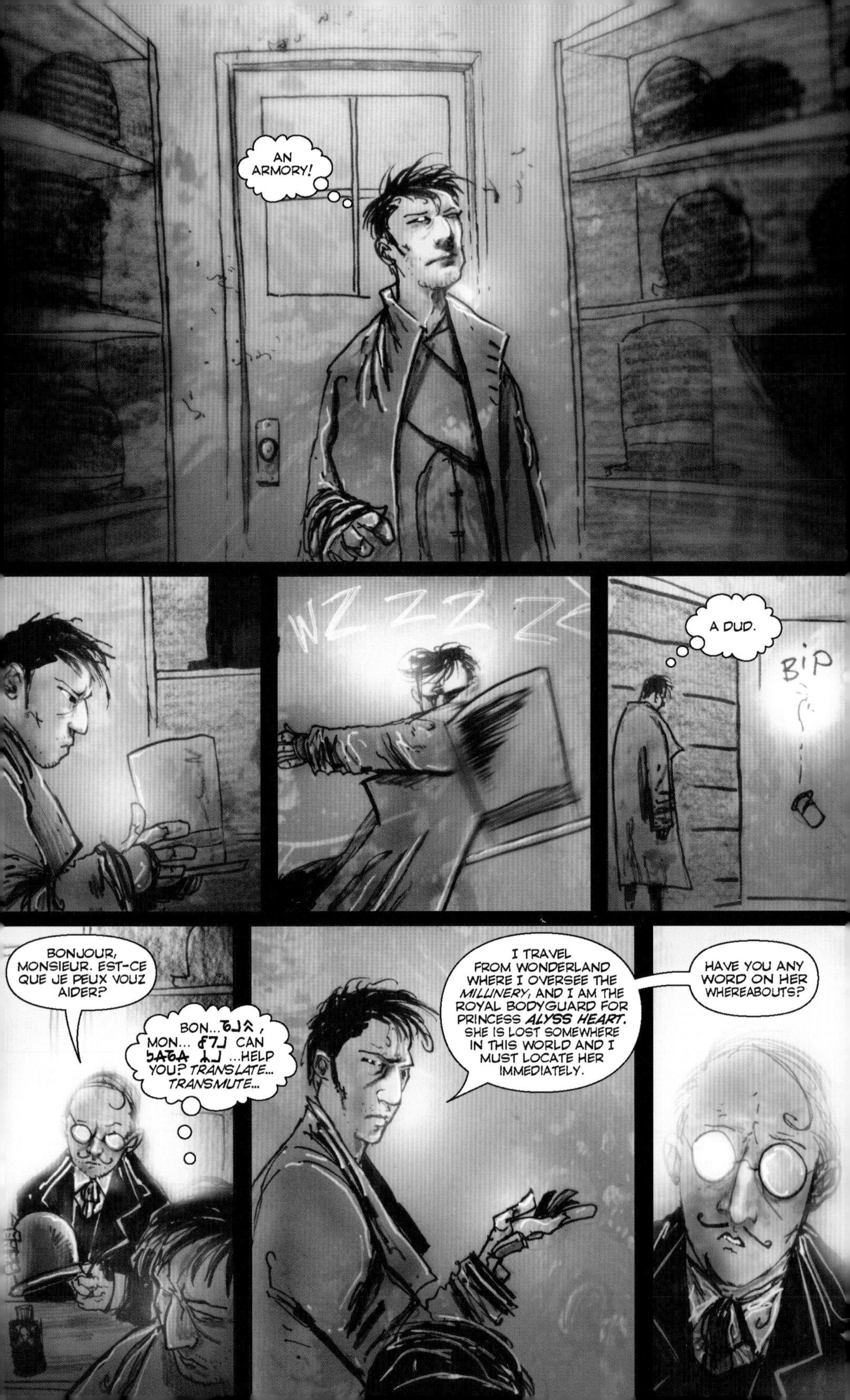
AN ARMORY!
WZZZZZ
A DUD.
BIP
BONJOUR, MONSIEUR. EST-CE QUE JE PEUX VOUZ AIDER?
BON... , MON... CAN ...HELP YOU? TRANSLATE... TRANSMUTE...
I TRAVEL FROM WONDERLAND WHERE I OVERSEE THE MILLINERY, AND I AM THE ROYAL BODYGUARD FOR PRINCESS ALYSS HEART. SHE IS LOST SOMEWHERE IN THIS WORLD AND I MUST LOCATE HER IMMEDIATELY.
HAVE YOU ANY WORD ON HER WHEREABOUTS?

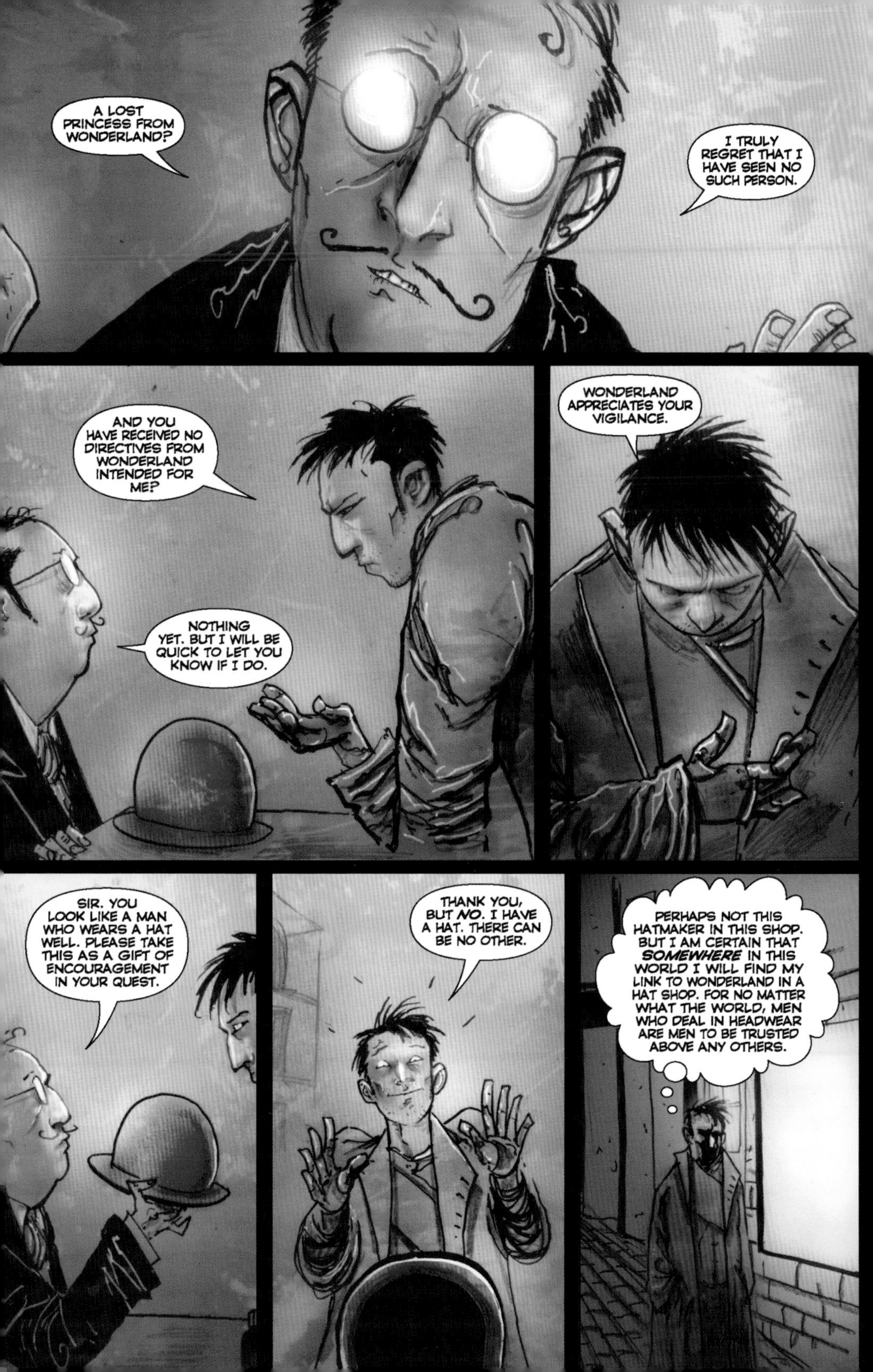
A LOST PRINCESS FROM WONDERLAND?
I TRULY REGRET THAT I HAVE SEEN NO SUCH PERSON.
AND YOU HAVE RECEIVED NO DIRECTIVES FROM WONDERLAND INTENDED FOR ME?
NOTHING YET. BUT I WILL BE QUICK TO LET YOU KNOW IF I DO.
WONDERLAND APPRECIATES YOUR VIGILANCE.
SIR. YOU LOOK LIKE A MAN WHO WEARS A HAT WELL. PLEASE TAKE THIS AS A GIFT OF ENCOURAGEMENT IN YOUR QUEST.
THANK YOU, BUT NO. I HAVE A HAT. THERE CAN BE NO OTHER.
PERHAPS NOT THIS HATMAKER IN THIS SHOP. BUT I AM CERTAIN THAT SOMEWHERE IN THIS WORLD I WILL FIND MY LINK TO WONDERLAND IN A HAT SHOP. FOR NO MATTER WHAT THE WORLD, MEN WHO DEAL IN HEADWEAR ARE MEN TO BE TRUSTED ABOVE ANY OTHERS.

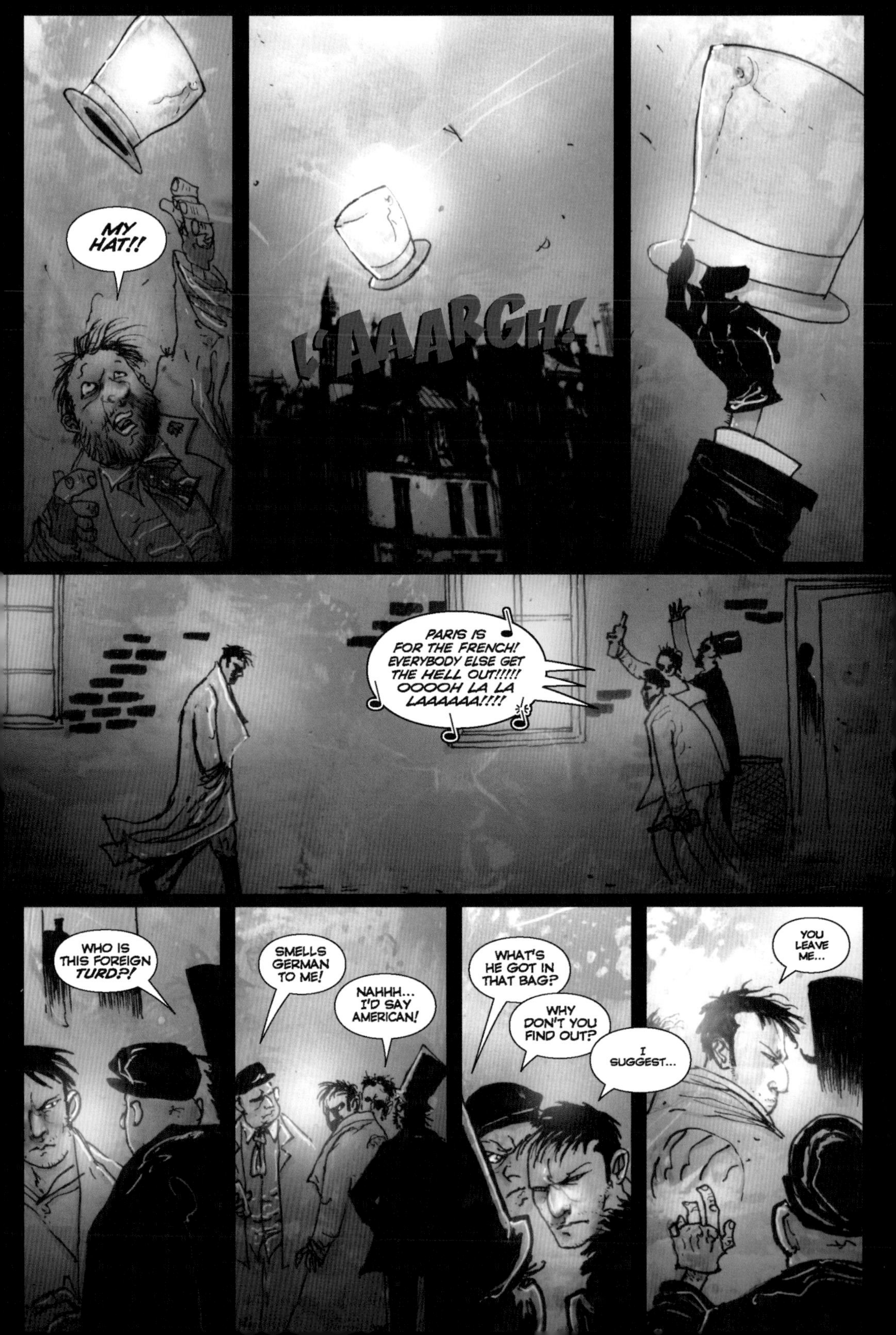
MY HAT!!
L'AAARGH!
PARIS IS FOR THE FRENCH! EVERYBODY ELSE GET THE HELL OUT!!!!! OOOOH LA LA LAAAAAAA!!!!
WHO IS THIS FOREIGN TURD?!
SMELLS GERMAN TO ME!
NAHHH... I'D SAY AMERICAN!
WHAT'S HE GOT IN THAT BAG?
WHY DON'T YOU FIND OUT?
I SUGGEST...
YOU LEAVE ME...

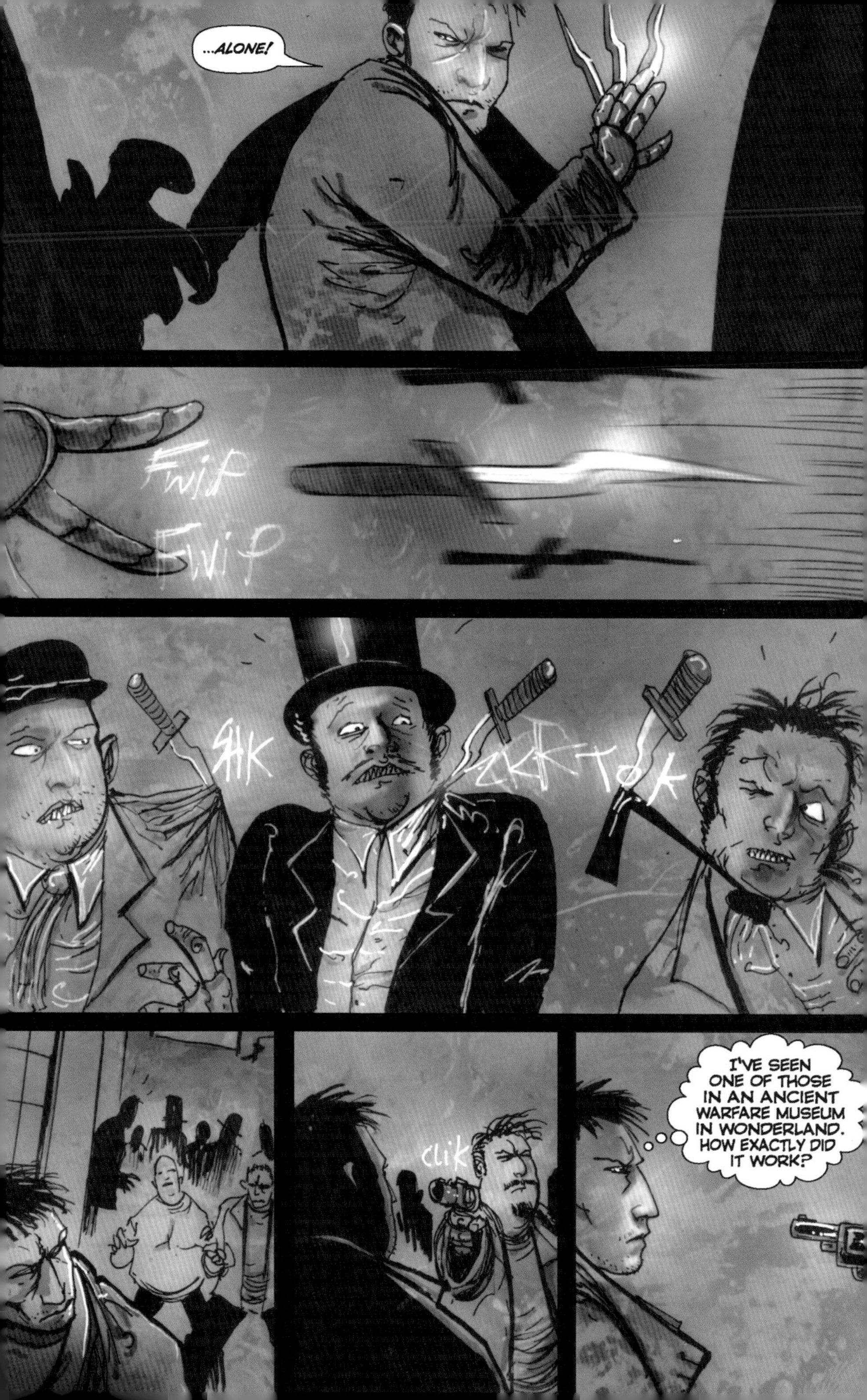
...ALONE!
FWIP
FWIP
SHK
CKRTOK
CLIK
I'VE SEEN ONE OF THOSE IN AN ANCIENT WARFARE MUSEUM IN WONDERLAND. HOW EXACTLY DID IT WORK?

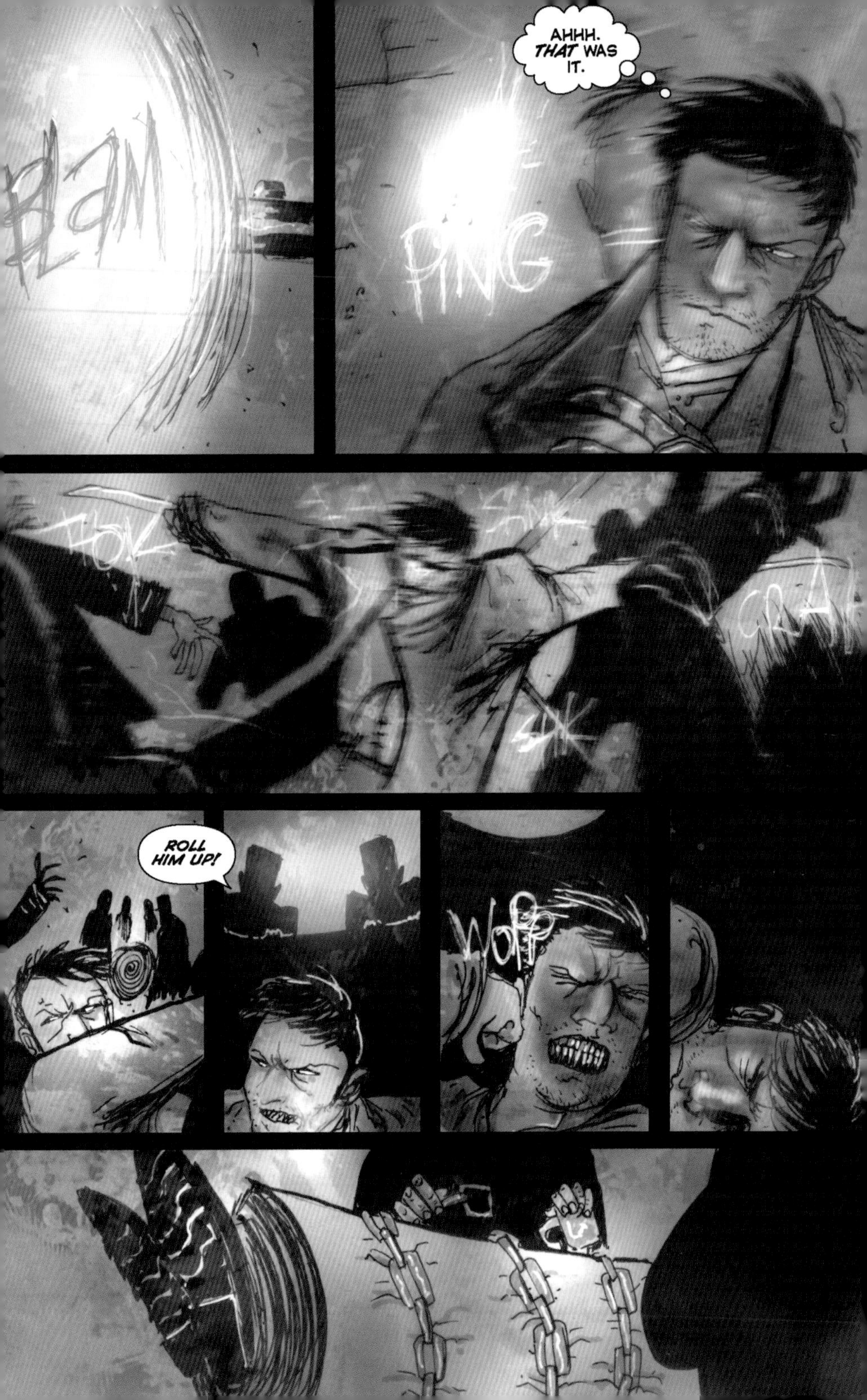
BLAM
AHHH. THAT WAS IT.
PING
ROLL HIM UP!
WOPP

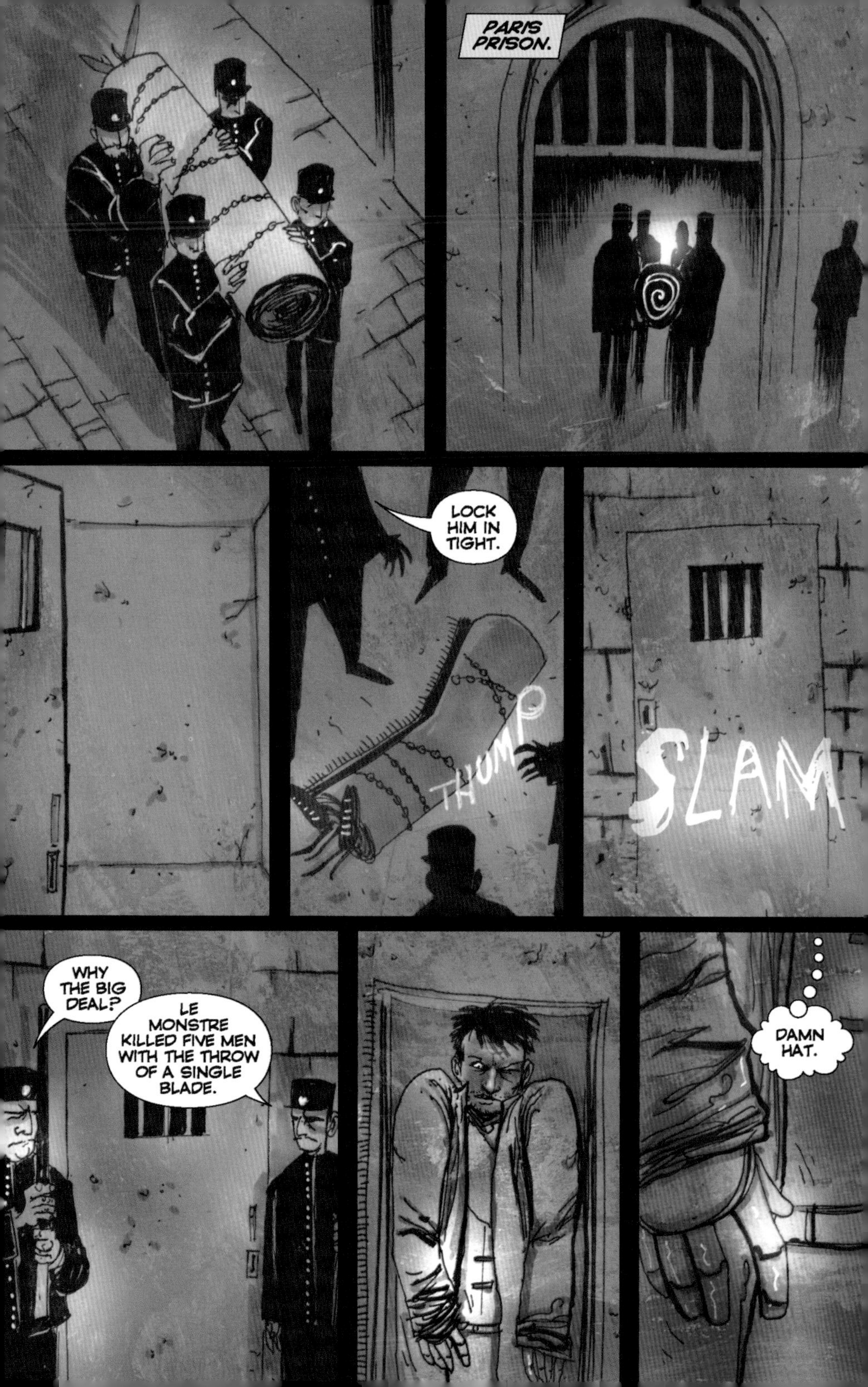
PARIS PRISON.
LOCK HIM IN TIGHT.
THUMP
SLAM
WHY THE BIG DEAL?
LE MONSTRE KILLED FIVE MEN WITH THE THROW OF A SINGLE BLADE.
...
DAMN HAT.

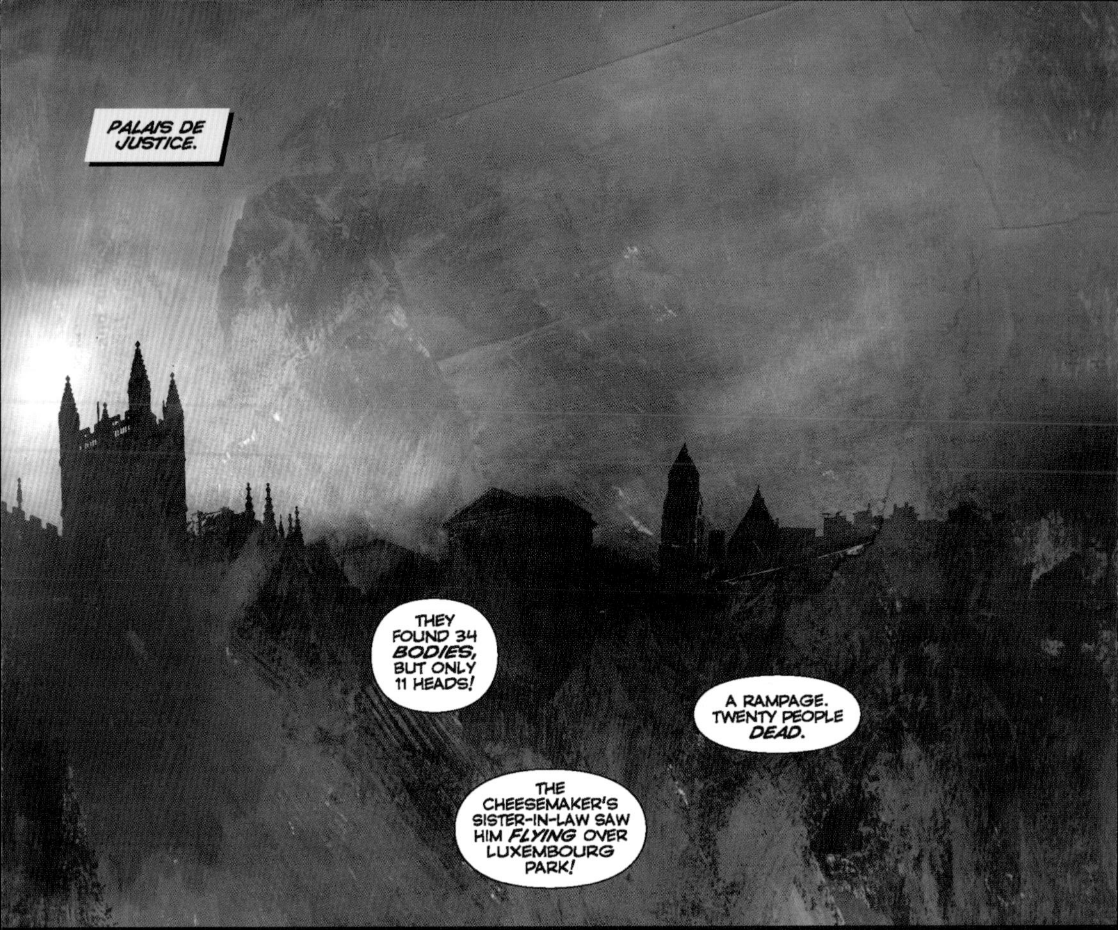
PALAIS DE JUSTICE.
THEY FOUND 34 BODIES, BUT ONLY 11 HEADS!
A RAMPAGE. TWENTY PEOPLE DEAD.
THE CHEESEMAKER'S SISTER-IN-LAW SAW HIM FLYING OVER LUXEMBOURG PARK!

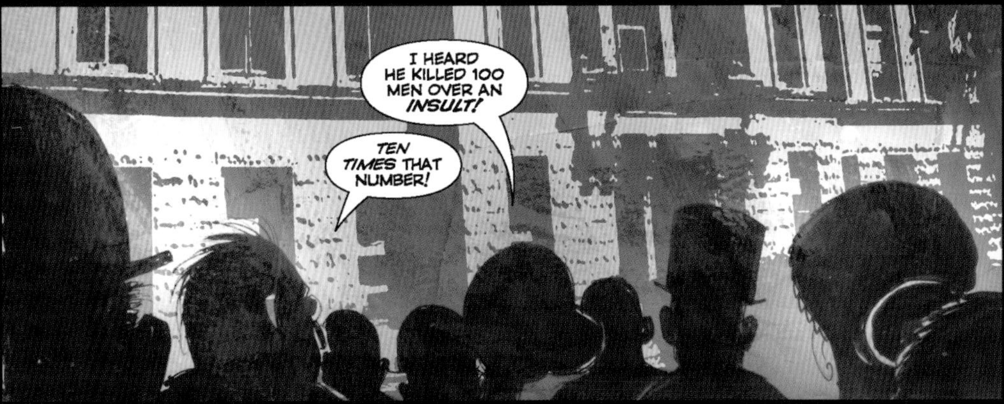
I HEARD HE KILLED 100 MEN OVER AN INSULT!
TEN TIMES THAT NUMBER!

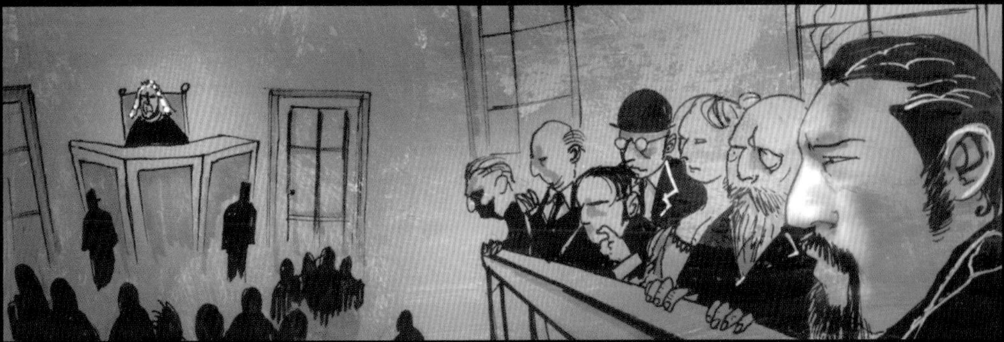

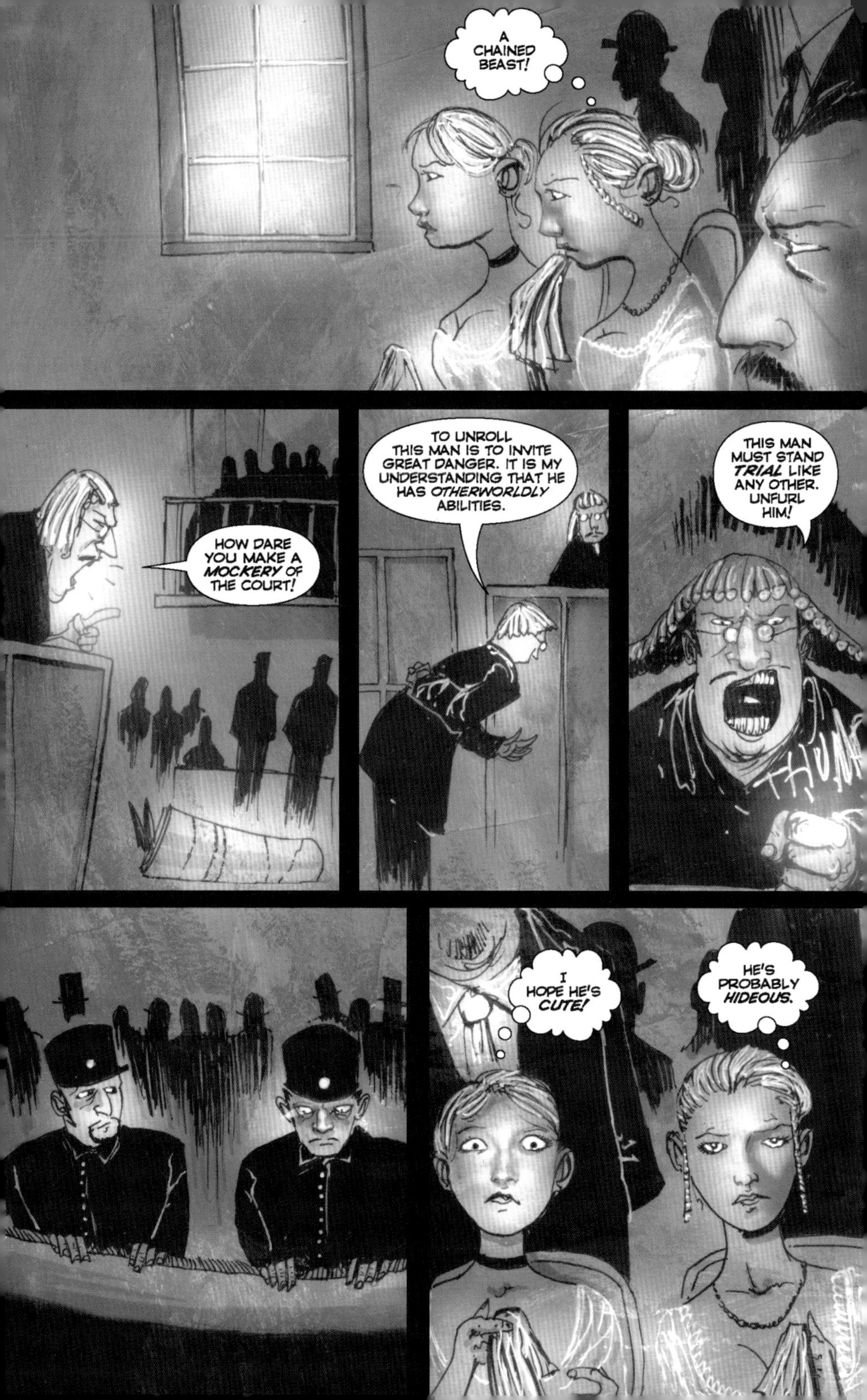
A CHAINED BEAST!
HOW DARE YOU MAKE A MOCKERY OF THE COURT!
TO UNROLL THIS MAN IS TO INVITE GREAT DANGER. IT IS MY UNDERSTANDING THAT HE HAS OTHERWORLDLY ABILITIES.
THIS MAN MUST STAND TRIAL LIKE ANY OTHER. UNFURL HIM!
THUMP
I HOPE HE'S CUTE!
HE'S PROBABLY HIDEOUS.

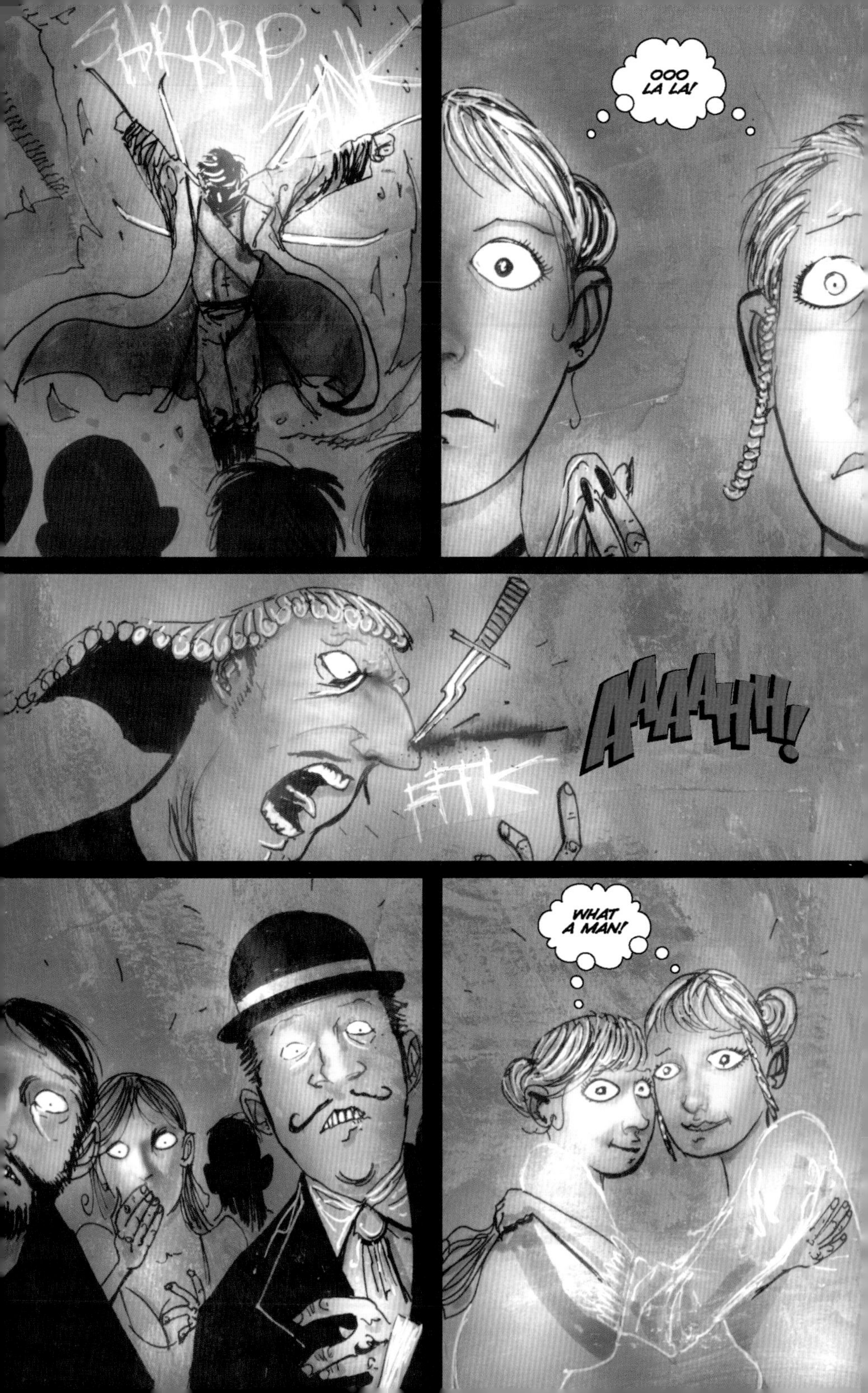
OOO LA LA!
AAAAHH!
WHAT A MAN!

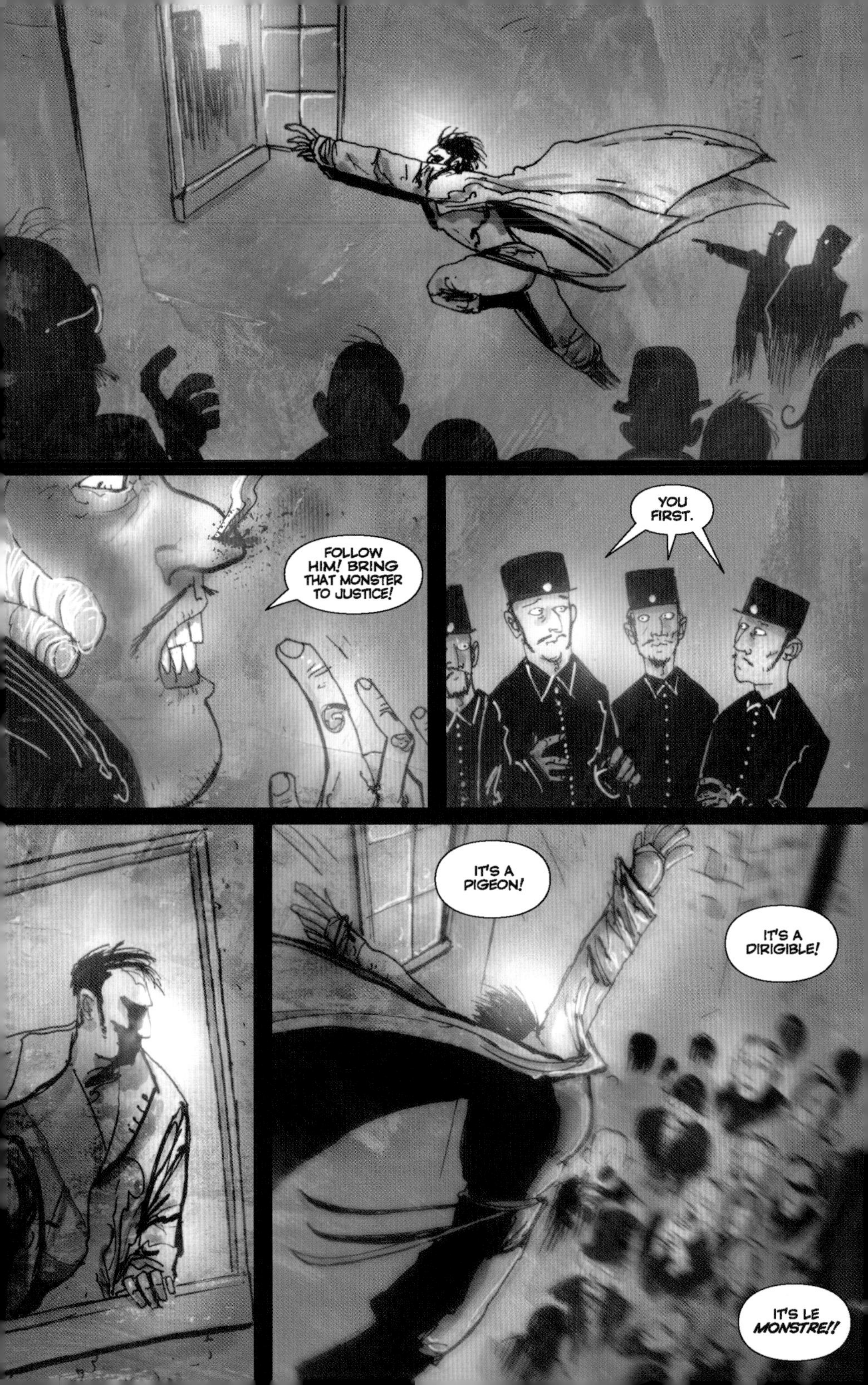
FOLLOW HIM! BRING THAT MONSTER TO JUSTICE!
YOU FIRST.
IT'S A PIGEON!
IT'S A DIRIGIBLE!
IT'S LE MONSTRE!!

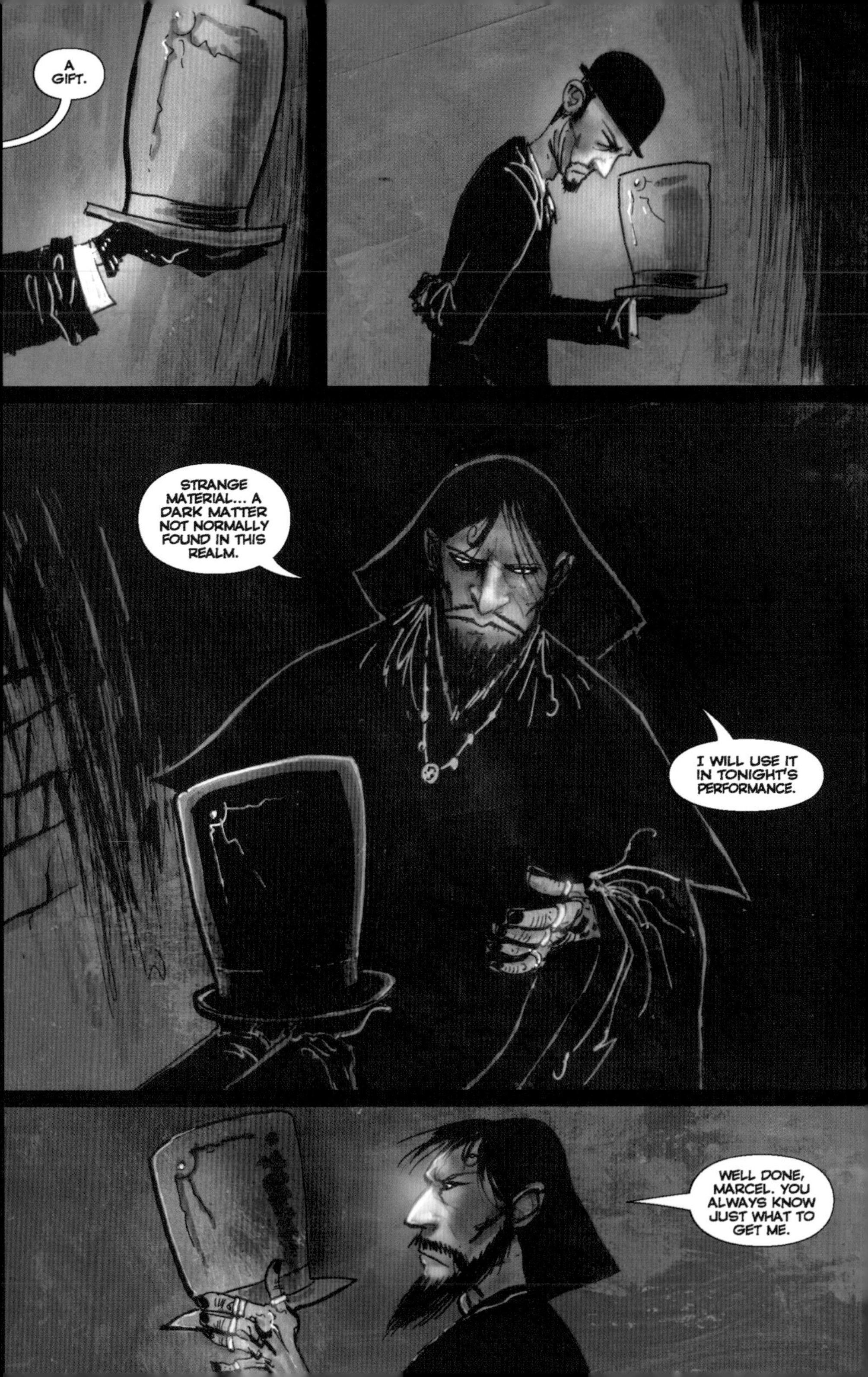
A GIFT.
STRANGE MATERIAL... A DARK MATTER NOT NORMALLY FOUND IN THIS REALM.
I WILL USE IT IN TONIGHT'S PERFORMANCE.
WELL DONE, MARCEL. YOU ALWAYS KNOW JUST WHAT TO GET ME.

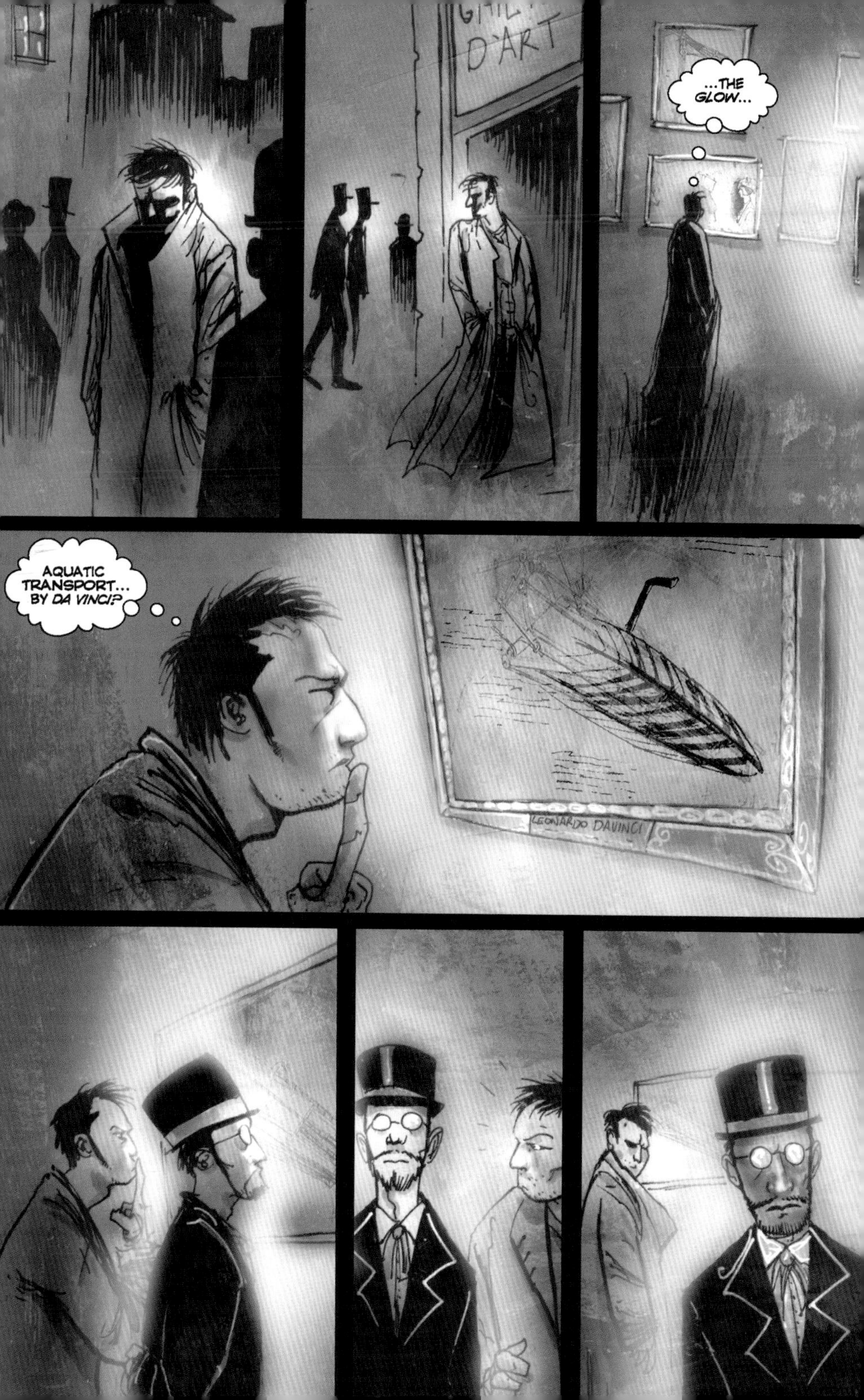
GALERIE D'ART
...THE GLOW...
AQUATIC TRANSPORT... BY DA VINCI?
LEONARDO DA VINCI

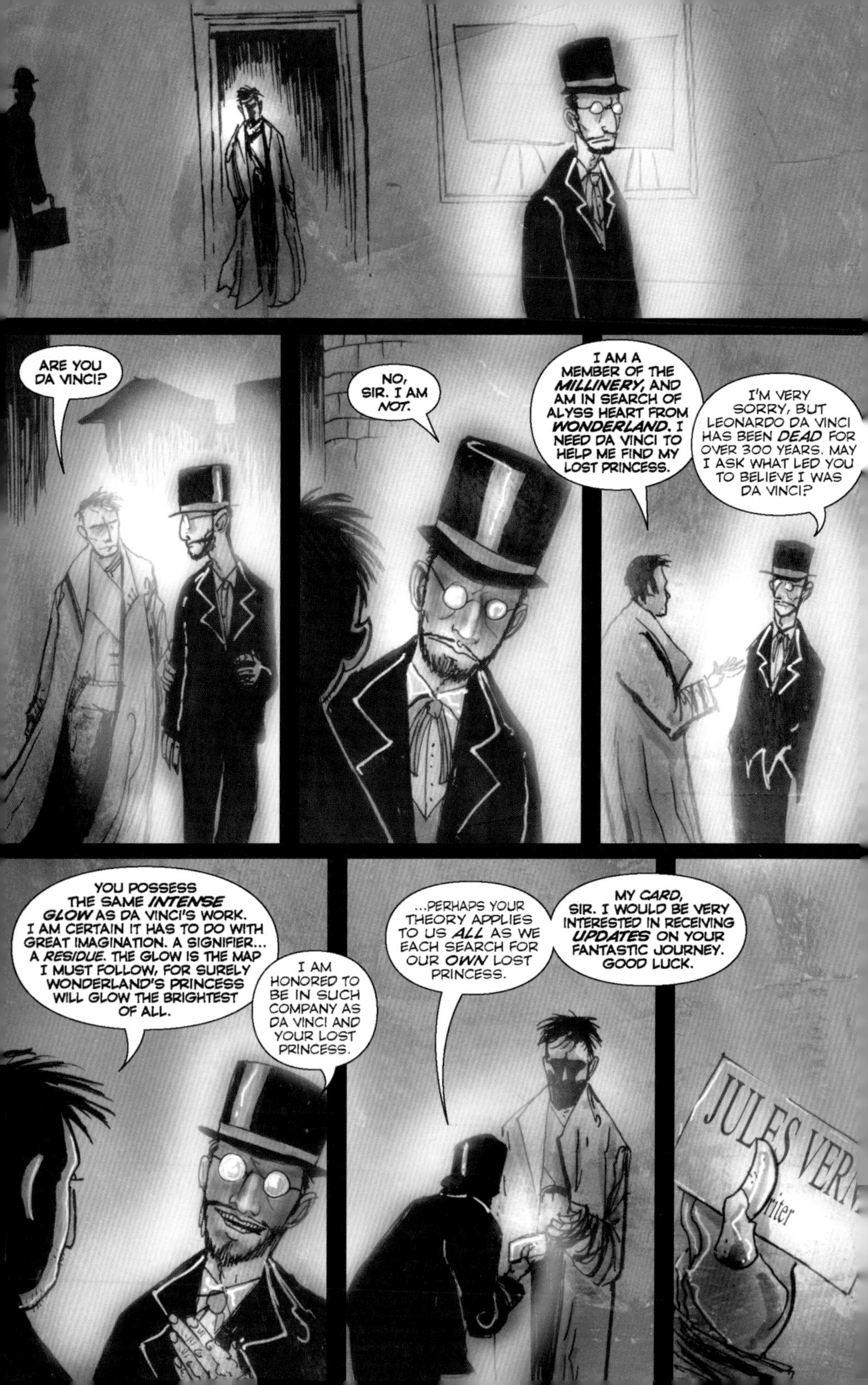

ARE YOU DA VINCI?
NO, SIR. I AM NOT.
I AM A MEMBER OF THE MILLINERY, AND AM IN SEARCH OF ALYSS HEART FROM WONDERLAND. I NEED DA VINCI TO HELP ME FIND MY LOST PRINCESS.
I'M VERY SORRY, BUT LEONARDO DA VINCI HAS BEEN DEAD FOR OVER 300 YEARS. MAY I ASK WHAT LED YOU TO BELIEVE I WAS DA VINCI?
YOU POSSESS THE SAME INTENSE GLOW AS DA VINCI'S WORK. I AM CERTAIN IT HAS TO DO WITH GREAT IMAGINATION. A SIGNIFIER... A RESIDUE. THE GLOW IS THE MAP I MUST FOLLOW, FOR SURELY WONDERLAND'S PRINCESS WILL GLOW THE BRIGHTEST OF ALL.
I AM HONORED TO BE IN SUCH COMPANY AS DA VINCI AND YOUR LOST PRINCESS.
...PERHAPS YOUR THEORY APPLIES TO US ALL AS WE EACH SEARCH FOR OUR OWN LOST PRINCESS.
MY CARD, SIR. I WOULD BE VERY INTERESTED IN RECEIVING UPDATES ON YOUR FANTASTIC JOURNEY. GOOD LUCK.
JULES VERN
riter

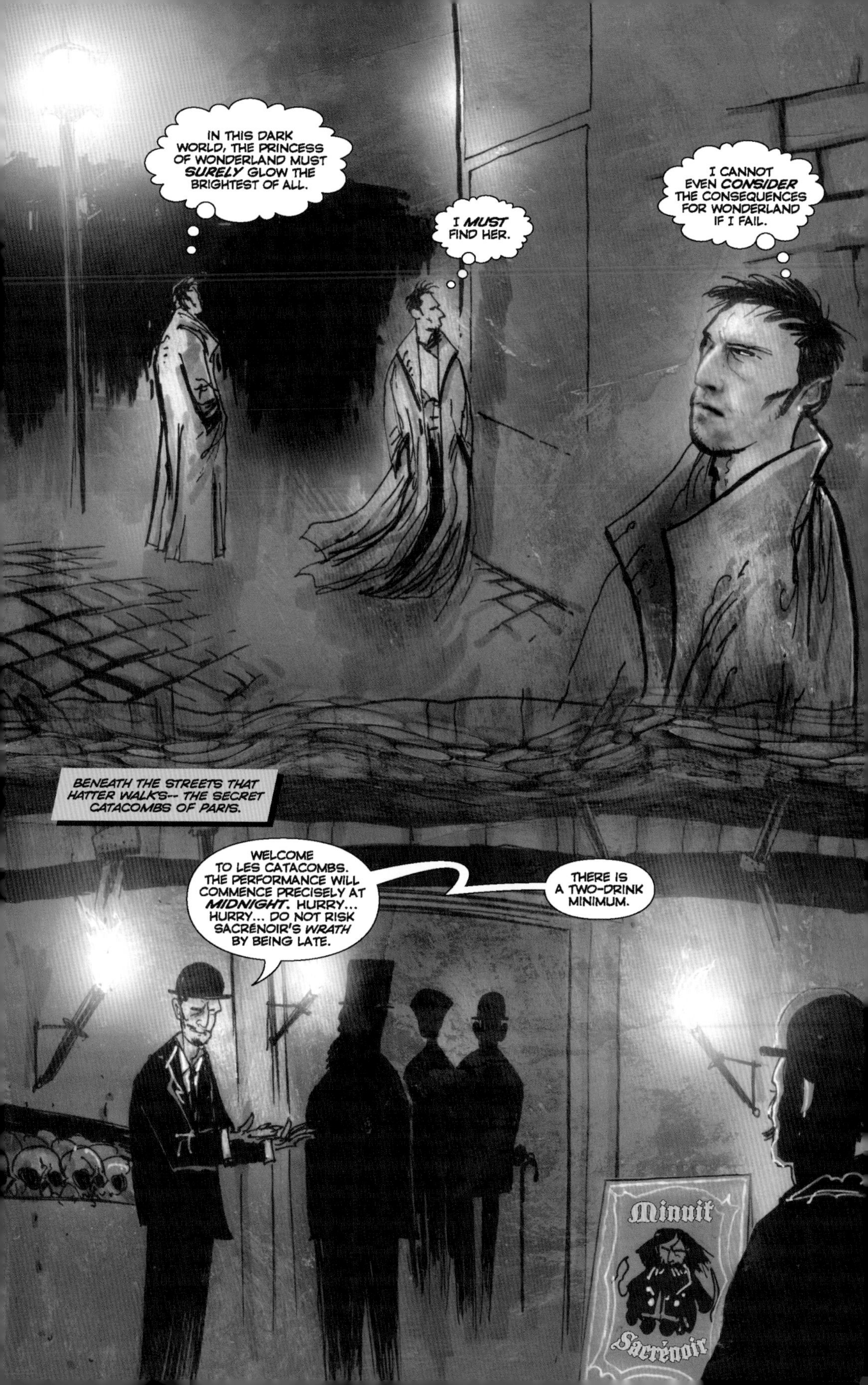
IN THIS DARK WORLD, THE PRINCESS OF WONDERLAND MUST SURELY GLOW THE BRIGHTEST OF ALL.
I MUST FIND HER.
I CANNOT EVEN CONSIDER THE CONSEQUENCES FOR WONDERLAND IF I FAIL.
BENEATH THE STREETS THAT HATTER WALKS-- THE SECRET CATACOMBS OF PARIS.
WELCOME TO LES CATACOMBS. THE PERFORMANCE WILL COMMENCE PRECISELY AT MIDNIGHT. HURRY... HURRY... DO NOT RISK SACRÉNOIR'S WRATH BY BEING LATE.
THERE IS A TWO-DRINK MINIMUM.
Minuit
Sacrénoir

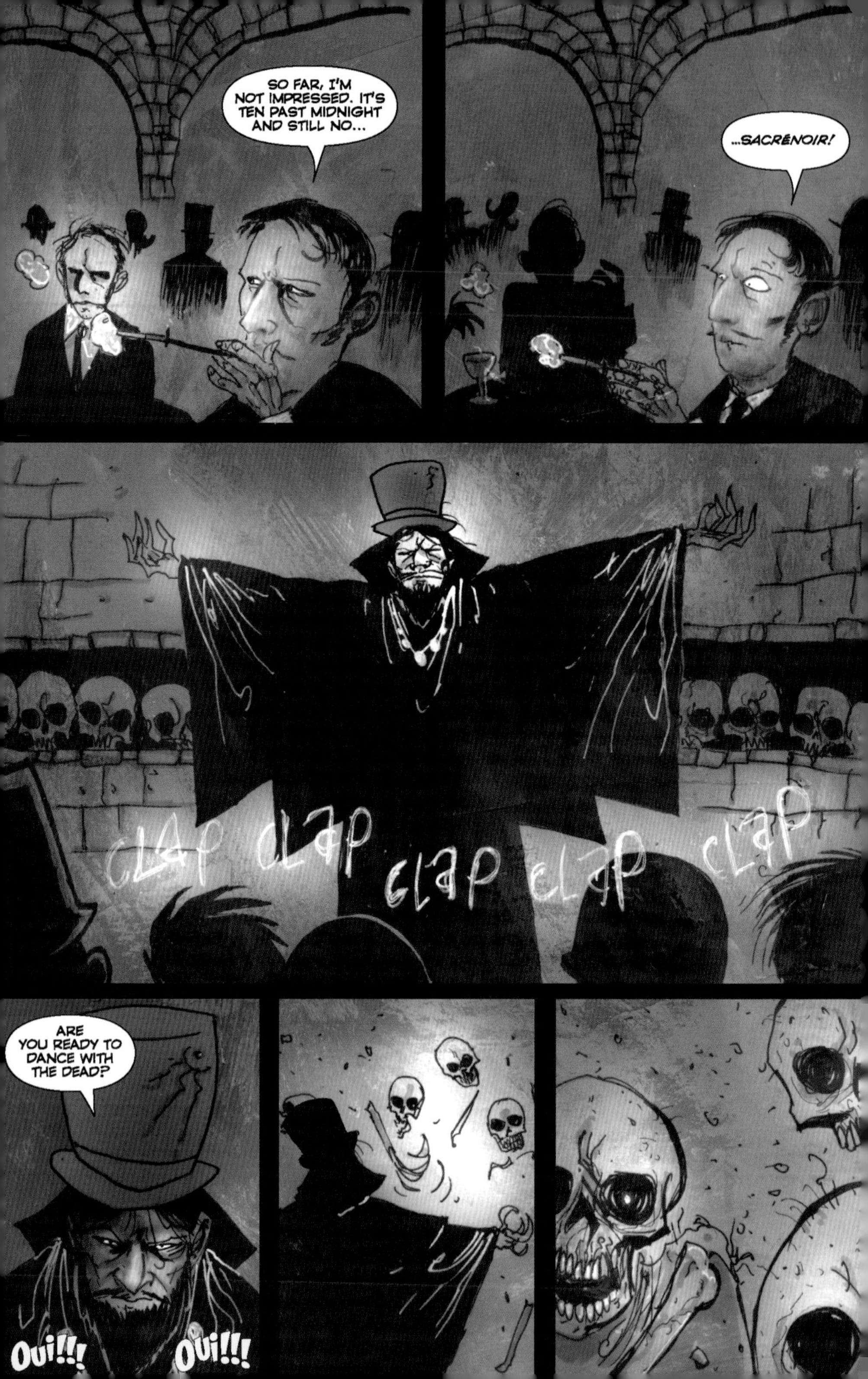

SO FAR, I'M NOT IMPRESSED. IT'S TEN PAST MIDNIGHT AND STILL NO...
...SACRÉNOIR!
CLAP CLAP CLAP CLAP CLAP
ARE YOU READY TO DANCE WITH THE DEAD?
OUI!!!
OUI!!!

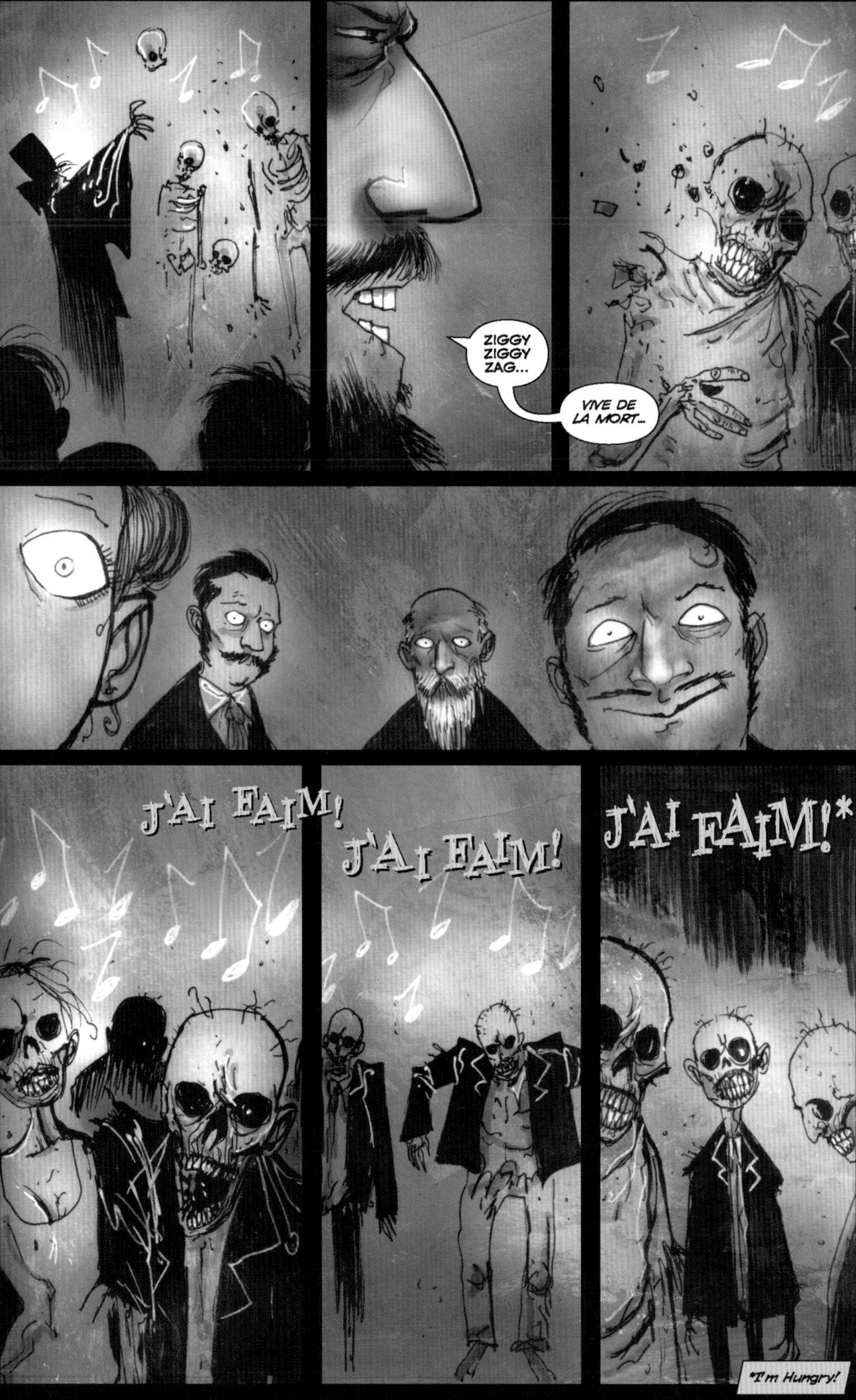
ZIGGY ZIGGY ZAG...
VIVE DE LA MORT...
J'AI FAIM!
J'AI FAIM!
J'AI FAIM!*
*I'm Hungry!

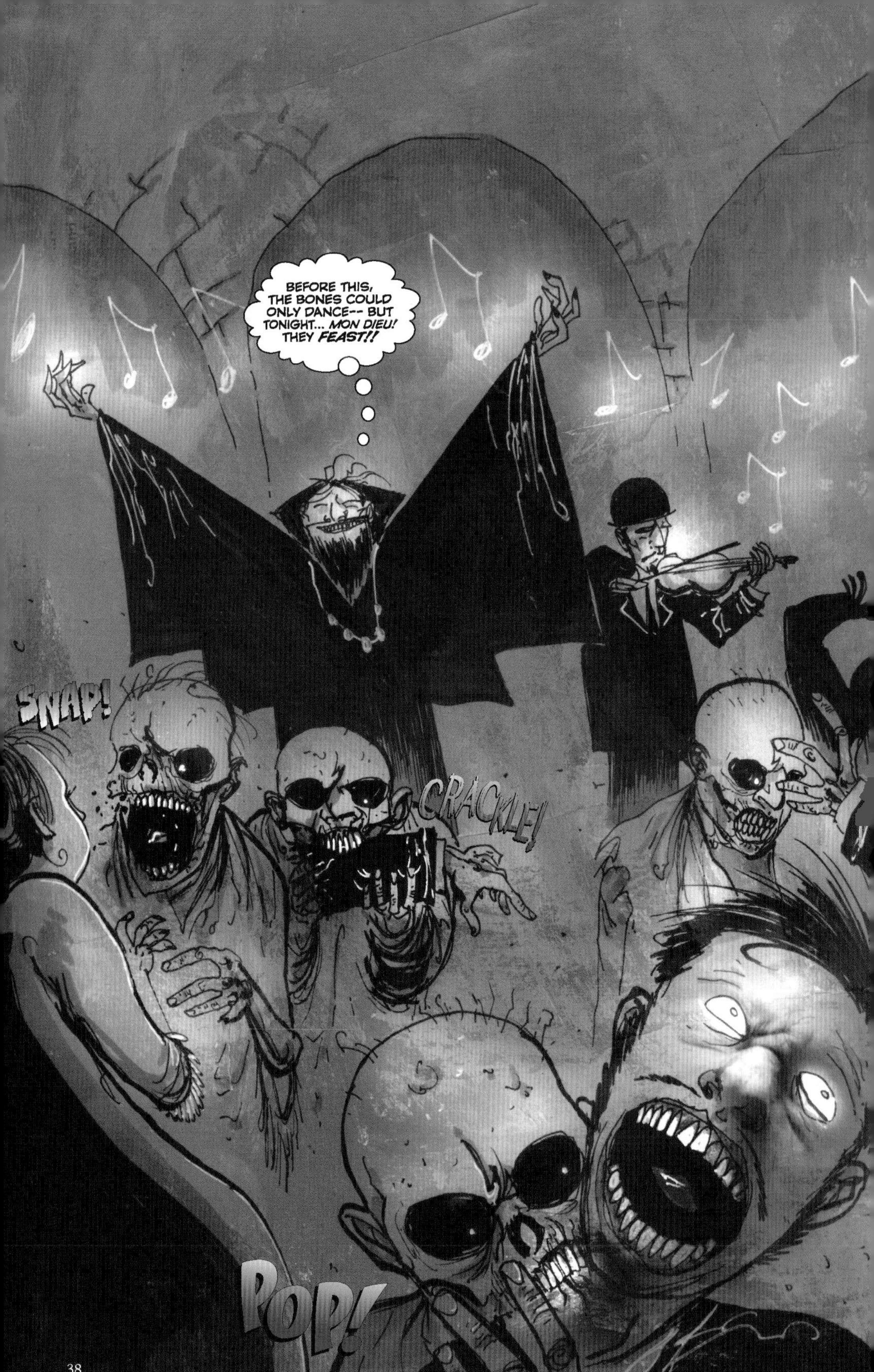

BEFORE THIS, THE BONES COULD ONLY DANCE-- BUT TONIGHT... *MON DIEU!* THEY ***FEAST!!***
SNAP!
CRACKLE!
POP!

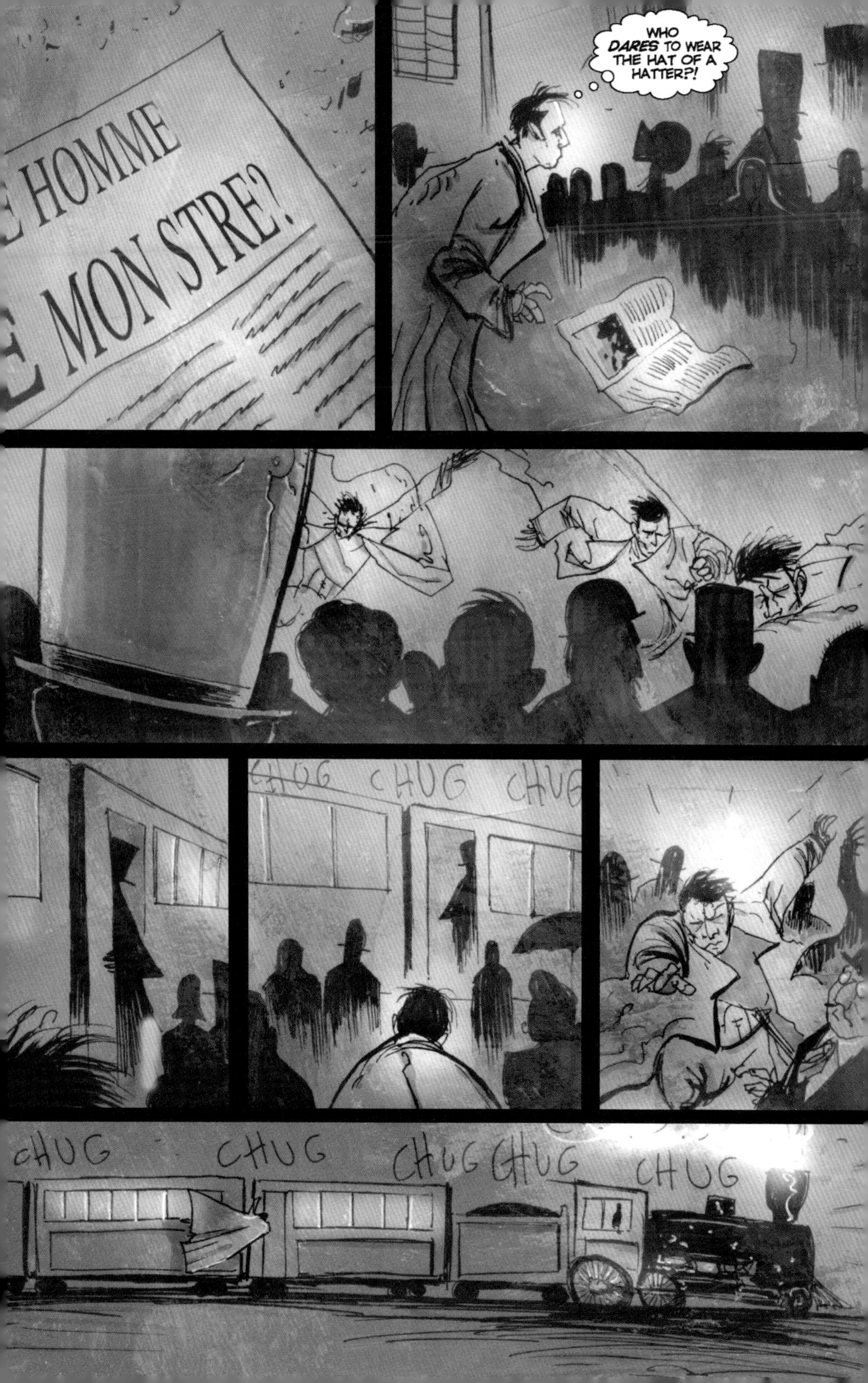

E HOMME
E MONSTRE?
WHO DARES TO WEAR THE HAT OF A HATTER?!
CHUG CHUG CHUG
CHUG CHUG CHUG CHUG CHUG

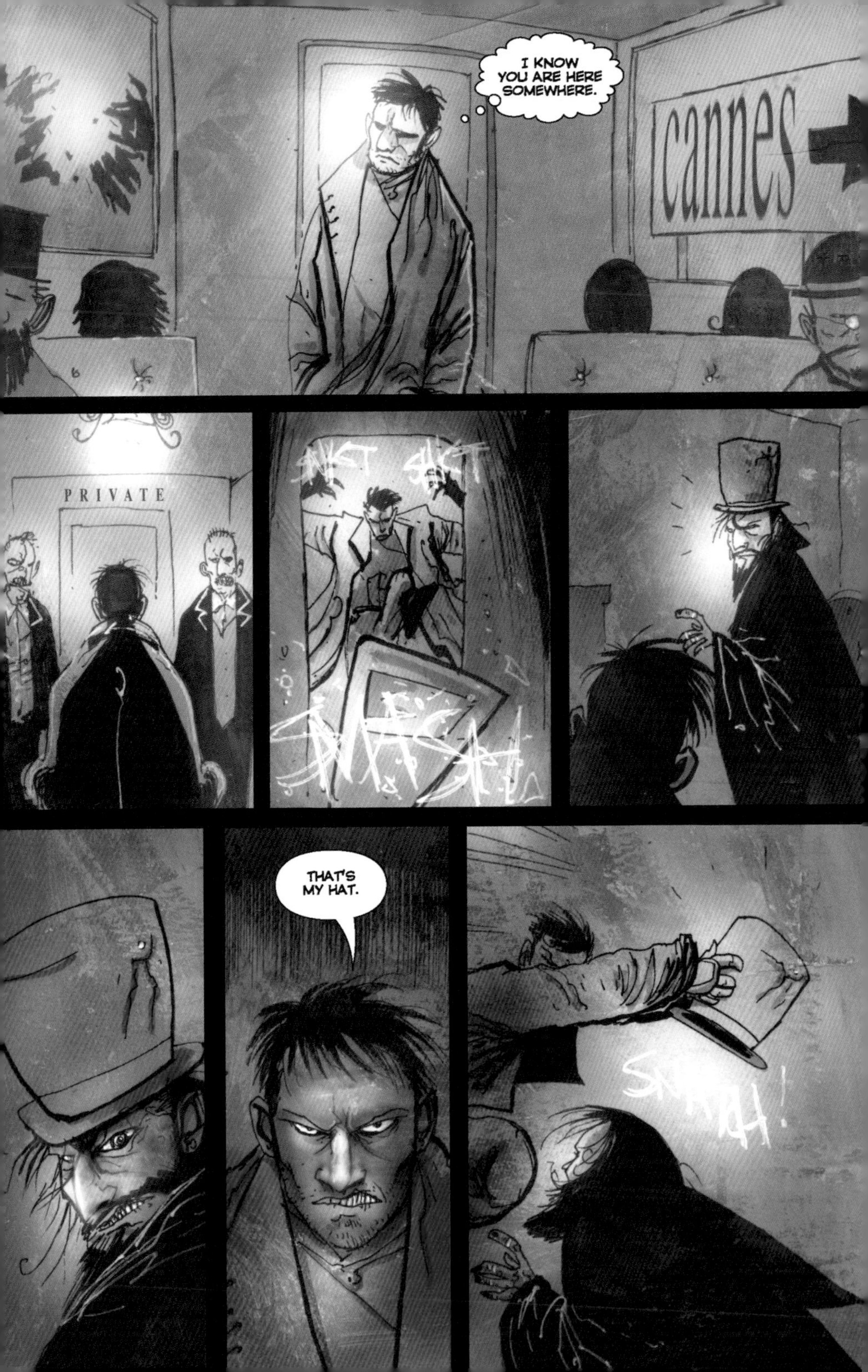
I KNOW YOU ARE HERE SOMEWHERE.
cannes
PRIVATE
THAT'S MY HAT.

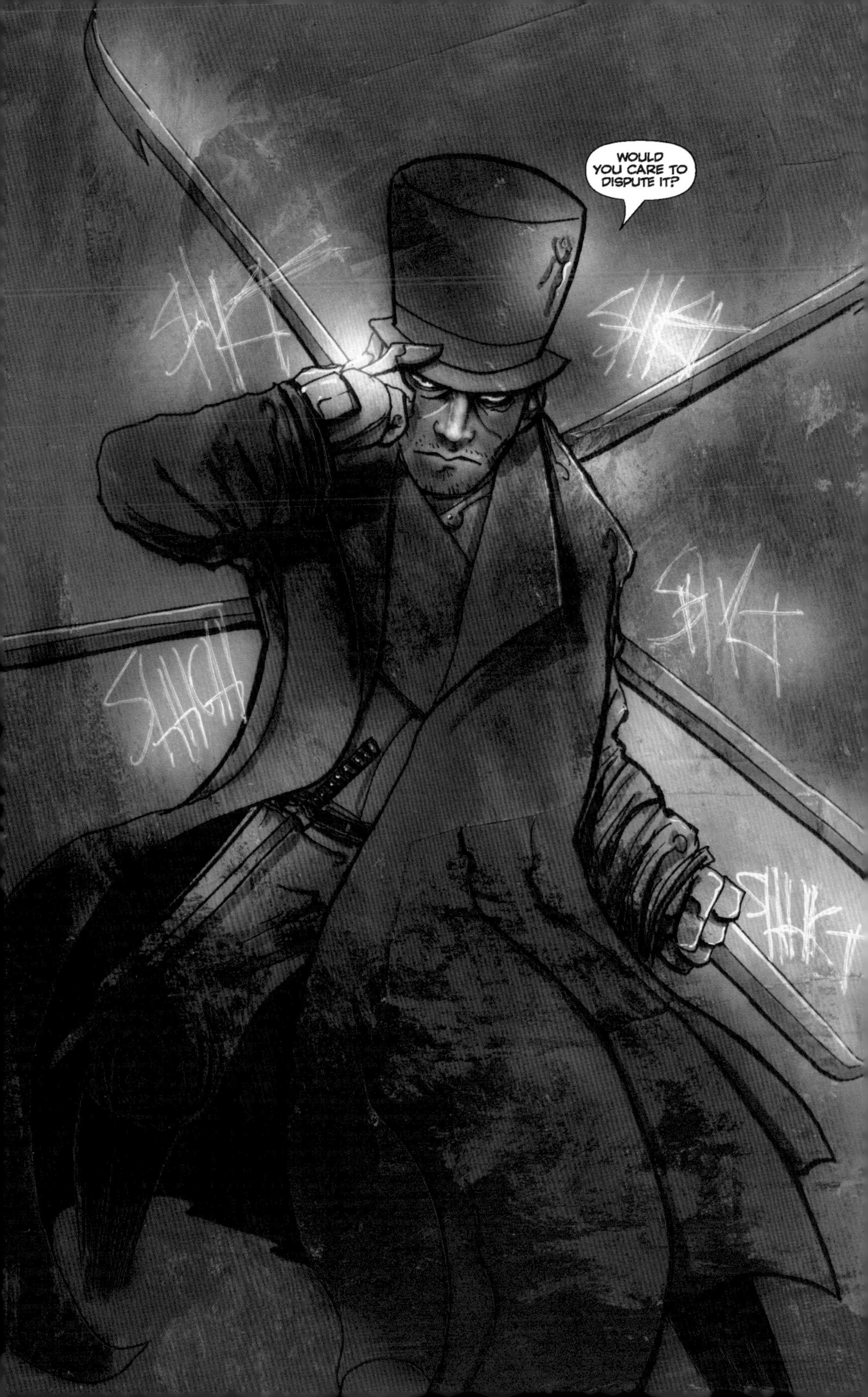
WOULD YOU CARE TO DISPUTE IT?

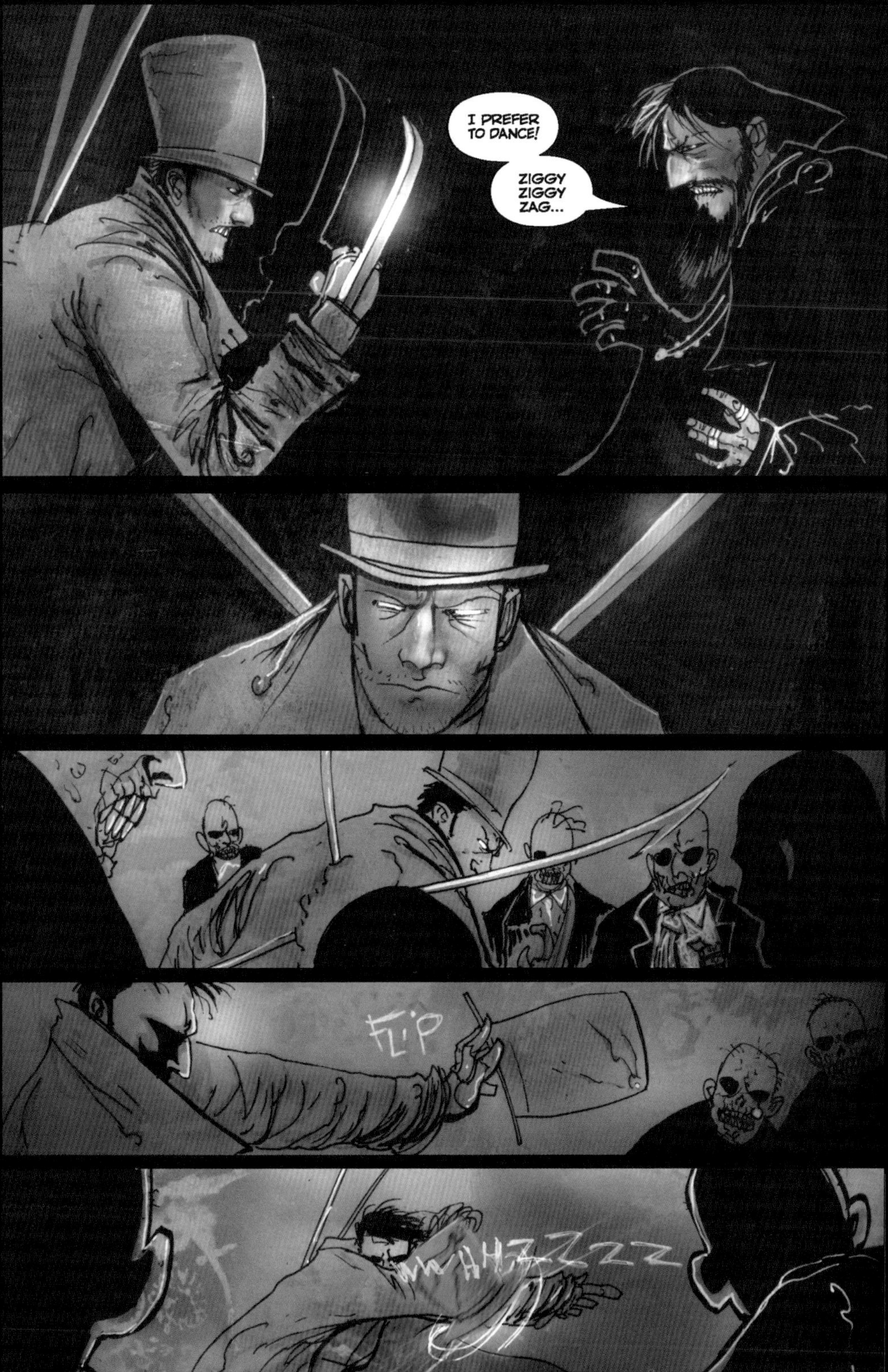
I PREFER TO DANCE!
ZIGGY ZIGGY ZAG...
FLIP
WWHHZZZZZ

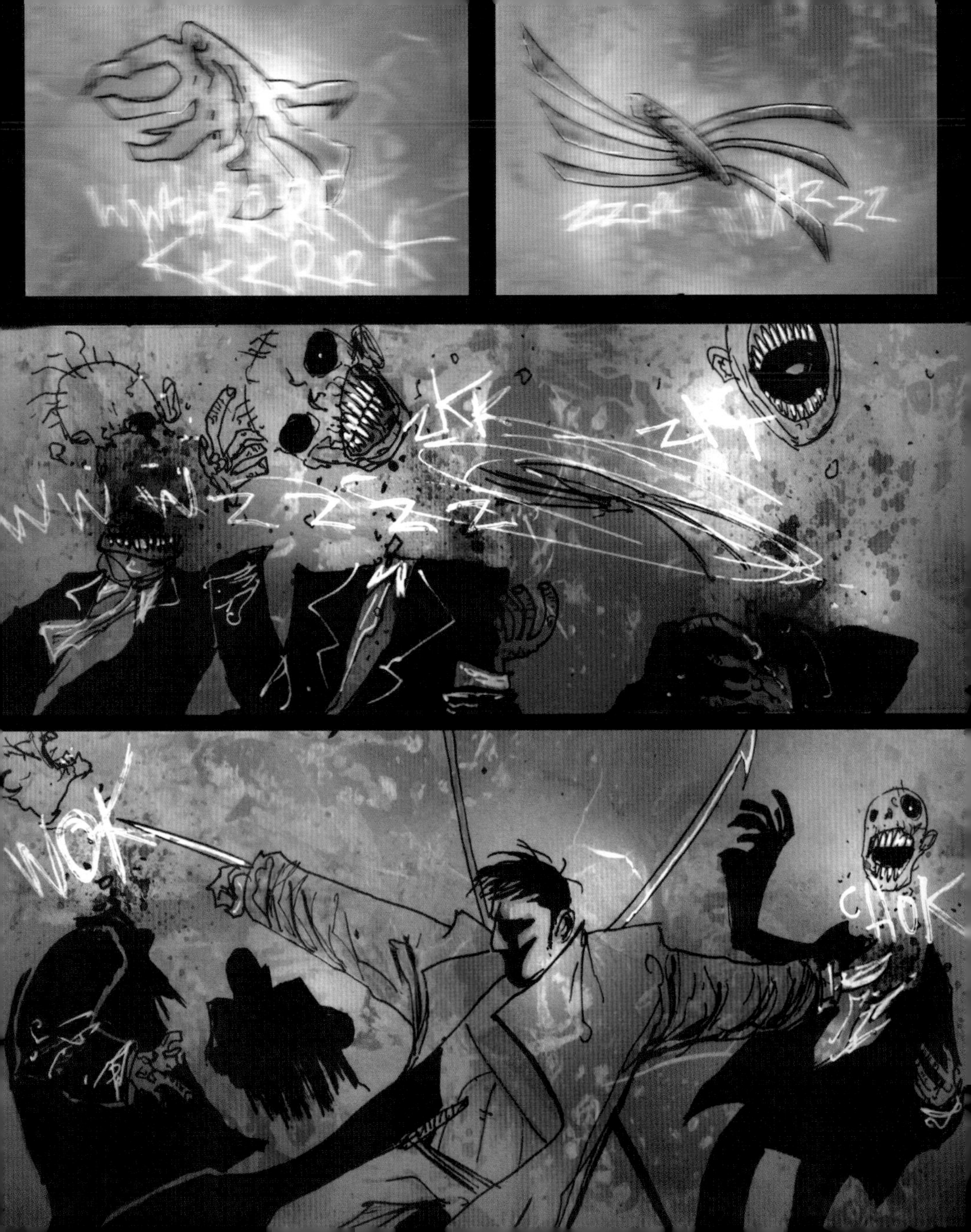
WOK
CHOK

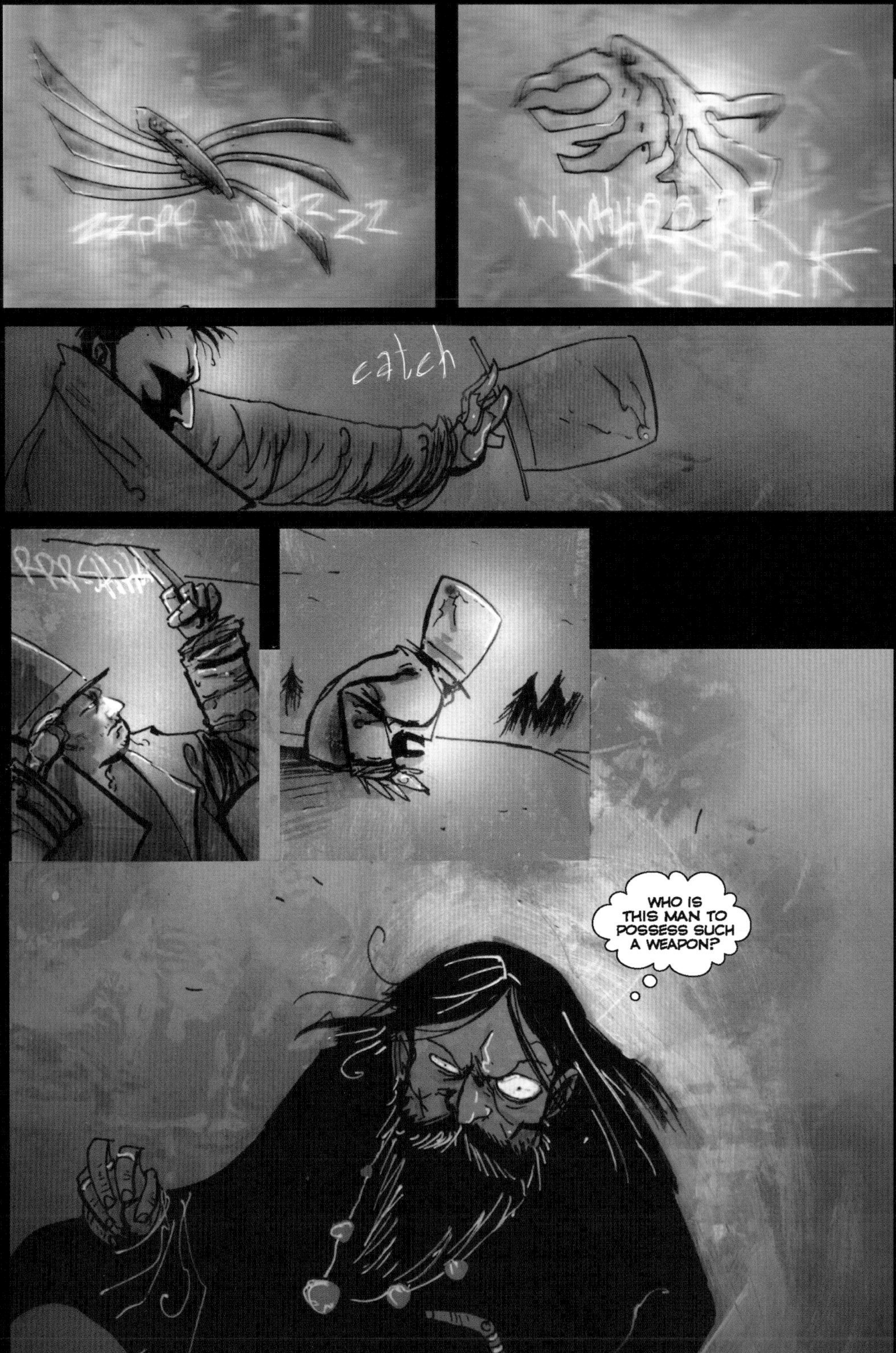
catch
WHO IS THIS MAN TO POSSESS SUCH A WEAPON?

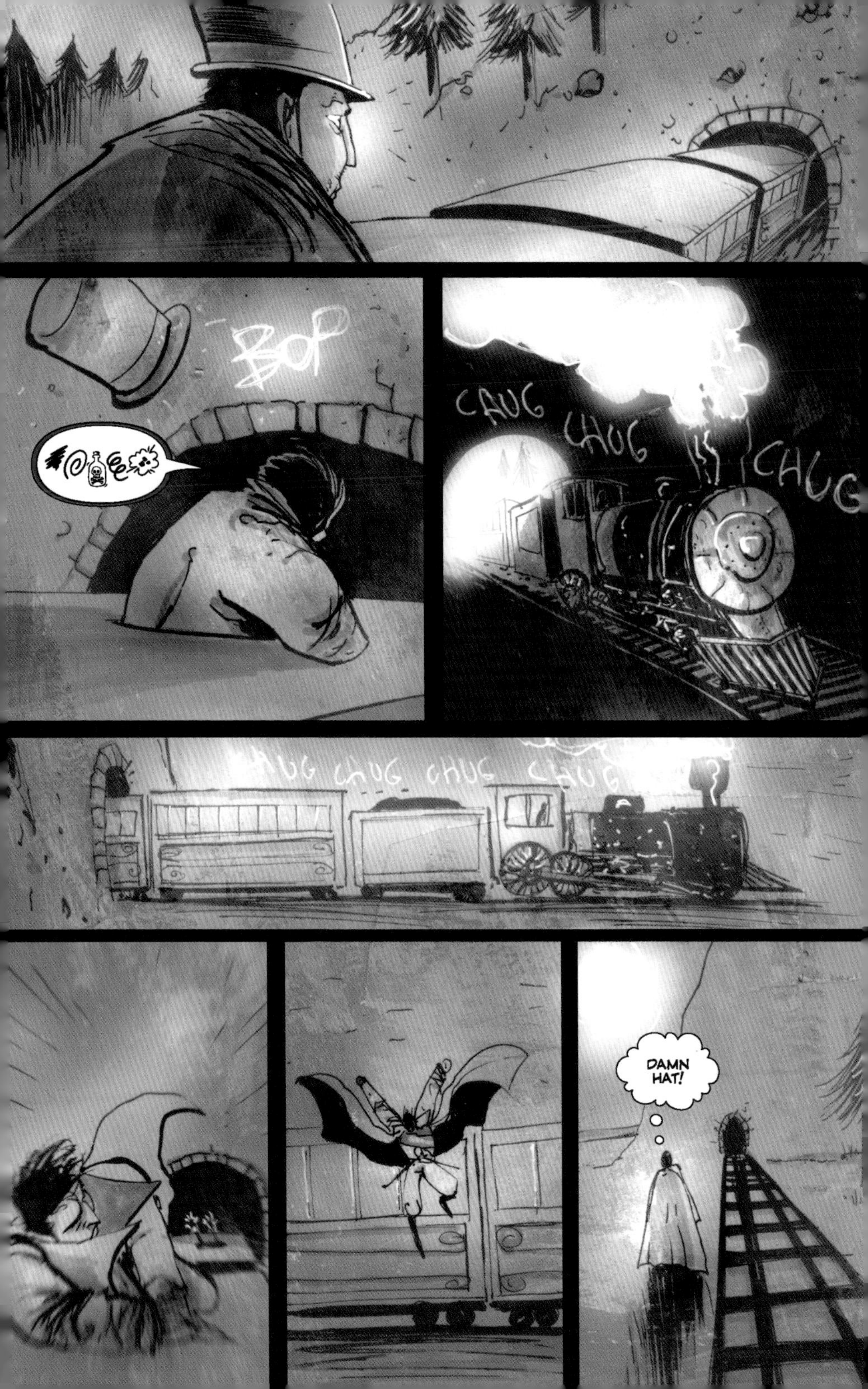
BOP
CHUG
CHUG
CHUG
CHUG CHUG CHUG CHUG
DAMN HAT!

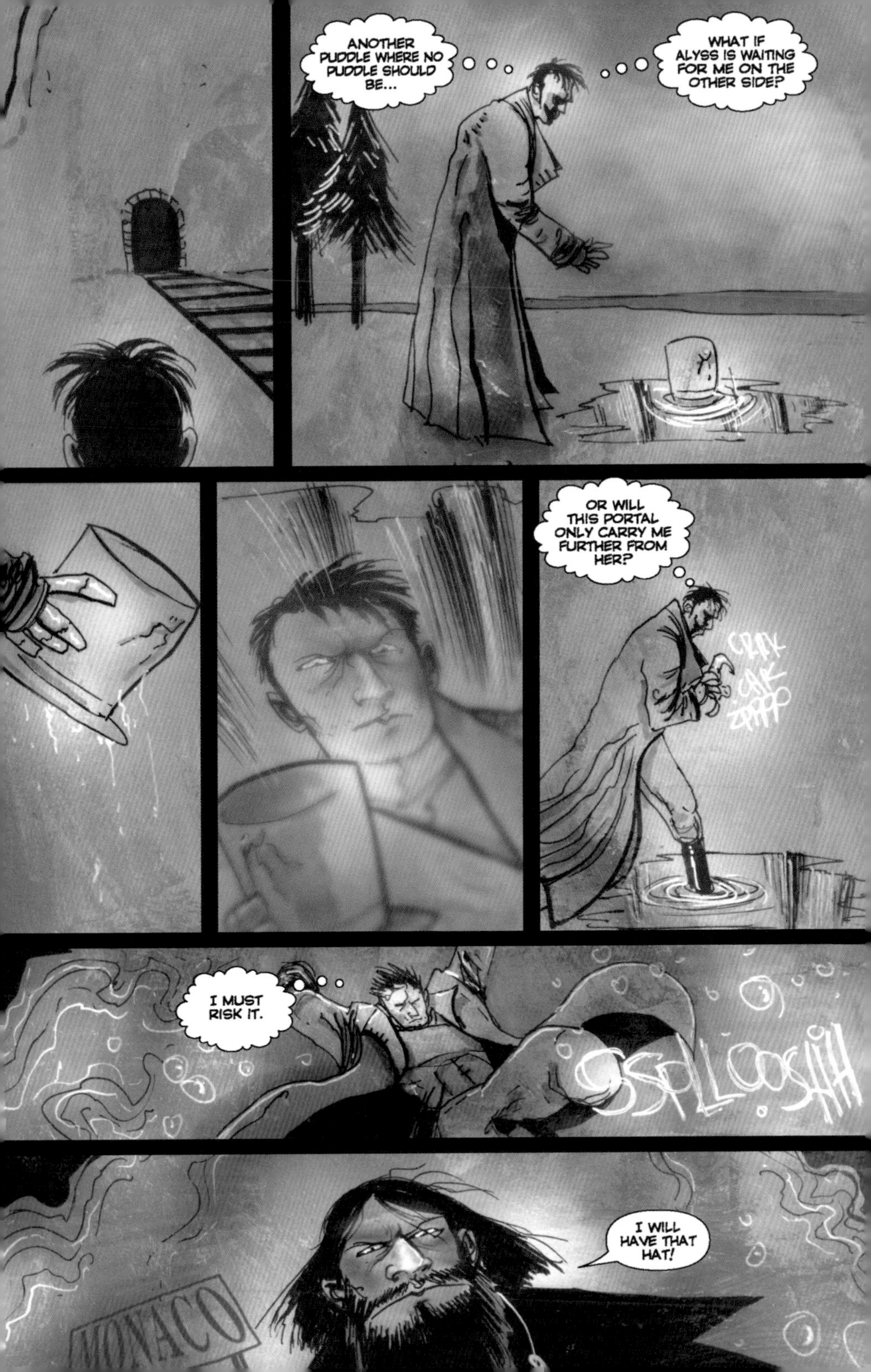
ANOTHER PUDDLE WHERE NO PUDDLE SHOULD BE...
WHAT IF ALYSS IS WAITING FOR ME ON THE OTHER SIDE?
OR WILL THIS PORTAL ONLY CARRY ME FURTHER FROM HER?
I MUST RISK IT.
SPLOOSHH
I WILL HAVE THAT HAT!
MONACO

Millinery
Code of Honor

One Hat One Hatter

Absolute Allegiance to White Imagination
and its ruling Queen

To Serve and Sustain White Imagination

To Master the Forging of Immaculate Blades

To Excel in Personal Combat

To Contain and Control All Emotion

If You Promise, You Must Fulfill

If at any time you sense yourself in danger of
breaking any of the tenets of the Millinery Code
you must immediately remove your Hat
from active service.

What dark world is this where those desiring the glow prey upon children? My hope of finding Princess Alyss is now mixed with terror as I realize there are entities in this far place just as deadly as those that forced her from her palace. No longer is it only the glow that will set my course, but the darkness as well, since to find her I must track the enemies of imagination who covet her every breath.

Children are the Juiciest

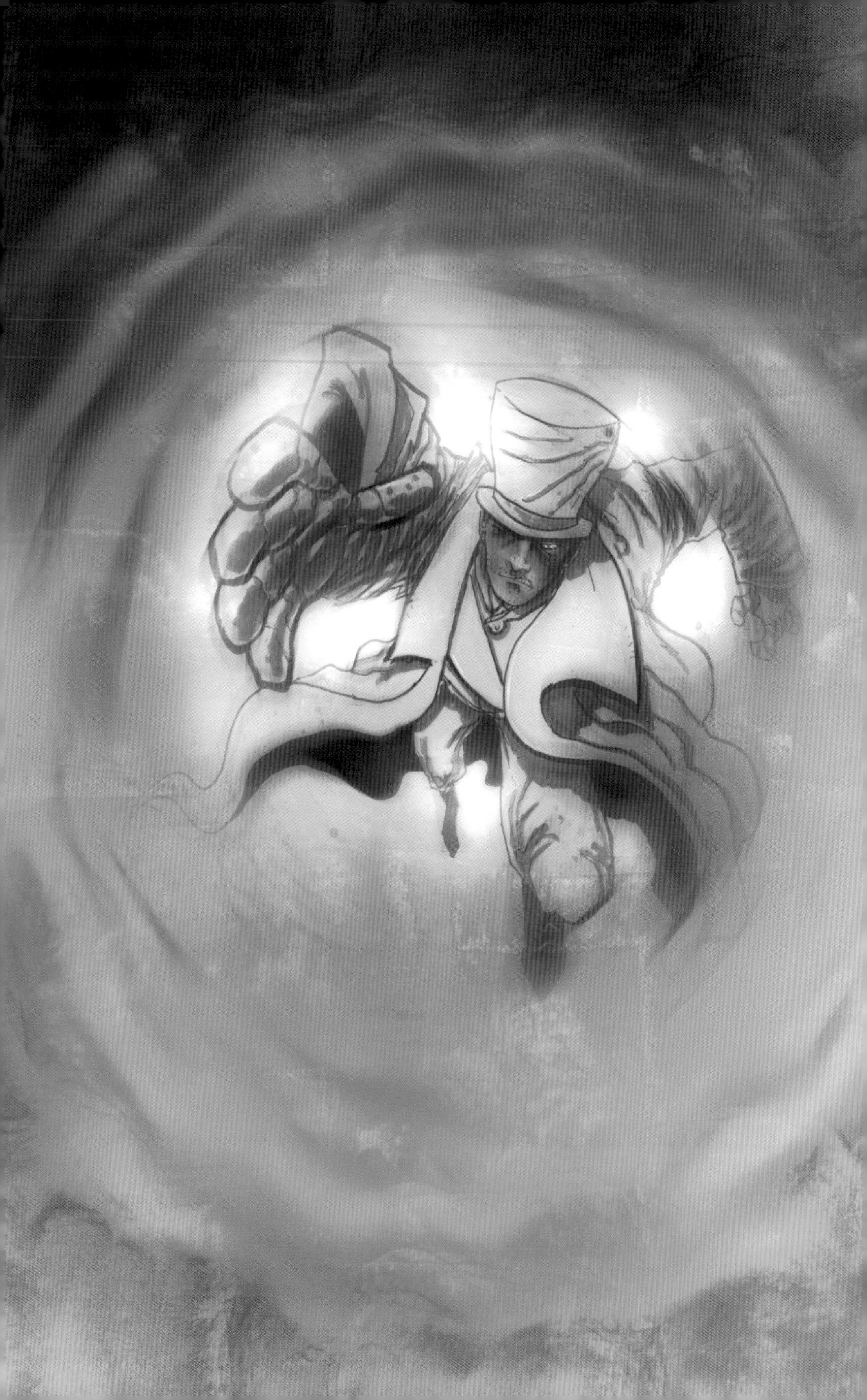

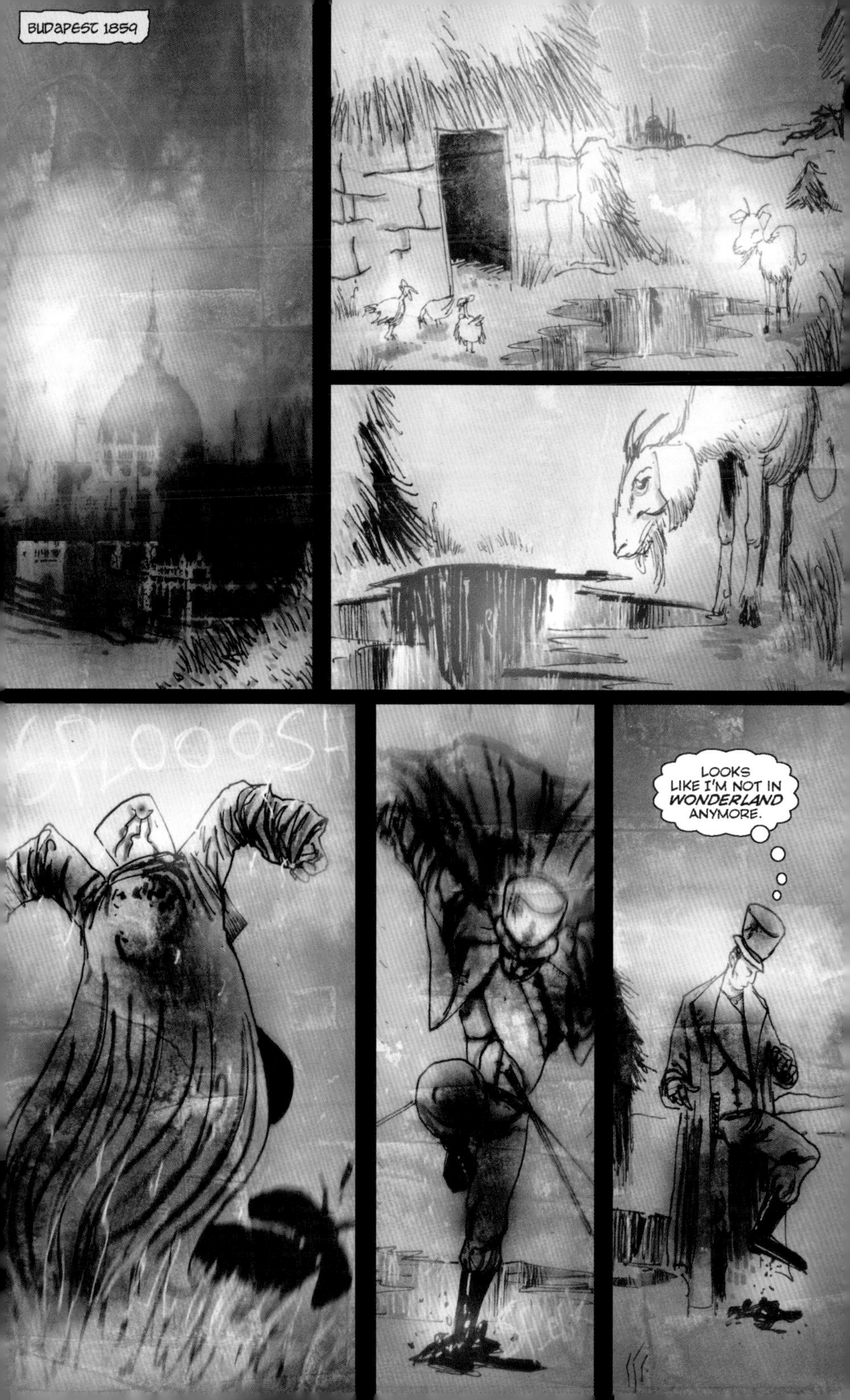
BUDAPEST 1859
SPLOOOSH
LOOKS LIKE I'M NOT IN WONDERLAND ANYMORE.

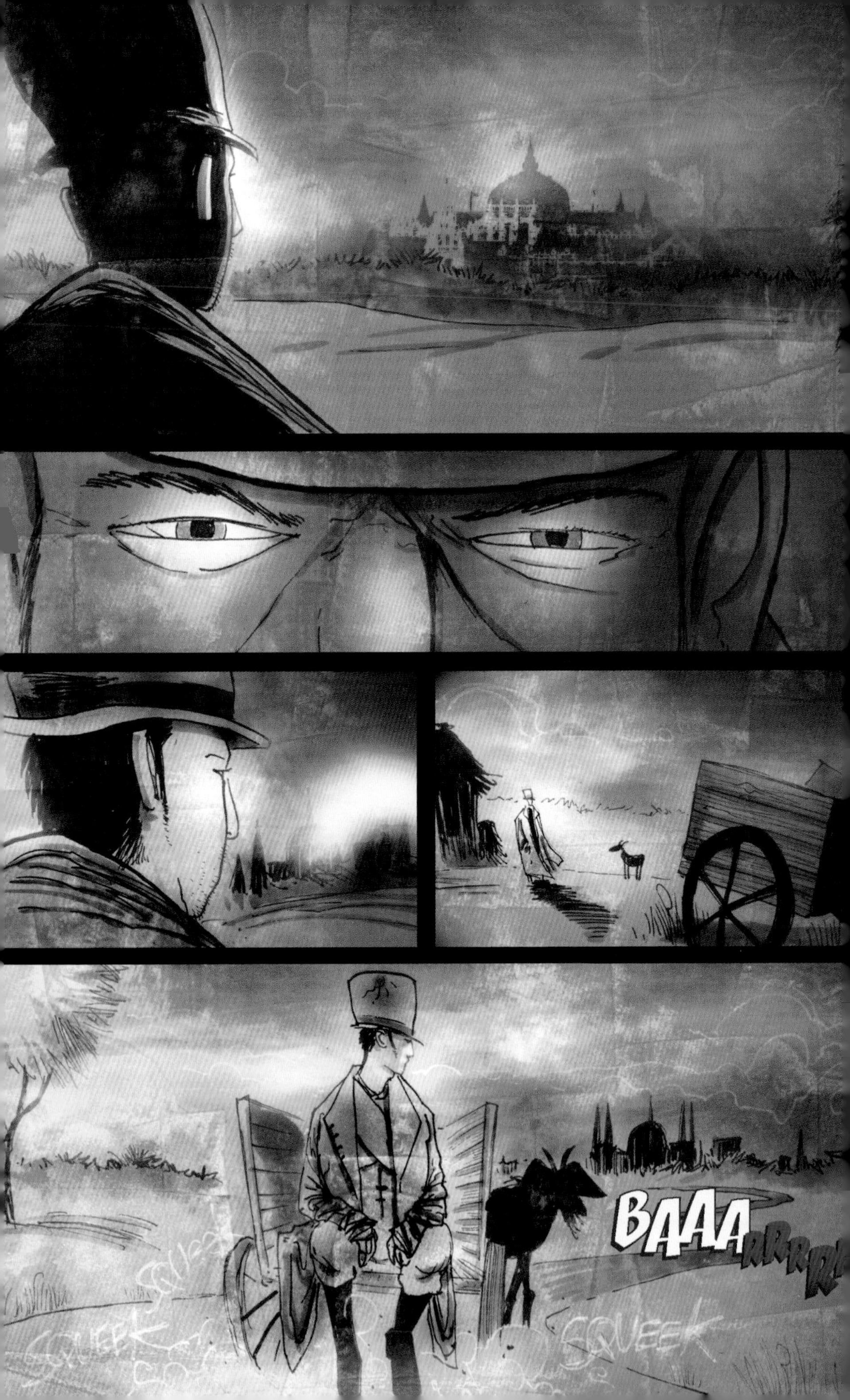
BAAARRRR
SQUEEK

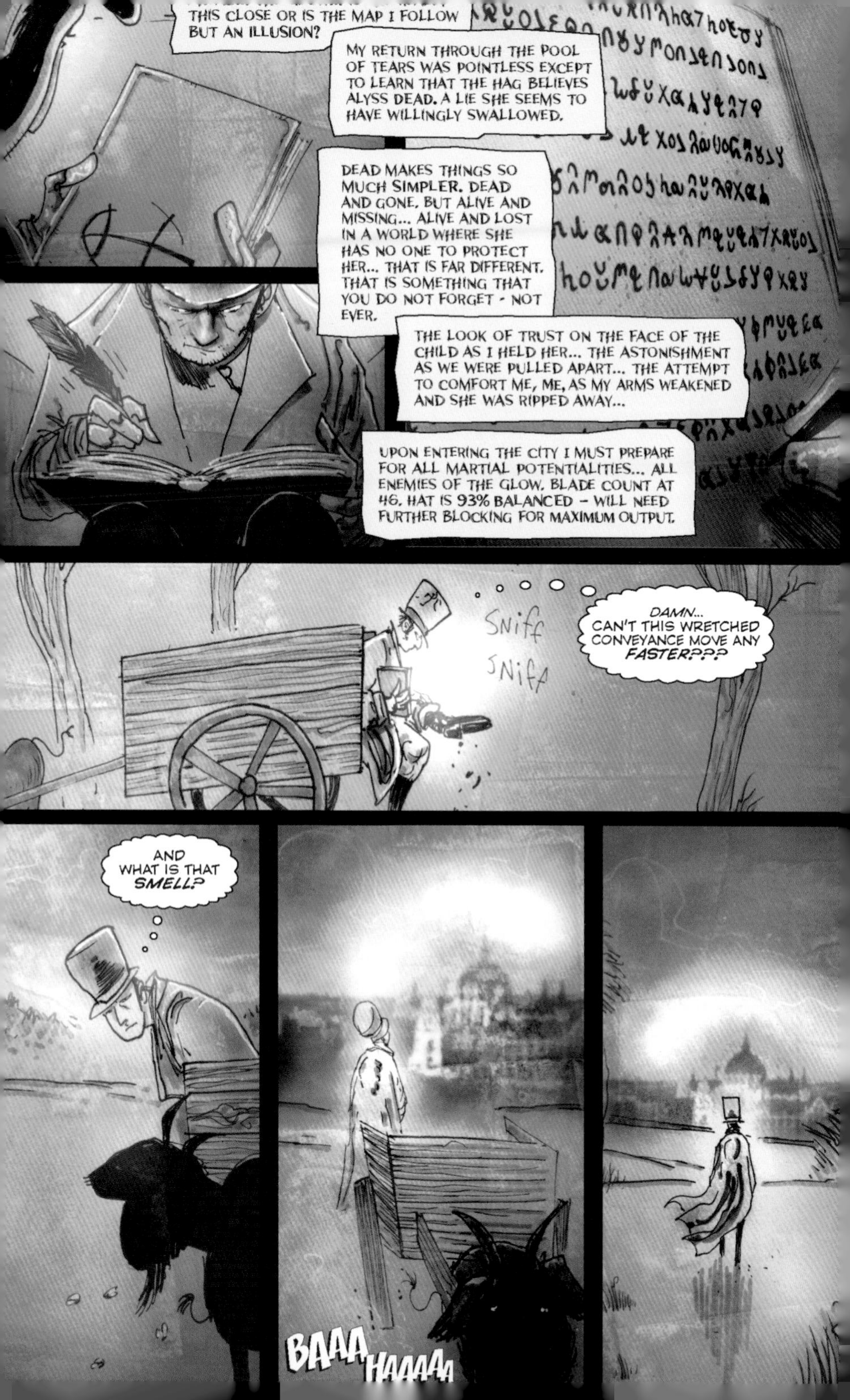
THIS CLOSE OR IS THE MAP I FOLLOW BUT AN ILLUSION?
MY RETURN THROUGH THE POOL OF TEARS WAS POINTLESS EXCEPT TO LEARN THAT THE HAG BELIEVES ALYSS DEAD. A LIE SHE SEEMS TO HAVE WILLINGLY SWALLOWED.
DEAD MAKES THINGS SO MUCH SIMPLER. DEAD AND GONE. BUT ALIVE AND MISSING... ALIVE AND LOST IN A WORLD WHERE SHE HAS NO ONE TO PROTECT HER... THAT IS FAR DIFFERENT. THAT IS SOMETHING THAT YOU DO NOT FORGET - NOT EVER.
THE LOOK OF TRUST ON THE FACE OF THE CHILD AS I HELD HER... THE ASTONISHMENT AS WE WERE PULLED APART... THE ATTEMPT TO COMFORT ME, ME, AS MY ARMS WEAKENED AND SHE WAS RIPPED AWAY...
UPON ENTERING THE CITY I MUST PREPARE FOR ALL MARTIAL POTENTIALITIES... ALL ENEMIES OF THE GLOW. BLADE COUNT AT 46. HAT IS 93% BALANCED - WILL NEED FURTHER BLOCKING FOR MAXIMUM OUTPUT.
SNiff
SNiff
DAMN... CAN'T THIS WRETCHED CONVEYANCE MOVE ANY FASTER???
AND WHAT IS THAT SMELL?
BAAAHAAAAA

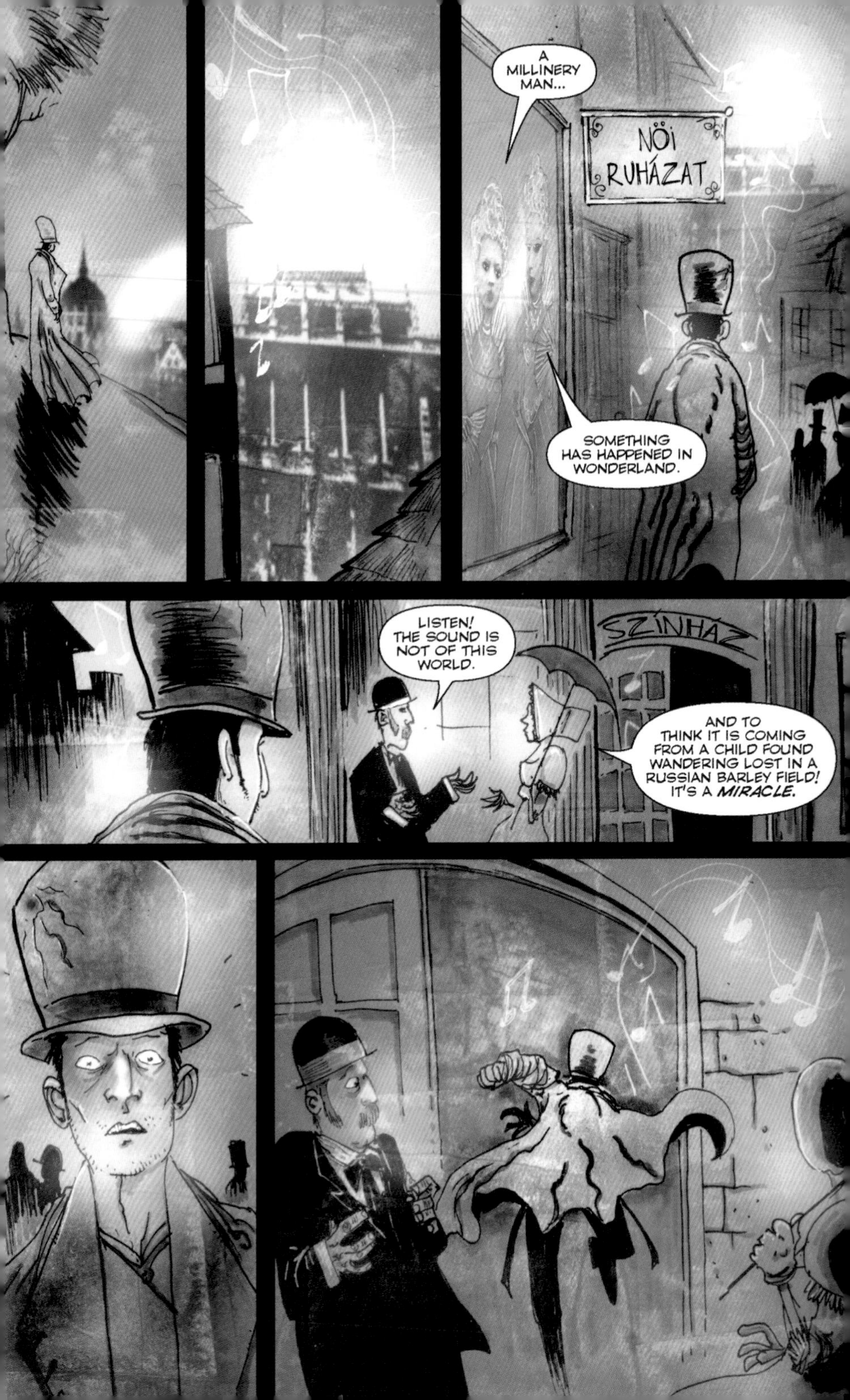
A MILLINERY MAN...
NÖI RUHÁZAT
SOMETHING HAS HAPPENED IN WONDERLAND.
LISTEN! THE SOUND IS NOT OF THIS WORLD.
SZÍNHÁZ
AND TO THINK IT IS COMING FROM A CHILD FOUND WANDERING LOST IN A RUSSIAN BARLEY FIELD! IT'S A *MIRACLE*.

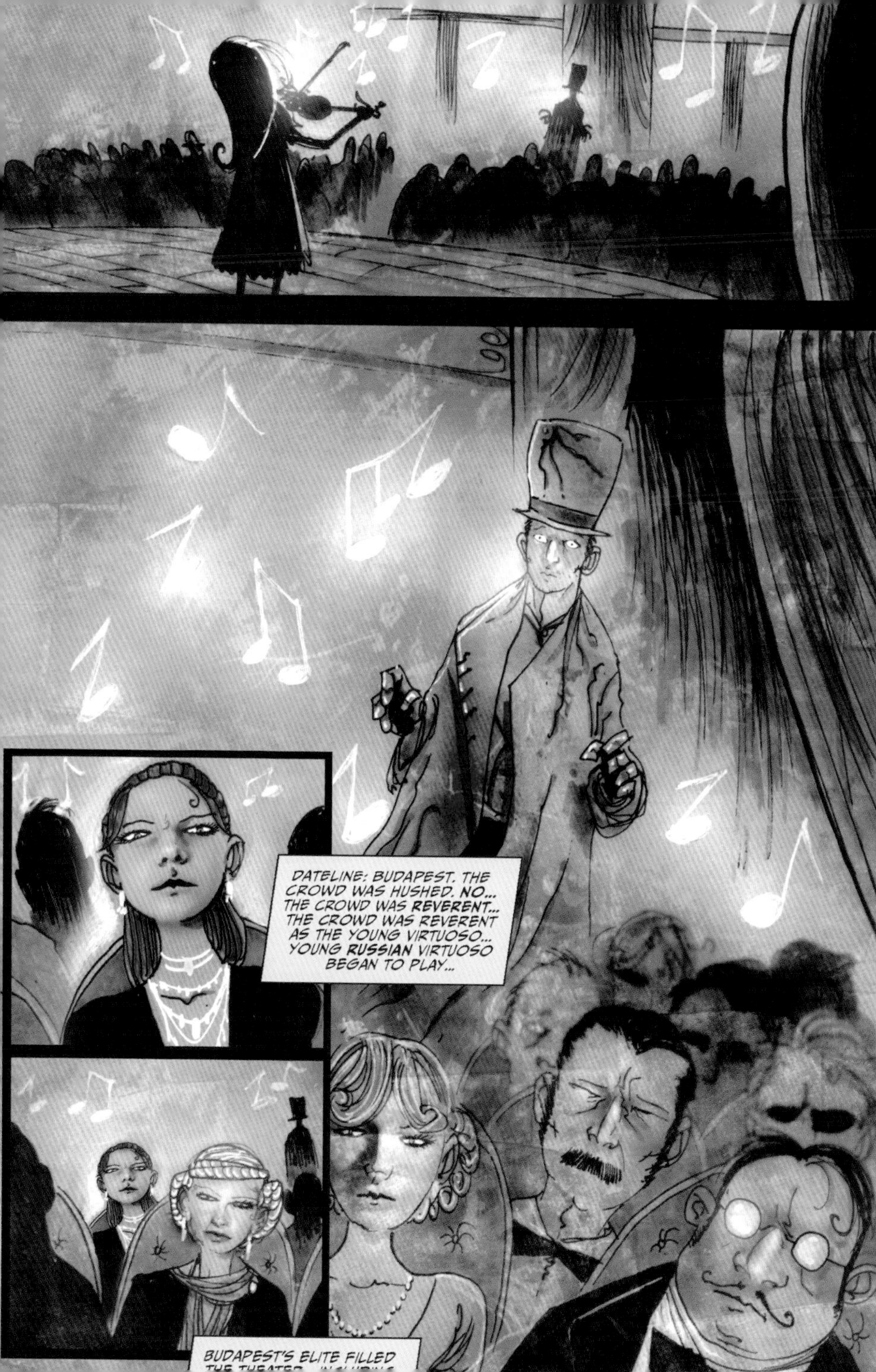
DATELINE: BUDAPEST. THE CROWD WAS HUSHED. NO... THE CROWD WAS REVERENT... ...THE CROWD WAS REVERENT AS THE YOUNG VIRTUOSO... YOUNG RUSSIAN VIRTUOSO BEGAN TO PLAY...
BUDAPEST'S ELITE FILLED

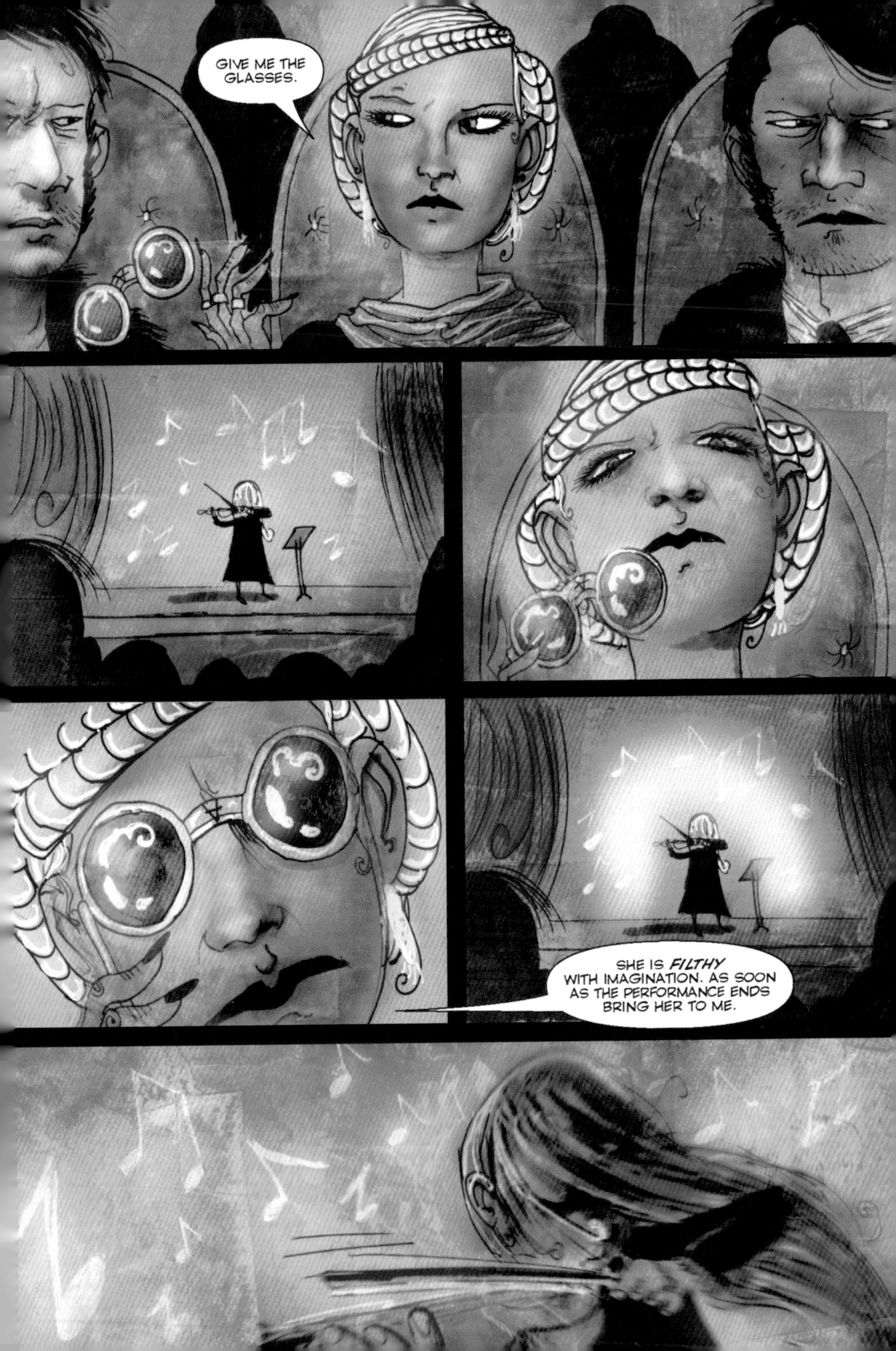
GIVE ME THE GLASSES.
SHE IS *FILTHY* WITH IMAGINATION. AS SOON AS THE PERFORMANCE ENDS BRING HER TO ME.

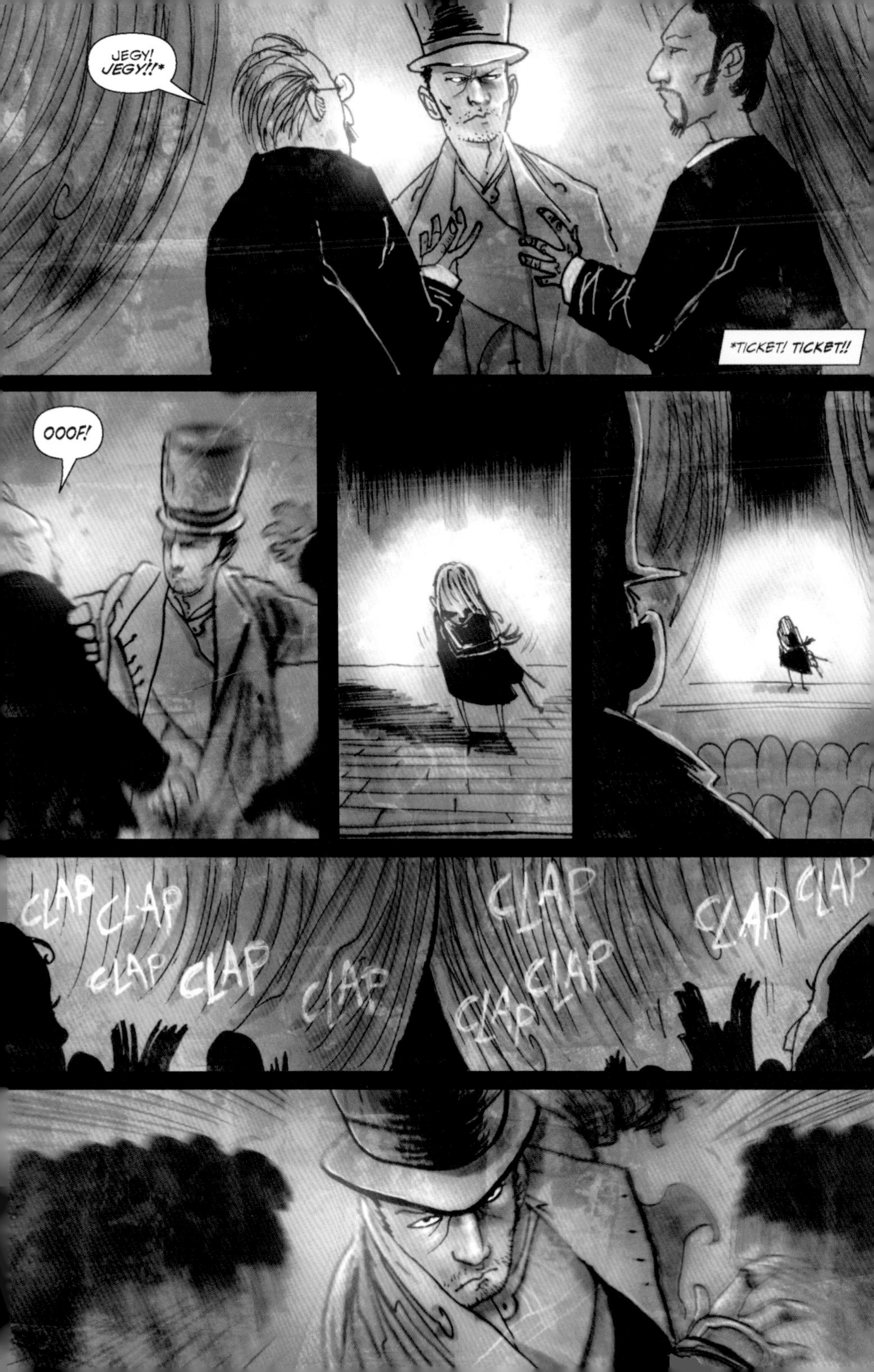
JEGY! JEGY!!*
*TICKET! TICKET!!
OOOF!
CLAP CLAP CLAP CLAP CLAP CLAP CLAP CLAP CLAP CLAP

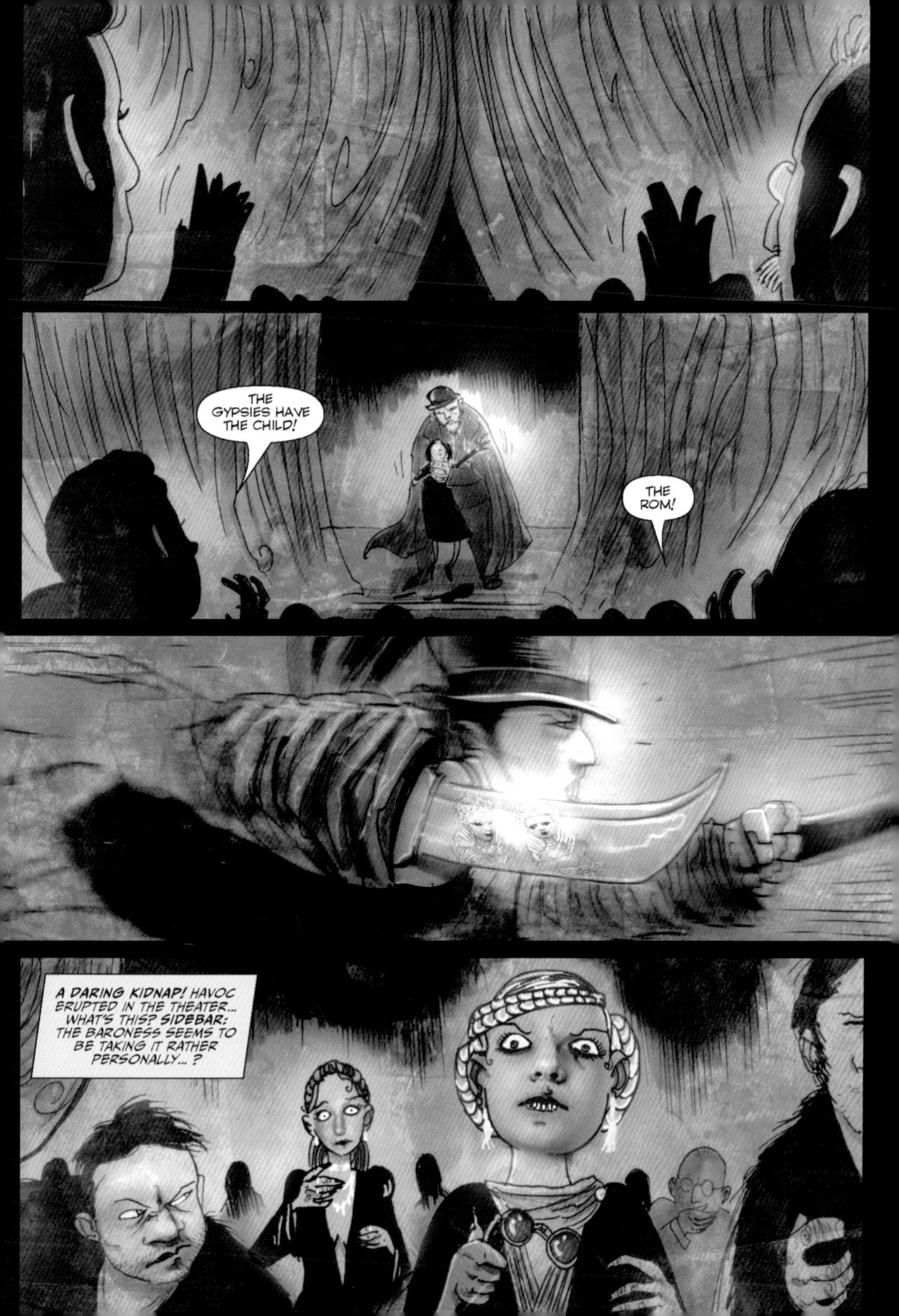
THE GYPSIES HAVE THE CHILD!
THE ROM!
A DARING KIDNAP! HAVOC ERUPTED IN THE THEATER... WHAT'S THIS? SIDEBAR: THE BARONESS SEEMS TO BE TAKING IT RATHER PERSONALLY... ?

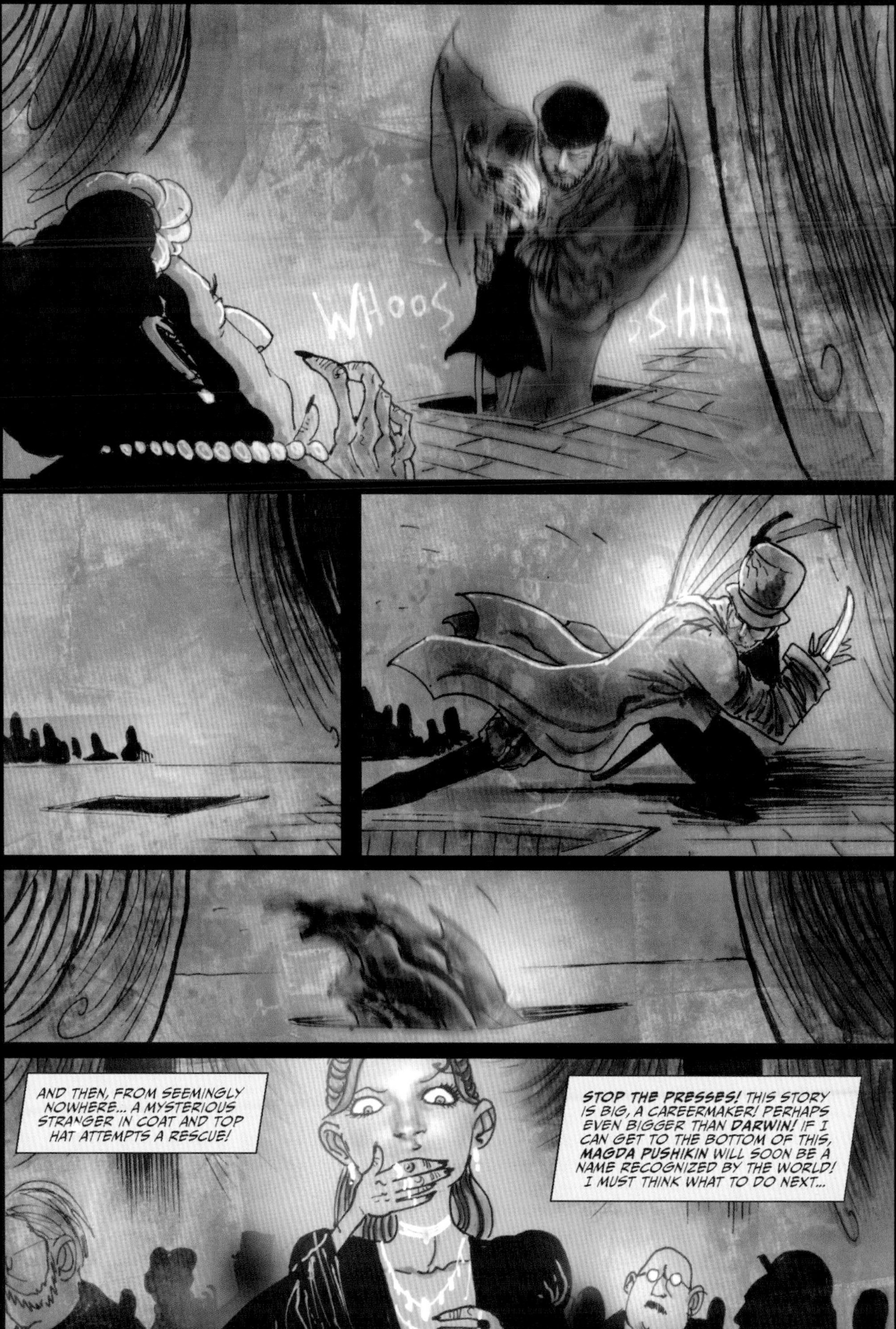
WHOOSSHH
AND THEN, FROM SEEMINGLY NOWHERE... A MYSTERIOUS STRANGER IN COAT AND TOP HAT ATTEMPTS A RESCUE!
STOP THE PRESSES! THIS STORY IS BIG, A CAREERMAKER! PERHAPS EVEN BIGGER THAN DARWIN! IF I CAN GET TO THE BOTTOM OF THIS, MAGDA PUSHIKIN WILL SOON BE A NAME RECOGNIZED BY THE WORLD! I MUST THINK WHAT TO DO NEXT...

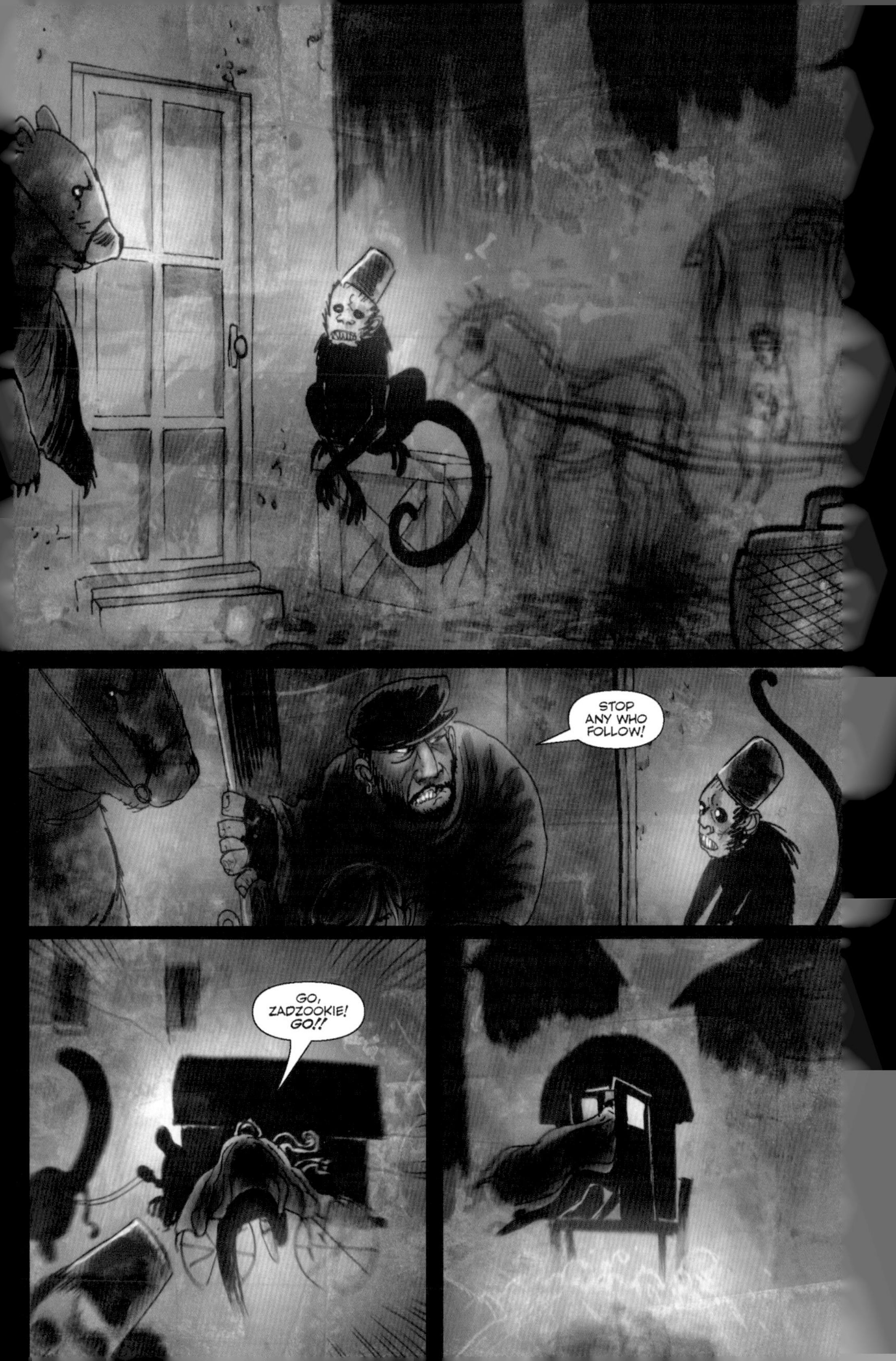
STOP ANY WHO FOLLOW!
GO, ZADZOOKIE! GO!!

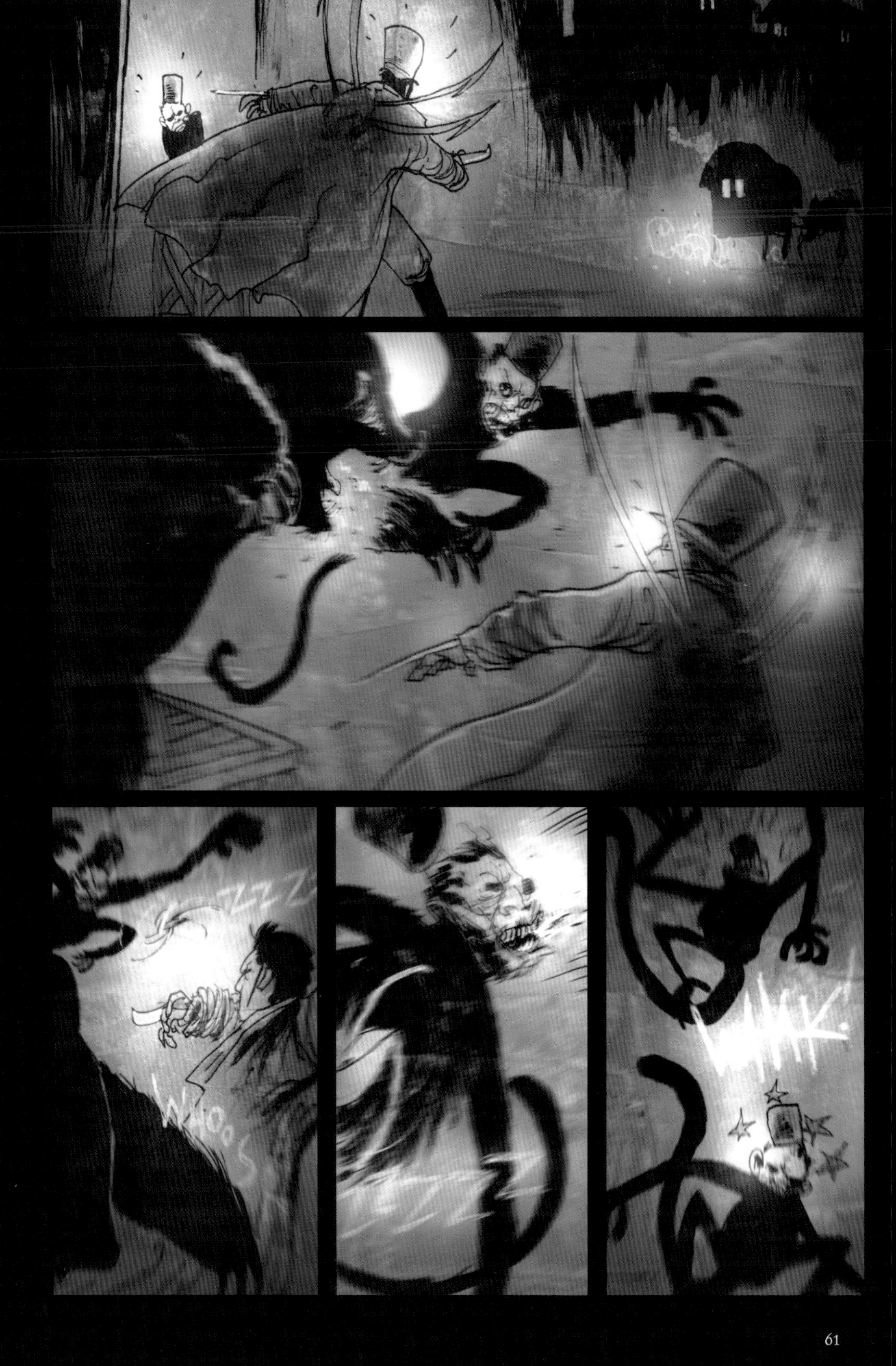
WHOOSH
WAK!

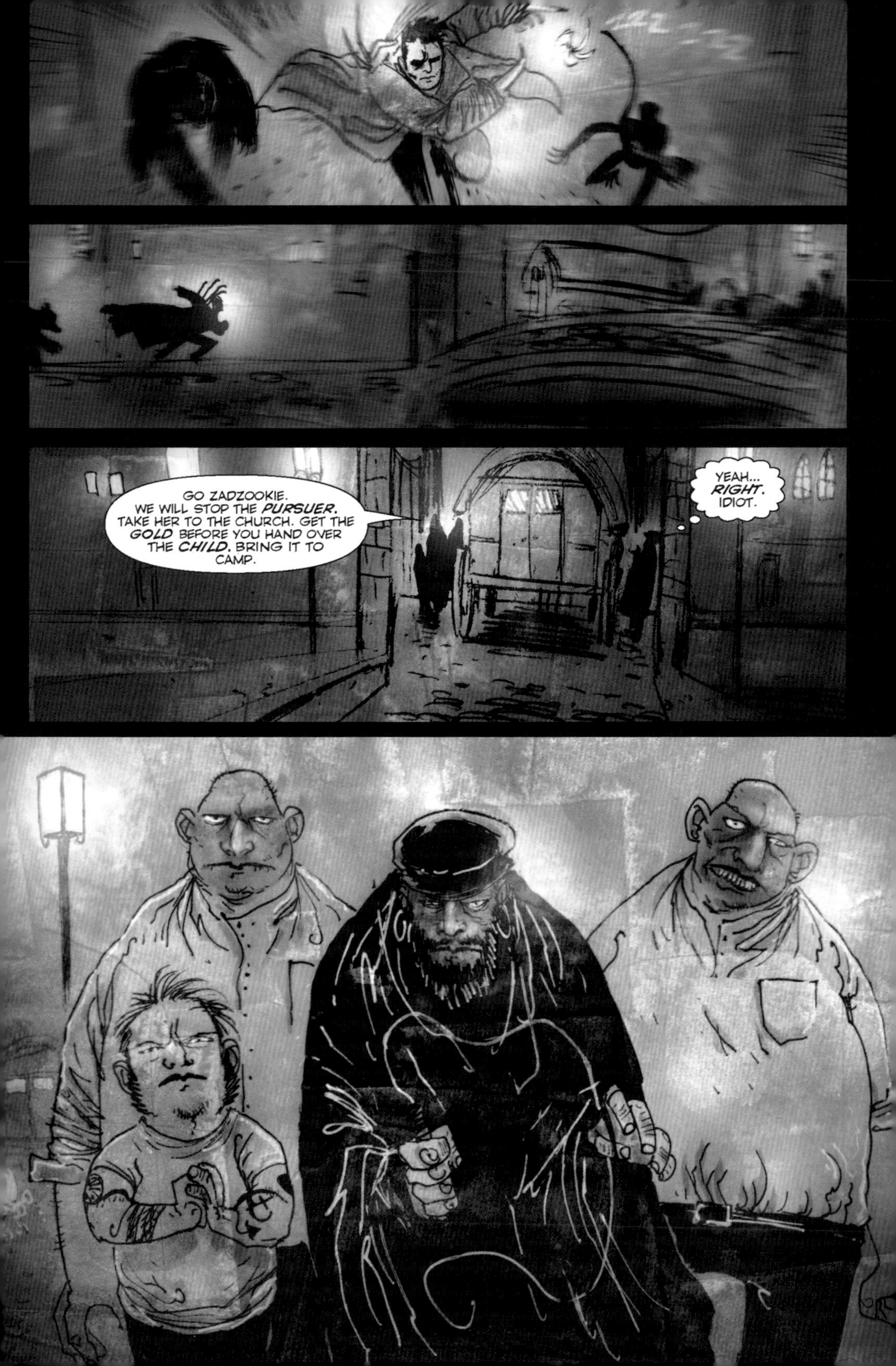
GO ZADZOOKIE. WE WILL STOP THE PURSUER. TAKE HER TO THE CHURCH. GET THE GOLD BEFORE YOU HAND OVER THE CHILD. BRING IT TO CAMP.
YEAH... RIGHT. IDIOT.

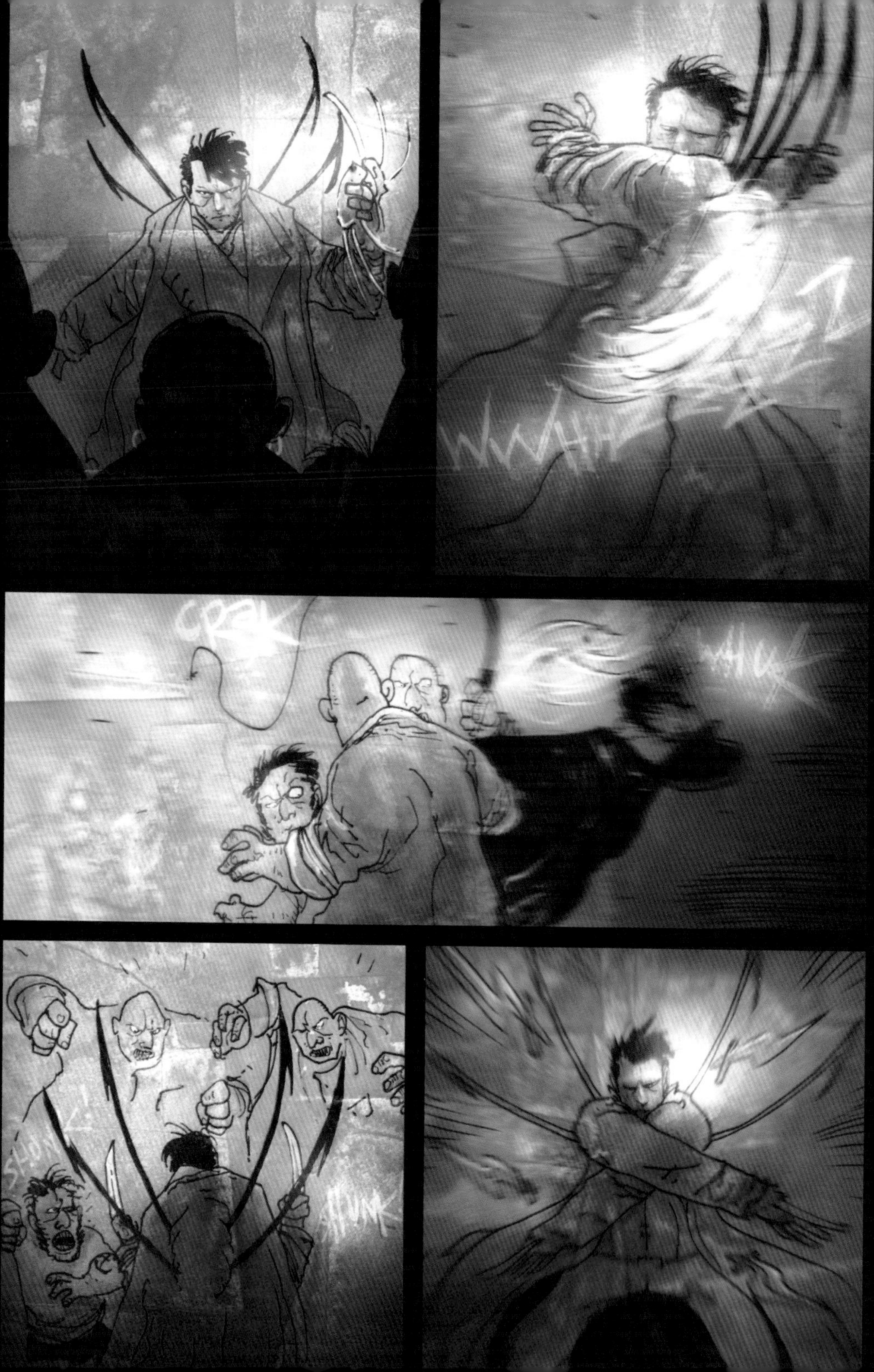

WWAHH
CRAK
SHUNK
SHUNK

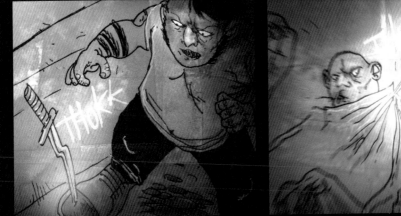

SKREEE WEEAAH WEAAA OOK OOK!? *

* YOU WANT SOME OF THIS, HATBOY?!

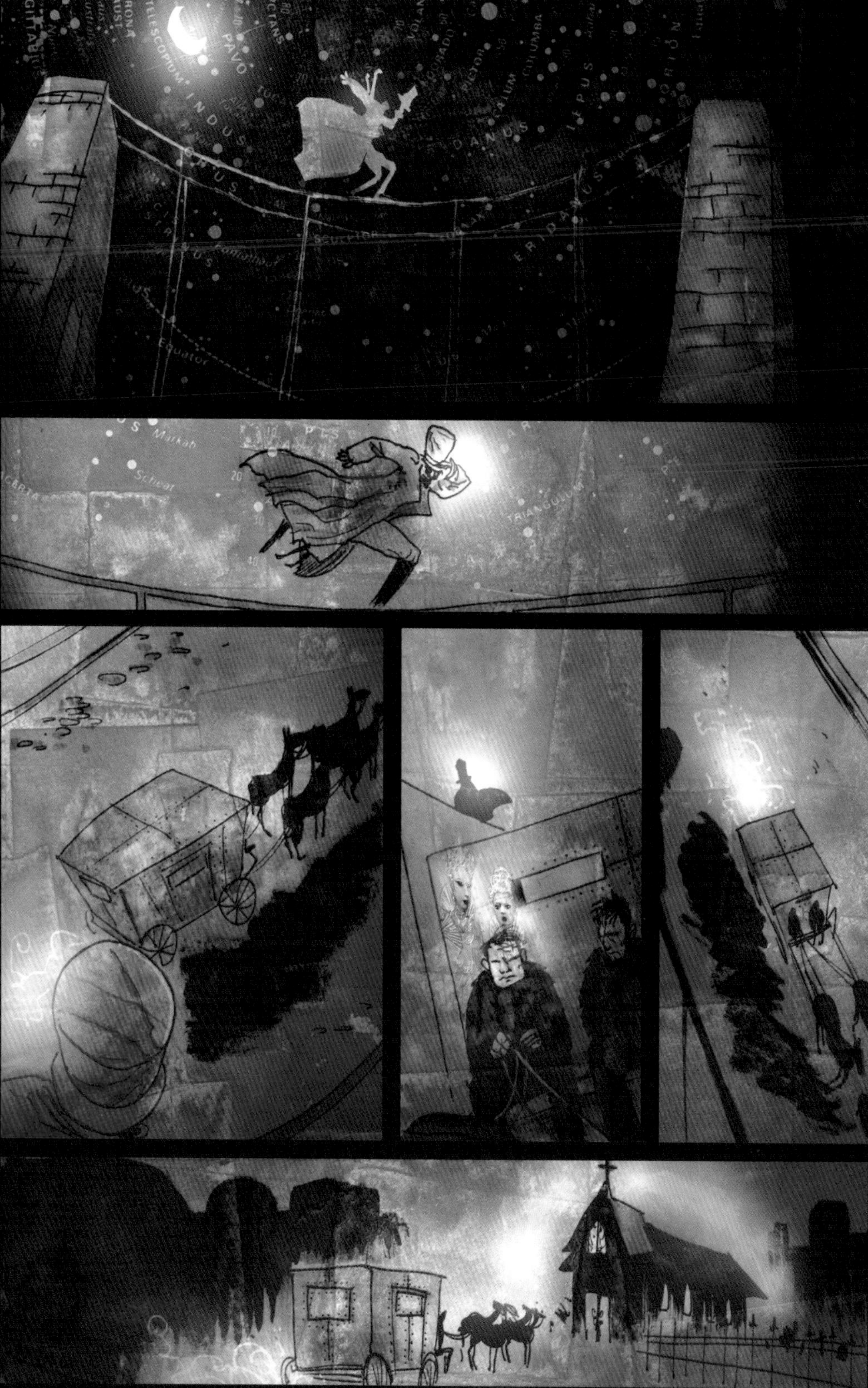

PAVO
INDUS
TELESCOPIUM
COLUMBA
PICTOR
CAELUM
LEPUS
ERIDANUS
Equator
Markab
Scheat
TRIANGULUM

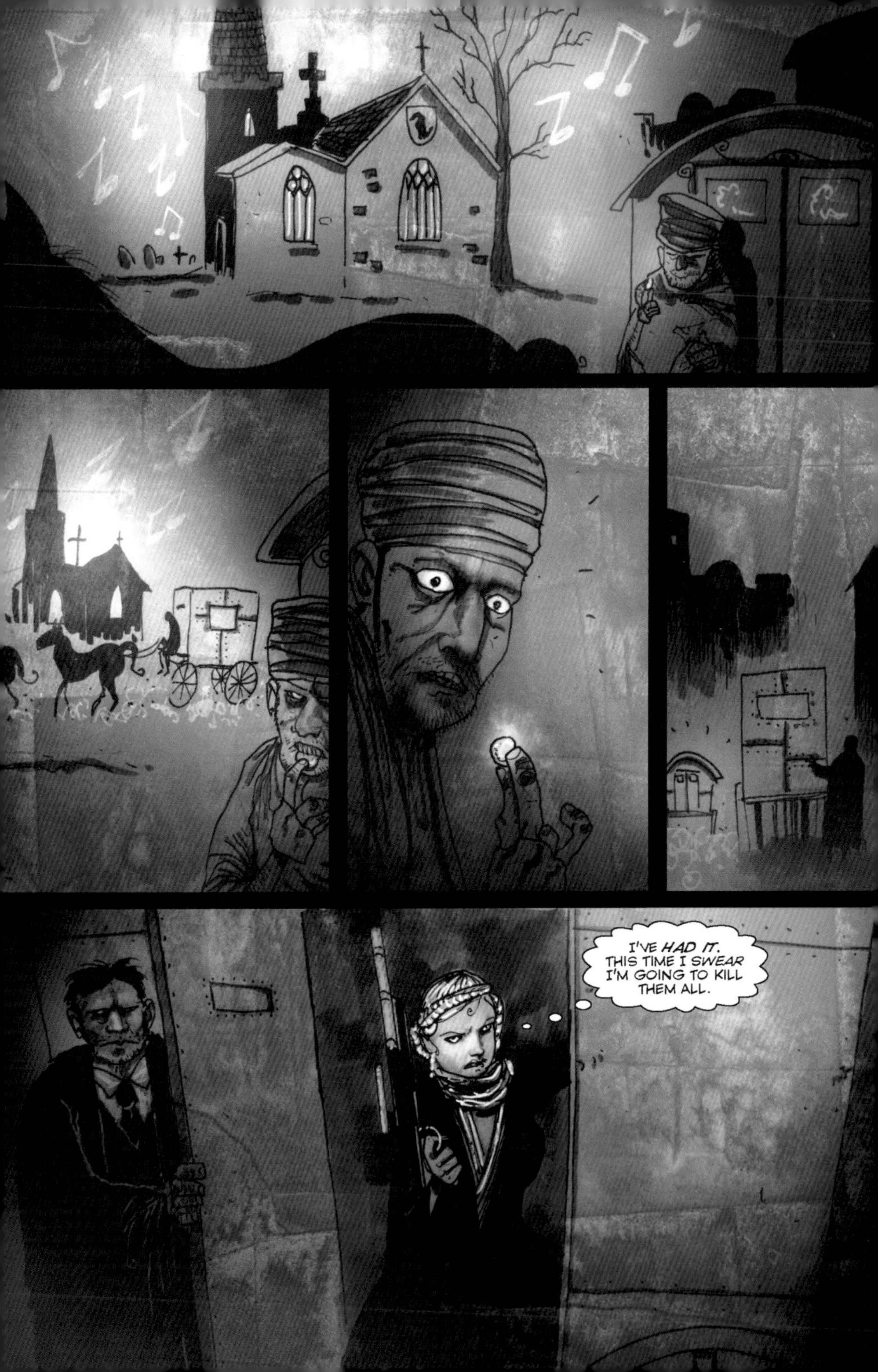
I'VE HAD IT. THIS TIME I SWEAR I'M GOING TO KILL THEM ALL.

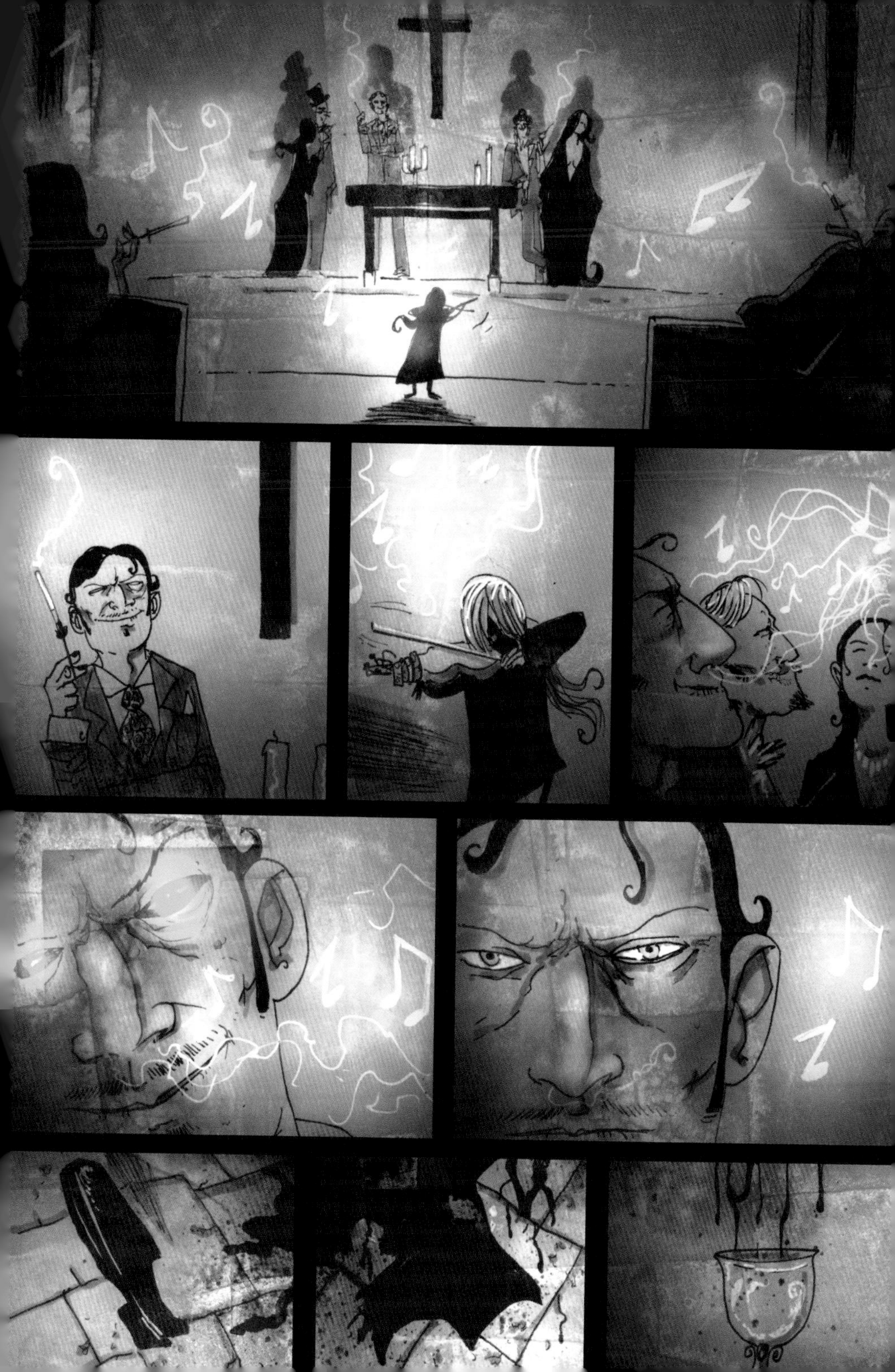

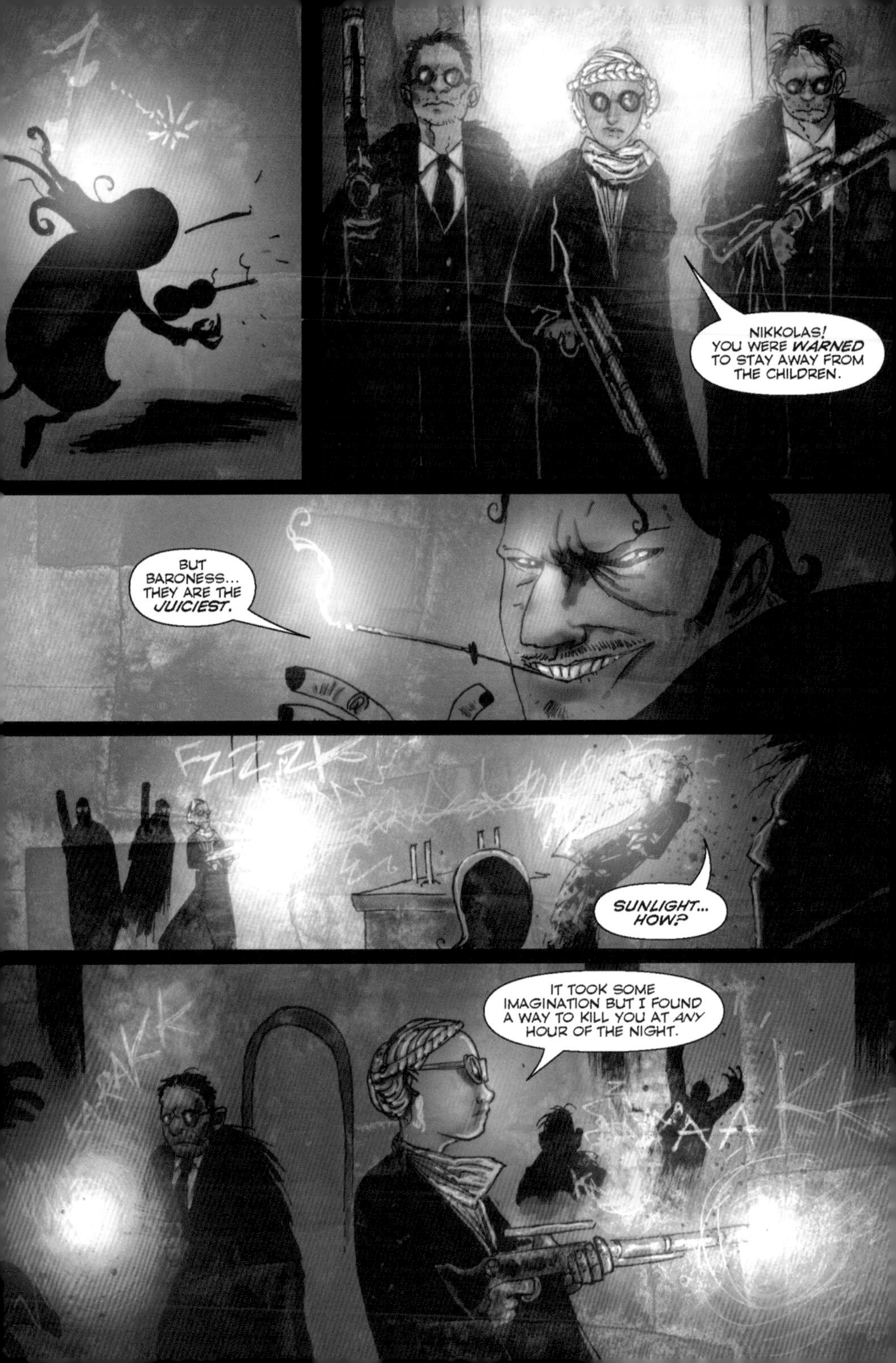
NIKKOLAS! YOU WERE *WARNED* TO STAY AWAY FROM THE CHILDREN.
BUT BARONESS... THEY ARE THE *JUICIEST*.
SUNLIGHT... HOW?
IT TOOK SOME IMAGINATION BUT I FOUND A WAY TO KILL YOU AT *ANY* HOUR OF THE NIGHT.

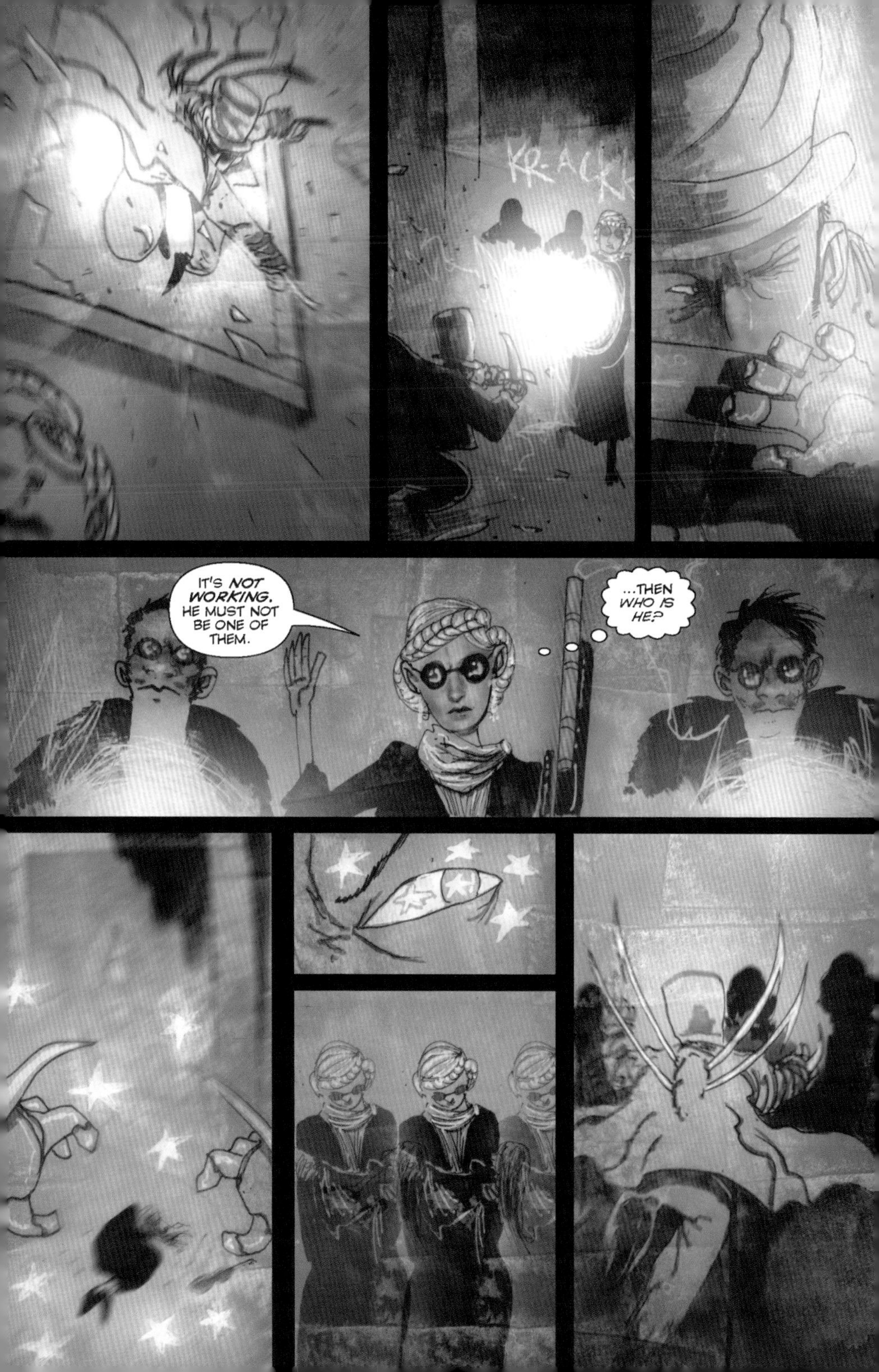
KR-ACKK
IT'S NOT WORKING. HE MUST NOT BE ONE OF THEM.
...THEN WHO IS HE?

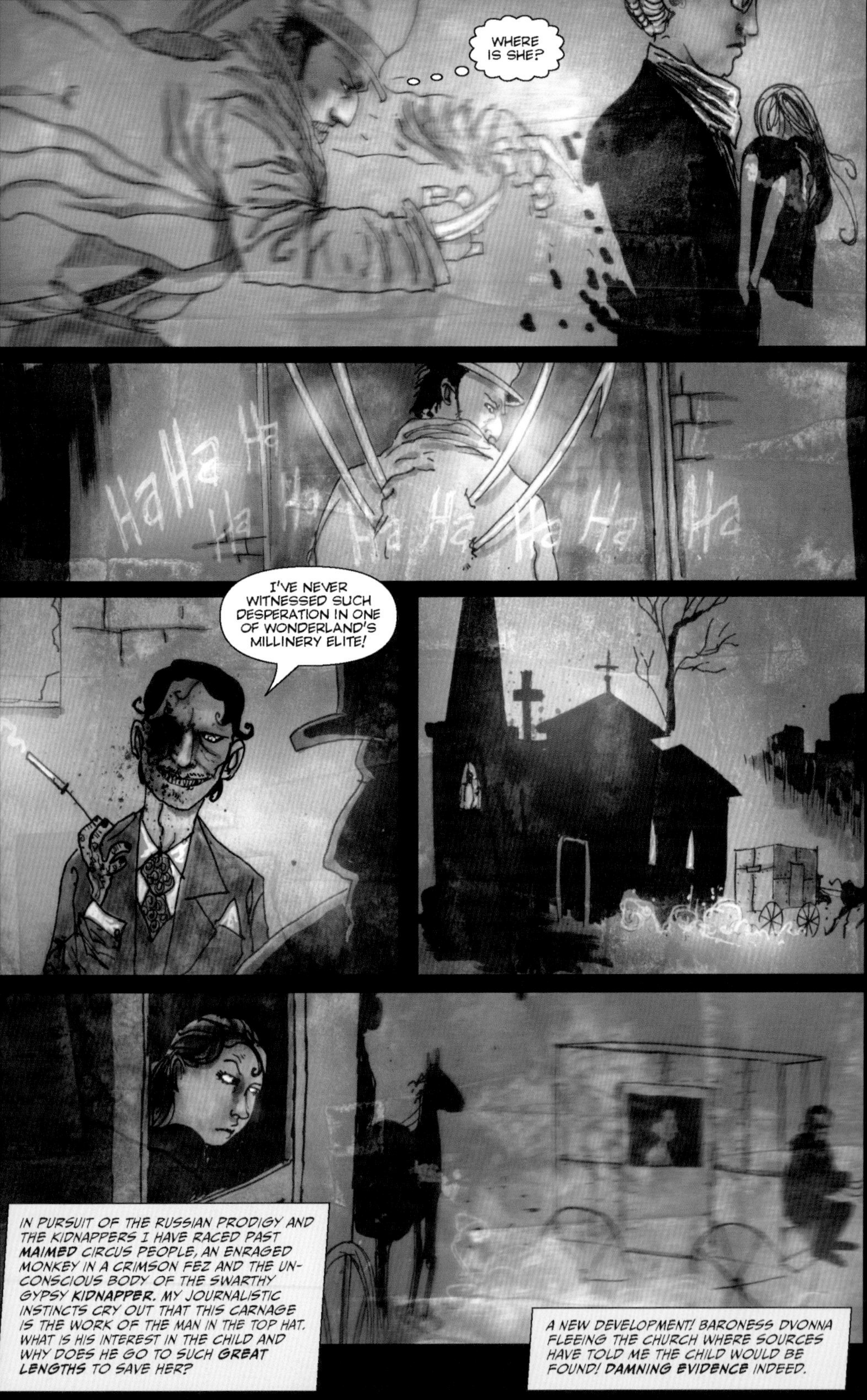
WHERE IS SHE?
I'VE NEVER WITNESSED SUCH DESPERATION IN ONE OF WONDERLAND'S MILLINERY ELITE!
IN PURSUIT OF THE RUSSIAN PRODIGY AND THE KIDNAPPERS I HAVE RACED PAST **MAIMED** CIRCUS PEOPLE, AN ENRAGED MONKEY IN A CRIMSON FEZ AND THE UN-CONSCIOUS BODY OF THE SWARTHY GYPSY **KIDNAPPER.** MY JOURNALISTIC INSTINCTS CRY OUT THAT THIS CARNAGE IS THE WORK OF THE MAN IN THE TOP HAT. WHAT IS HIS INTEREST IN THE CHILD AND WHY DOES HE GO TO SUCH **GREAT LENGTHS** TO SAVE HER?
A NEW DEVELOPMENT! BARONESS DVONNA FLEEING THE CHURCH WHERE SOURCES HAVE TOLD ME THE CHILD WOULD BE FOUND! **DAMNING EVIDENCE** INDEED.

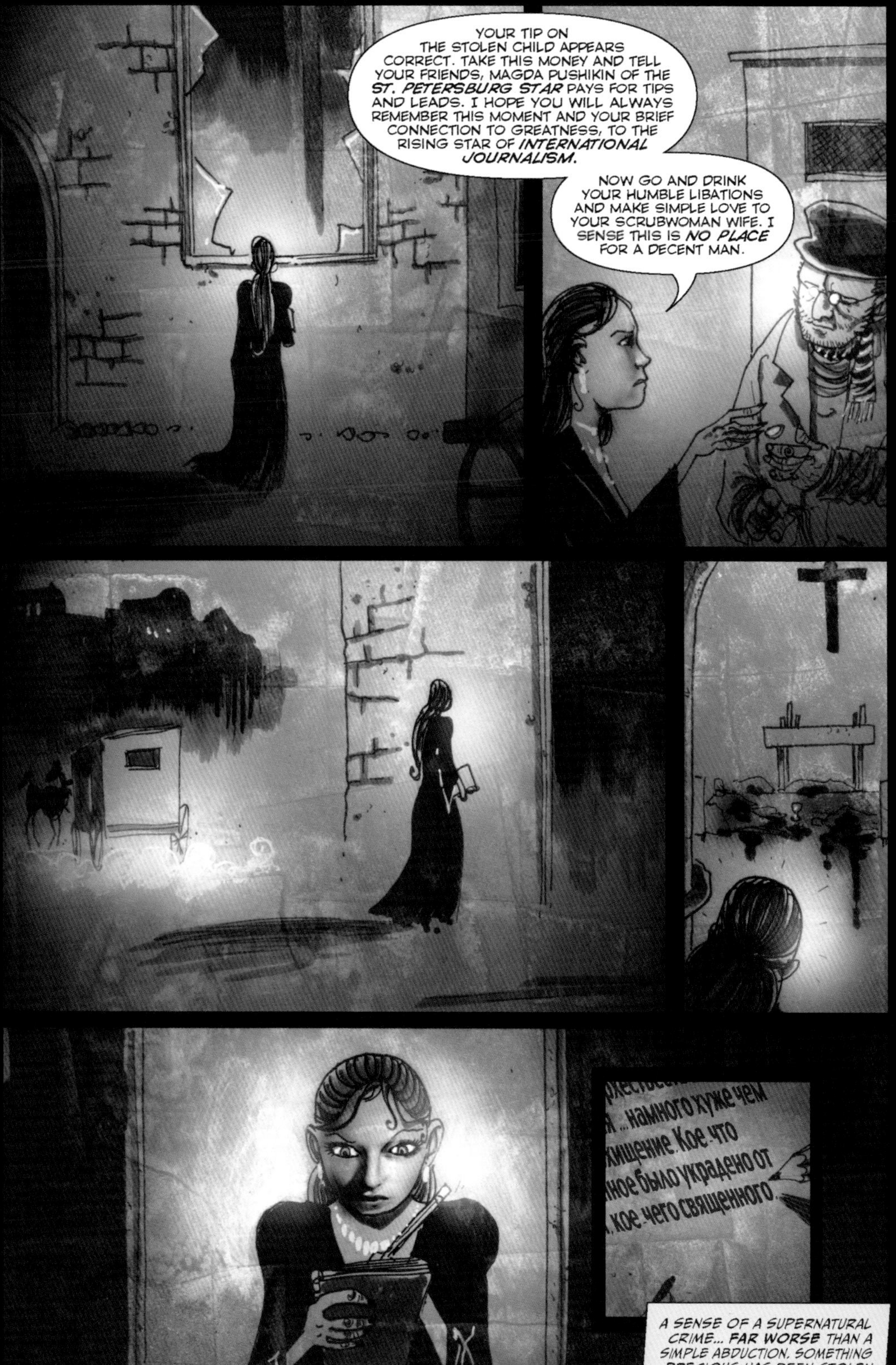
YOUR TIP ON THE STOLEN CHILD APPEARS CORRECT. TAKE THIS MONEY AND TELL YOUR FRIENDS, MAGDA PUSHIKIN OF THE ST. PETERSBURG STAR PAYS FOR TIPS AND LEADS. I HOPE YOU WILL ALWAYS REMEMBER THIS MOMENT AND YOUR BRIEF CONNECTION TO GREATNESS, TO THE RISING STAR OF INTERNATIONAL JOURNALISM.
NOW GO AND DRINK YOUR HUMBLE LIBATIONS AND MAKE SIMPLE LOVE TO YOUR SCRUBWOMAN WIFE. I SENSE THIS IS NO PLACE FOR A DECENT MAN.
намного хуже чем
хищение. Кое-что
ное было украдено от
Кое-чего священного.
A SENSE OF A SUPERNATURAL CRIME... FAR WORSE THAN A SIMPLE ABDUCTION. SOMETHING PRECIOUS HAS BEEN STOLEN IN THIS CHURCH...SOMETHING SACRED.

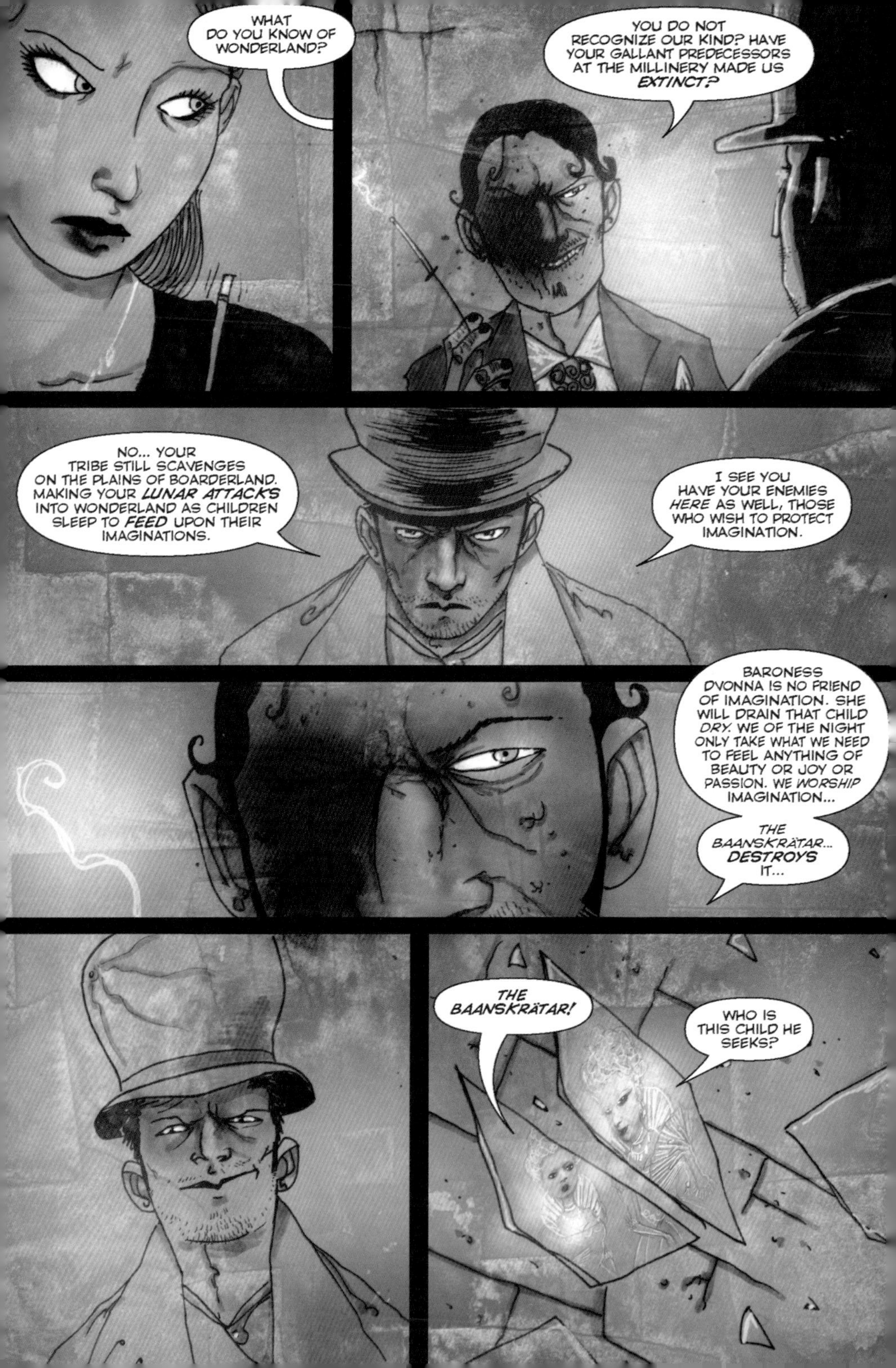
WHAT DO YOU KNOW OF WONDERLAND?
YOU DO NOT RECOGNIZE OUR KIND? HAVE YOUR GALLANT PREDECESSORS AT THE MILLINERY MADE US *EXTINCT?*
NO... YOUR TRIBE STILL SCAVENGES ON THE PLAINS OF BOARDERLAND. MAKING YOUR *LUNAR ATTACKS* INTO WONDERLAND AS CHILDREN SLEEP TO *FEED* UPON THEIR IMAGINATIONS.
I SEE YOU HAVE YOUR ENEMIES *HERE* AS WELL, THOSE WHO WISH TO PROTECT IMAGINATION.
BARONESS DVONNA IS NO FRIEND OF IMAGINATION. SHE WILL DRAIN THAT CHILD *DRY.* WE OF THE NIGHT ONLY TAKE WHAT WE NEED TO FEEL ANYTHING OF BEAUTY OR JOY OR PASSION. WE *WORSHIP* IMAGINATION...
THE BAANSKRÄTAR... ***DESTROYS*** IT...
THE BAANSKRÄTAR!
WHO IS THIS CHILD HE SEEKS?

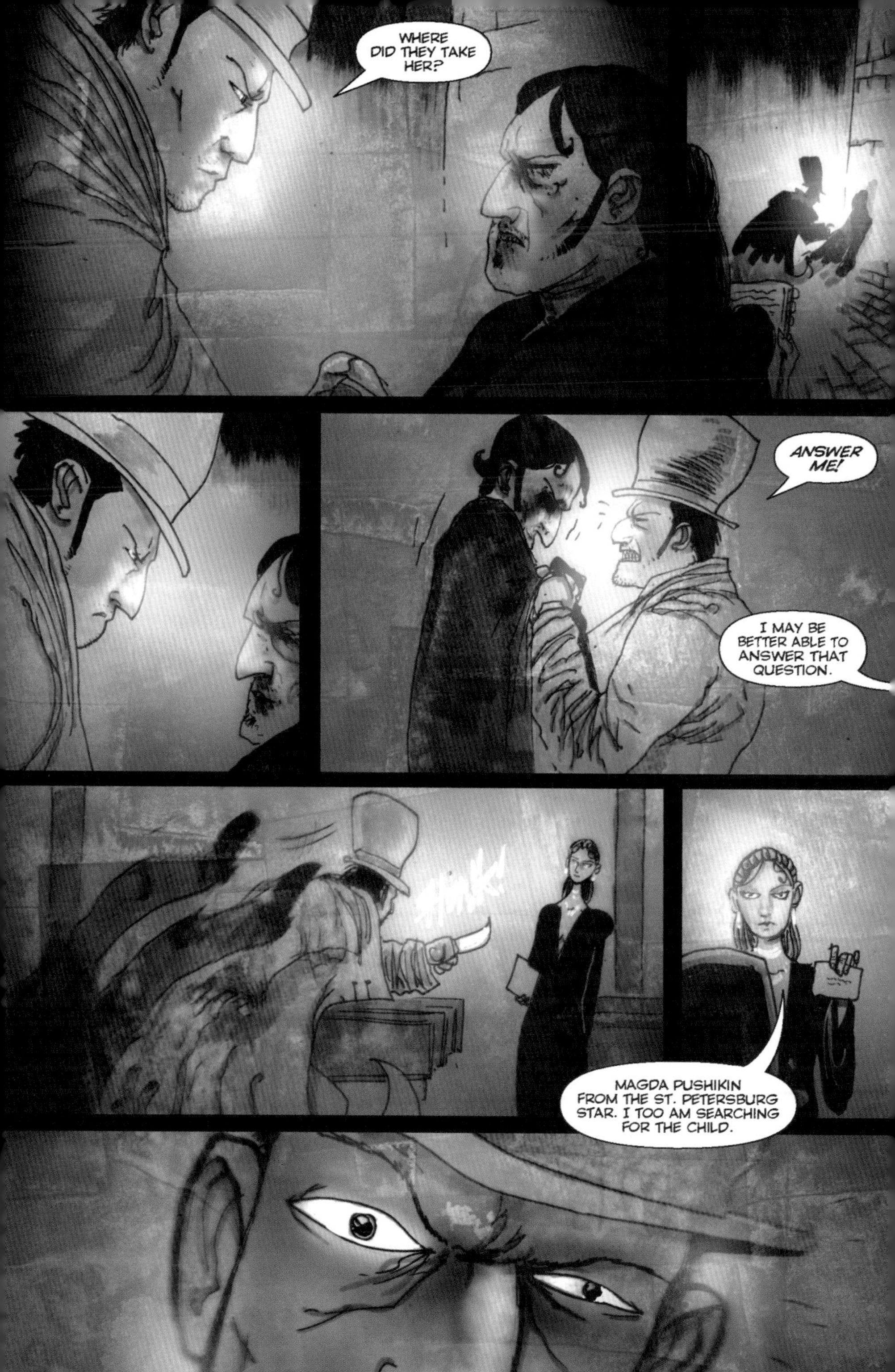
WHERE DID THEY TAKE HER?
ANSWER ME!
I MAY BE BETTER ABLE TO ANSWER THAT QUESTION.
MAGDA PUSHIKIN FROM THE ST. PETERSBURG STAR. I TOO AM SEARCHING FOR THE CHILD.

The palace attack came without warning.

As the Royal Bodyguard for the Queen of Hearts I had only one imperative: to guard my Queen. If I had stayed with her… if I had refused to leave Wonderland I could have saved my Queen's life. But she ordered me to go.

I did not leave her unprotected. Generals Doppel and Gänger and the Heart army, the mighty chessmen, the palace guard had all pledged to sacrifice their lives for hers. But I alone was her bodyguard!

What if Queen Genevieve sacrificed herself to save her daughter for nothing! It was her majesty's last wish that I take her daughter away and keep her safe. At this, I have failed. Queen Genevieve's death will be meaningless unless Alyss is found alive and returned to rule Wonderland.

The Queen is dead.

Long live the Queen.

Long live Alyss.

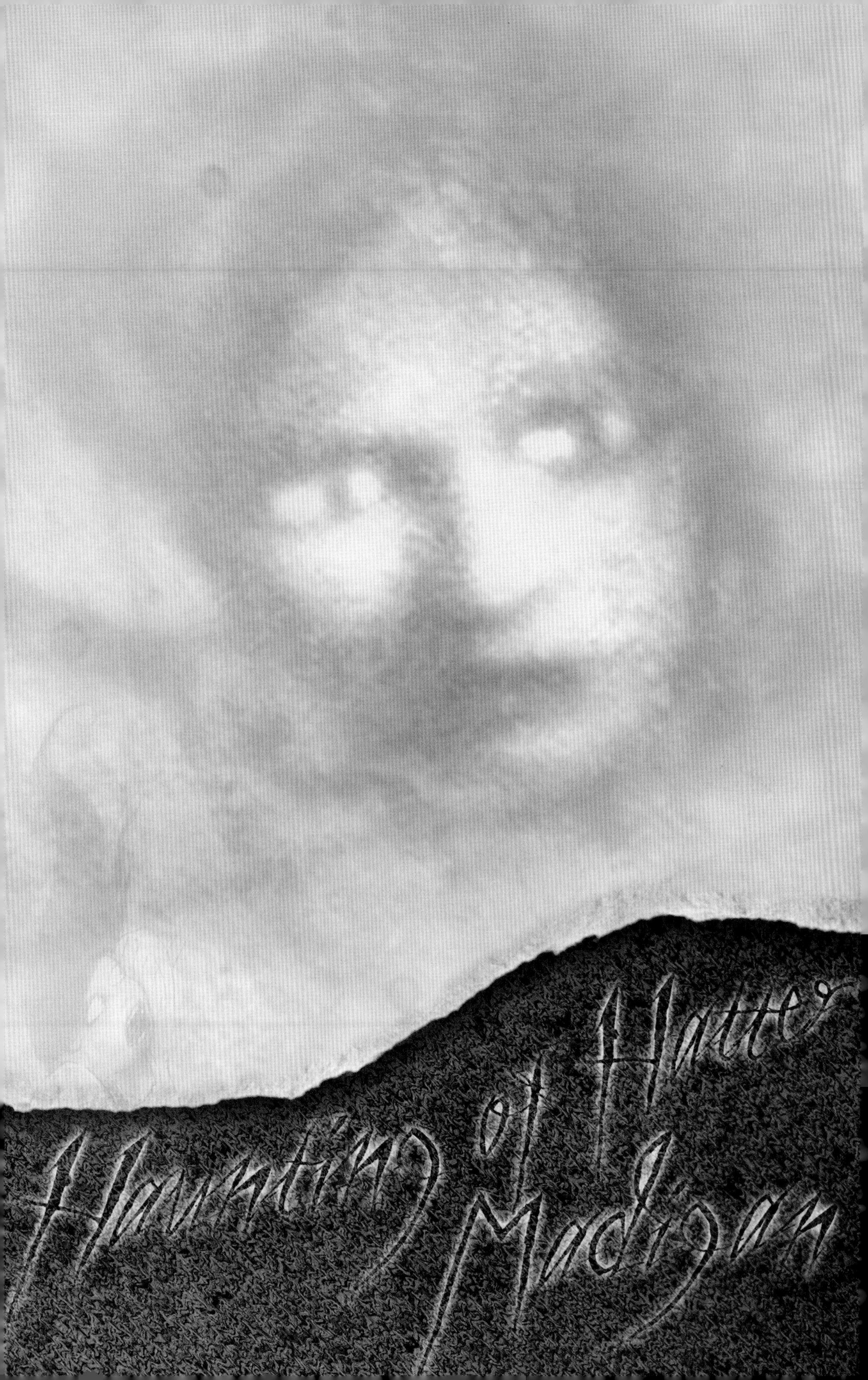
Haunting of Hatter Madigan

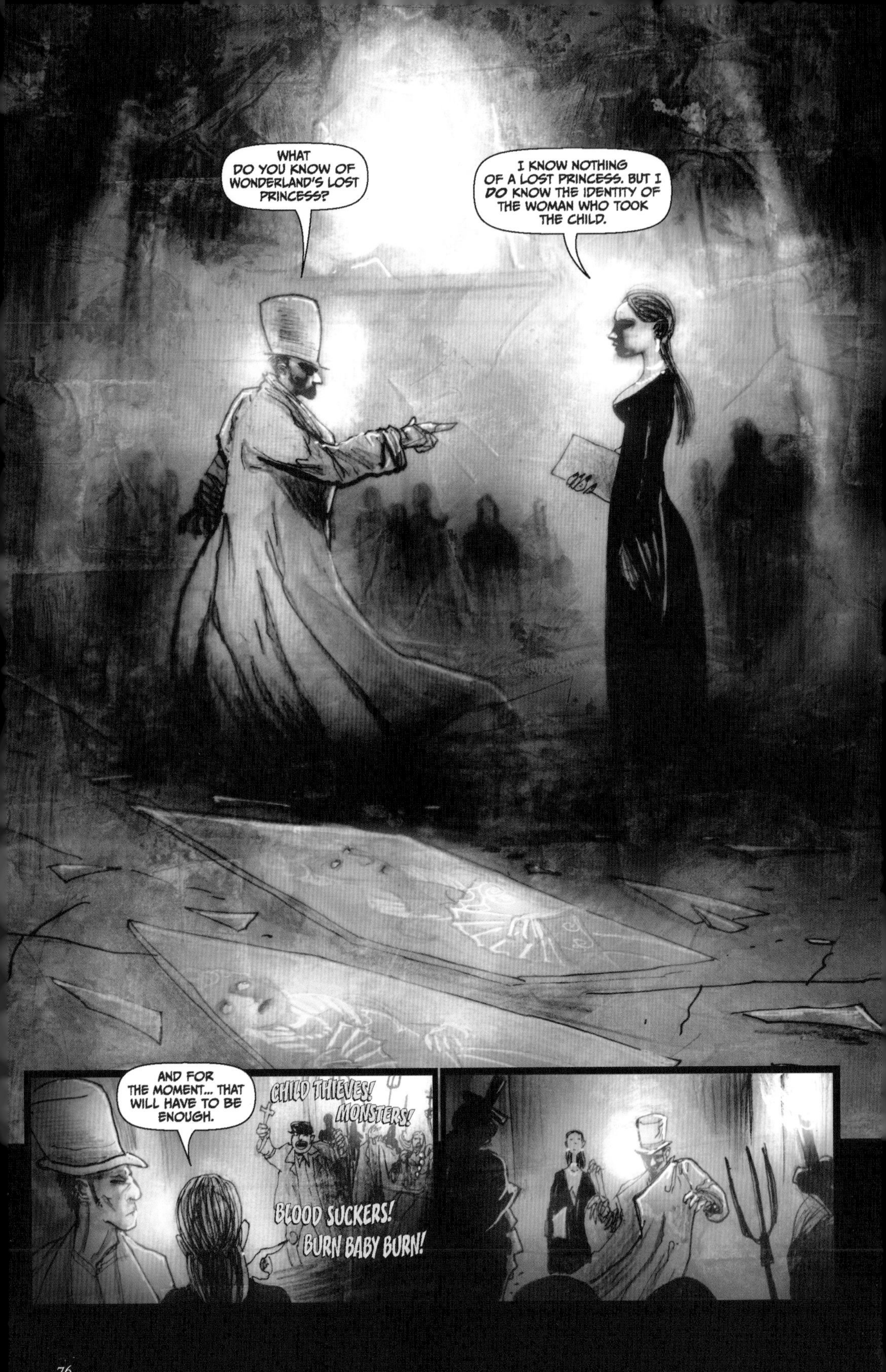
WHAT DO YOU KNOW OF WONDERLAND'S LOST PRINCESS?
I KNOW NOTHING OF A LOST PRINCESS. BUT I *DO* KNOW THE IDENTITY OF THE WOMAN WHO TOOK THE CHILD.
AND FOR THE MOMENT... THAT WILL HAVE TO BE ENOUGH.
CHILD THIEVES!
MONSTERS!
BLOOD SUCKERS!
BURN BABY BURN!

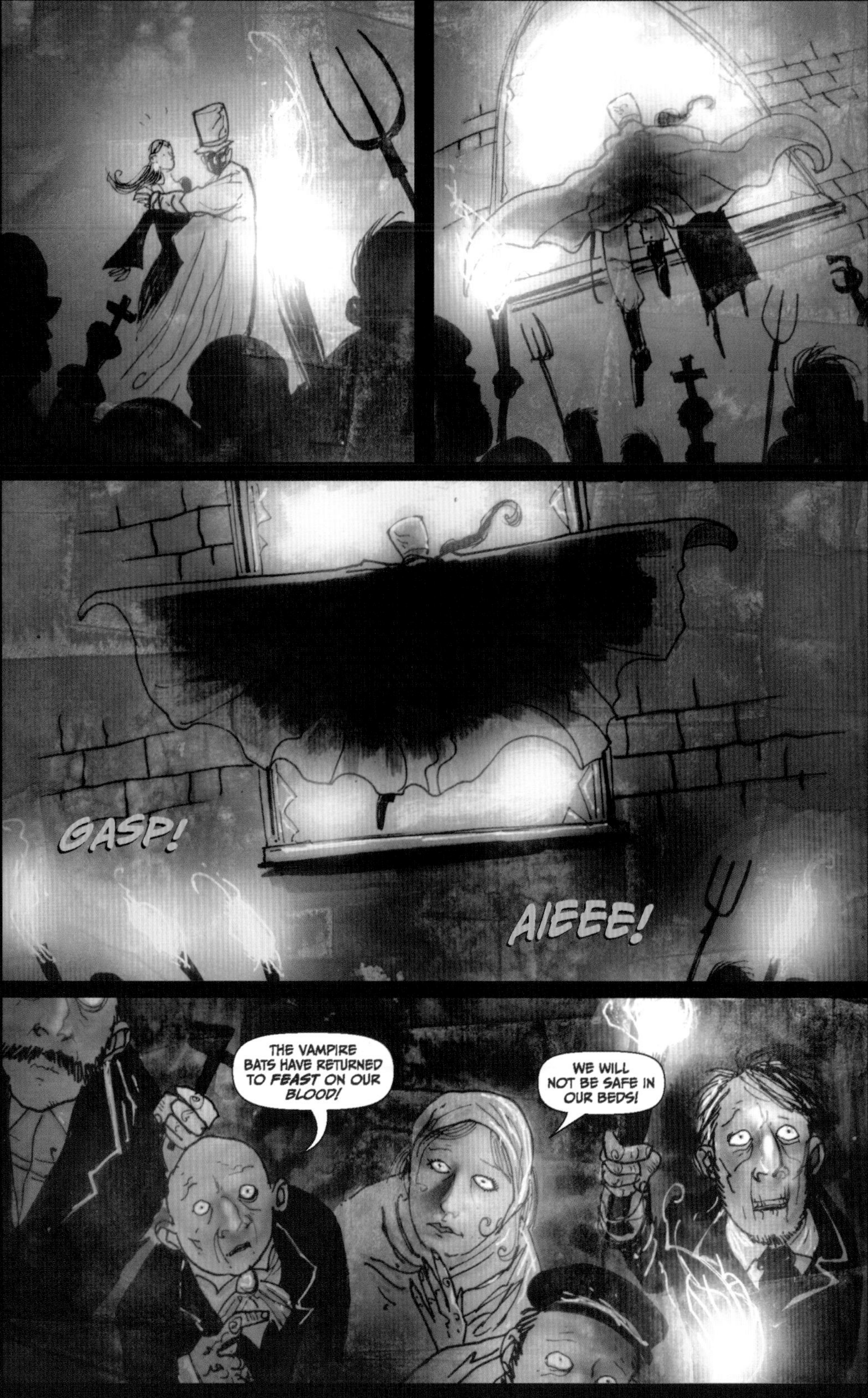
GASP!
AIEEE!
THE VAMPIRE BATS HAVE RETURNED TO FEAST ON OUR BLOOD!
WE WILL NOT BE SAFE IN OUR BEDS!

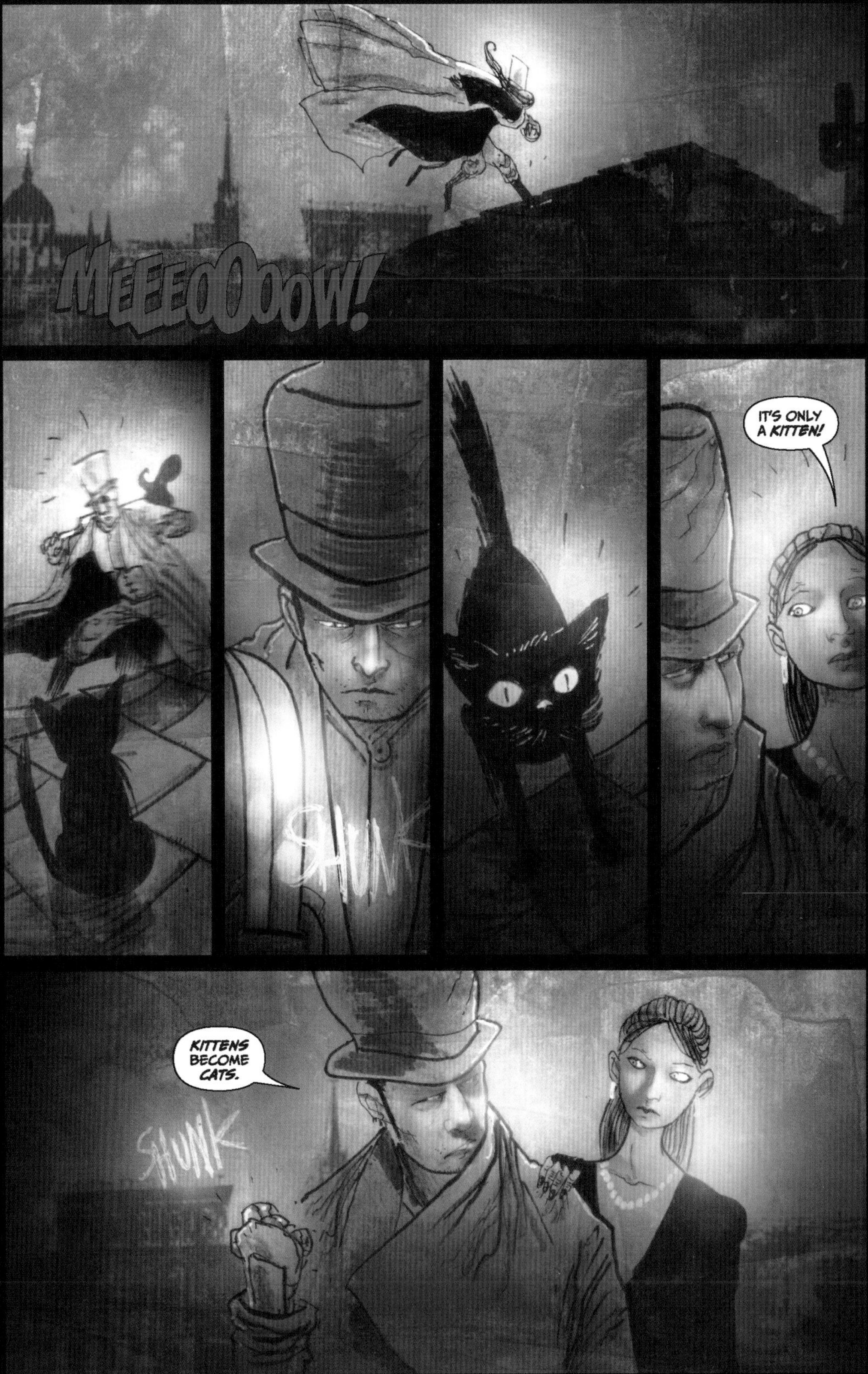
MEEEOOOoow!
SHUNK
IT'S ONLY A KITTEN!
KITTENS BECOME CATS.
SHUNK

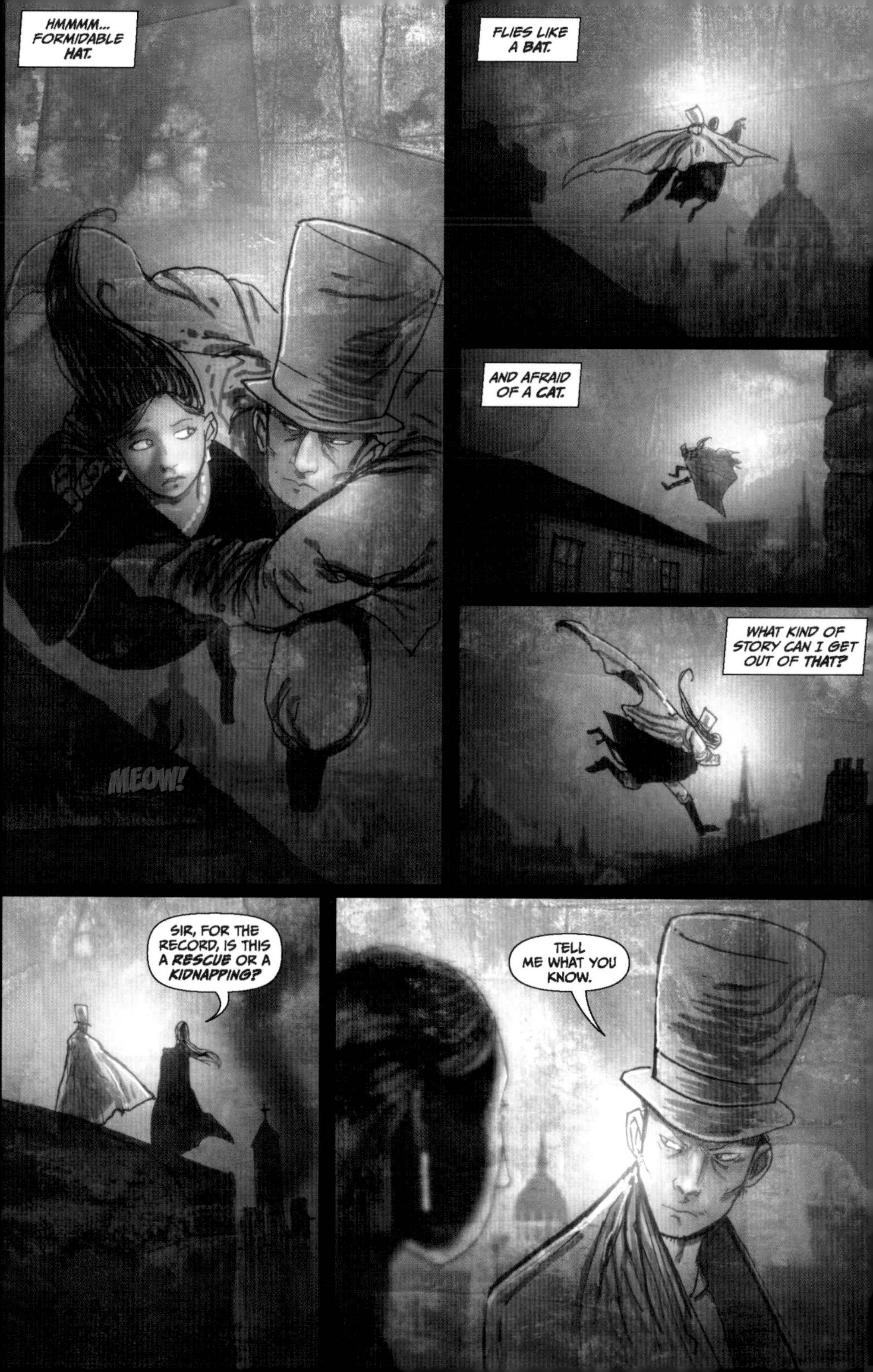
HMMMM... FORMIDABLE HAT.
MEOW!
FLIES LIKE A BAT.
AND AFRAID OF A CAT.
WHAT KIND OF STORY CAN I GET OUT OF THAT?
SIR, FOR THE RECORD, IS THIS A RESCUE OR A KIDNAPPING?
TELL ME WHAT YOU KNOW.

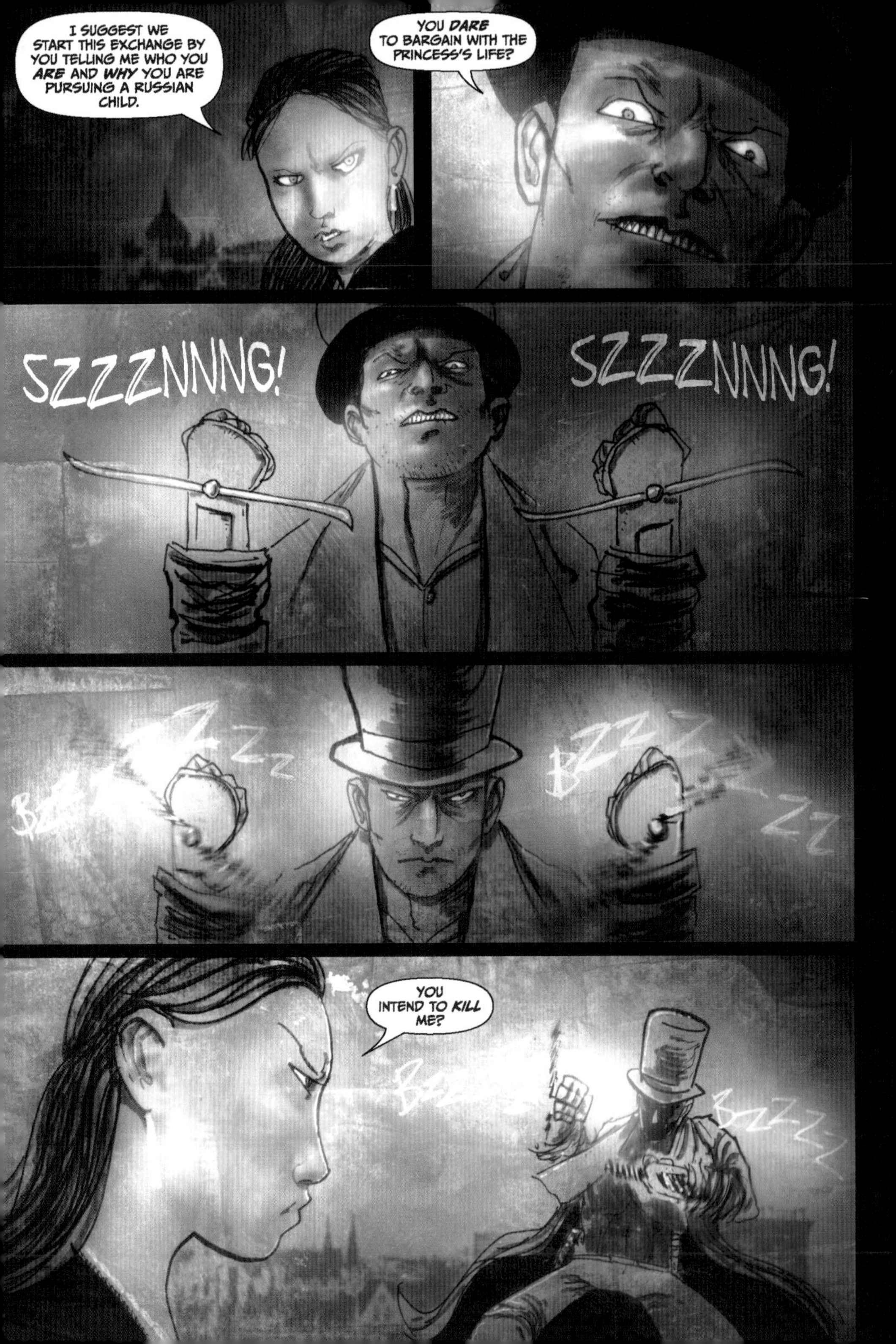
I SUGGEST WE START THIS EXCHANGE BY YOU TELLING ME WHO YOU *ARE* AND *WHY* YOU ARE PURSUING A RUSSIAN CHILD.
YOU *DARE* TO BARGAIN WITH THE PRINCESS'S LIFE?
SZZZNNNG!
SZZZNNNG!
YOU INTEND TO *KILL* ME?

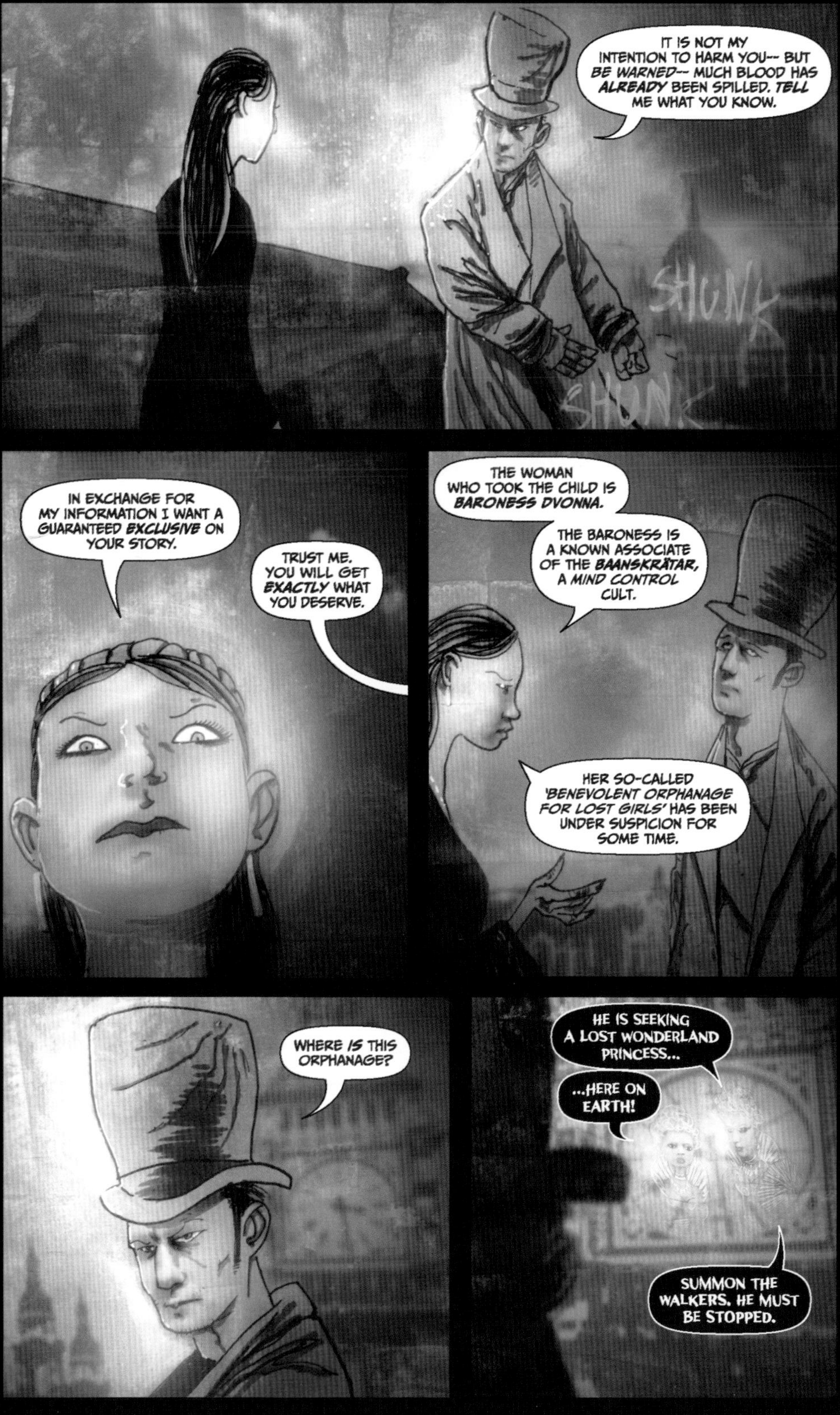
IT IS NOT MY INTENTION TO HARM YOU-- BUT *BE WARNED*-- MUCH BLOOD HAS ***ALREADY*** BEEN SPILLED. ***TELL*** ME WHAT YOU KNOW.
IN EXCHANGE FOR MY INFORMATION I WANT A GUARANTEED ***EXCLUSIVE*** ON YOUR STORY.
TRUST ME. YOU WILL GET ***EXACTLY*** WHAT YOU DESERVE.
THE WOMAN WHO TOOK THE CHILD IS ***BARONESS DVONNA.***
THE BARONESS IS A KNOWN ASSOCIATE OF THE ***BAANSKRÄTAR,*** A *MIND CONTROL* CULT.
HER SO-CALLED *'BENEVOLENT ORPHANAGE FOR LOST GIRLS'* HAS BEEN UNDER SUSPICION FOR SOME TIME.
WHERE *IS* THIS ORPHANAGE?
HE IS SEEKING A LOST WONDERLAND PRINCESS...
...HERE ON EARTH!
SUMMON THE WALKERS. HE MUST BE STOPPED.

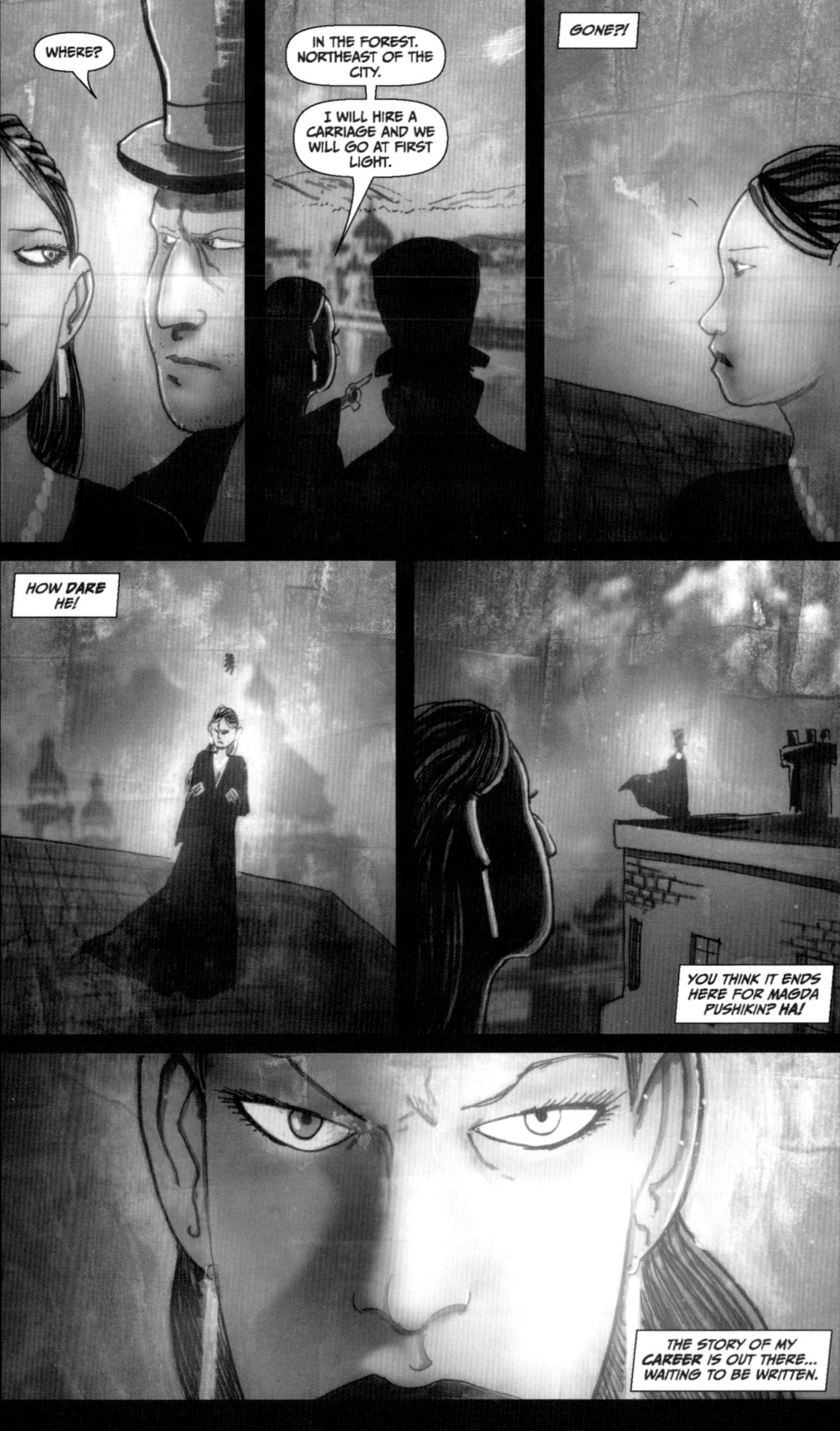
WHERE?
IN THE FOREST. NORTHEAST OF THE CITY.
I WILL HIRE A CARRIAGE AND WE WILL GO AT FIRST LIGHT.
GONE?!
HOW DARE HE!
YOU THINK IT ENDS HERE FOR MAGDA PUSHIKIN? HA!
THE STORY OF MY CAREER IS OUT THERE... WAITING TO BE WRITTEN.

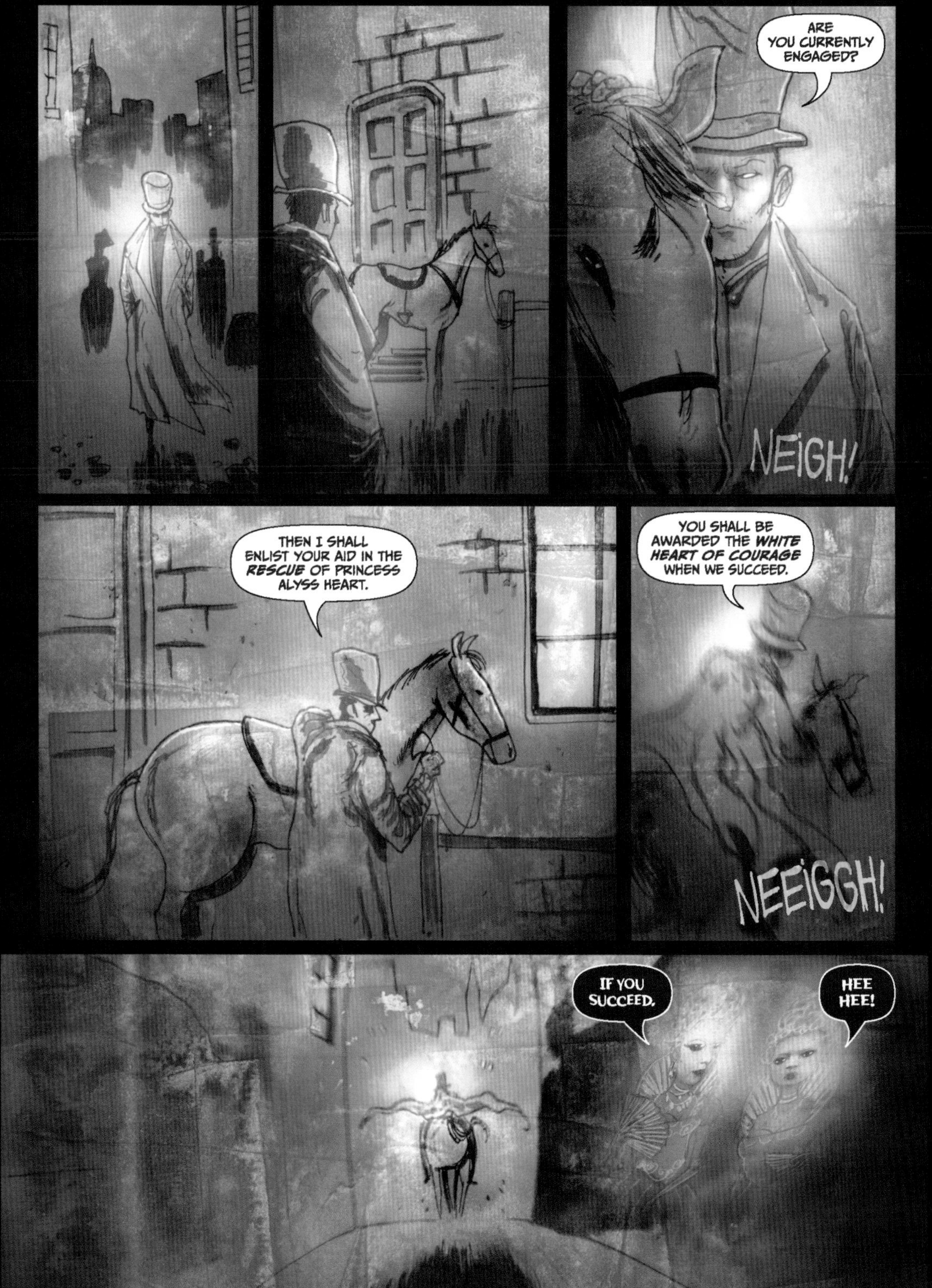
ARE YOU CURRENTLY ENGAGED?
NEIGH!
THEN I SHALL ENLIST YOUR AID IN THE RESCUE OF PRINCESS ALYSS HEART.
YOU SHALL BE AWARDED THE WHITE HEART OF COURAGE WHEN WE SUCCEED.
NEEIGGH!
IF YOU SUCCEED.
HEE HEE!

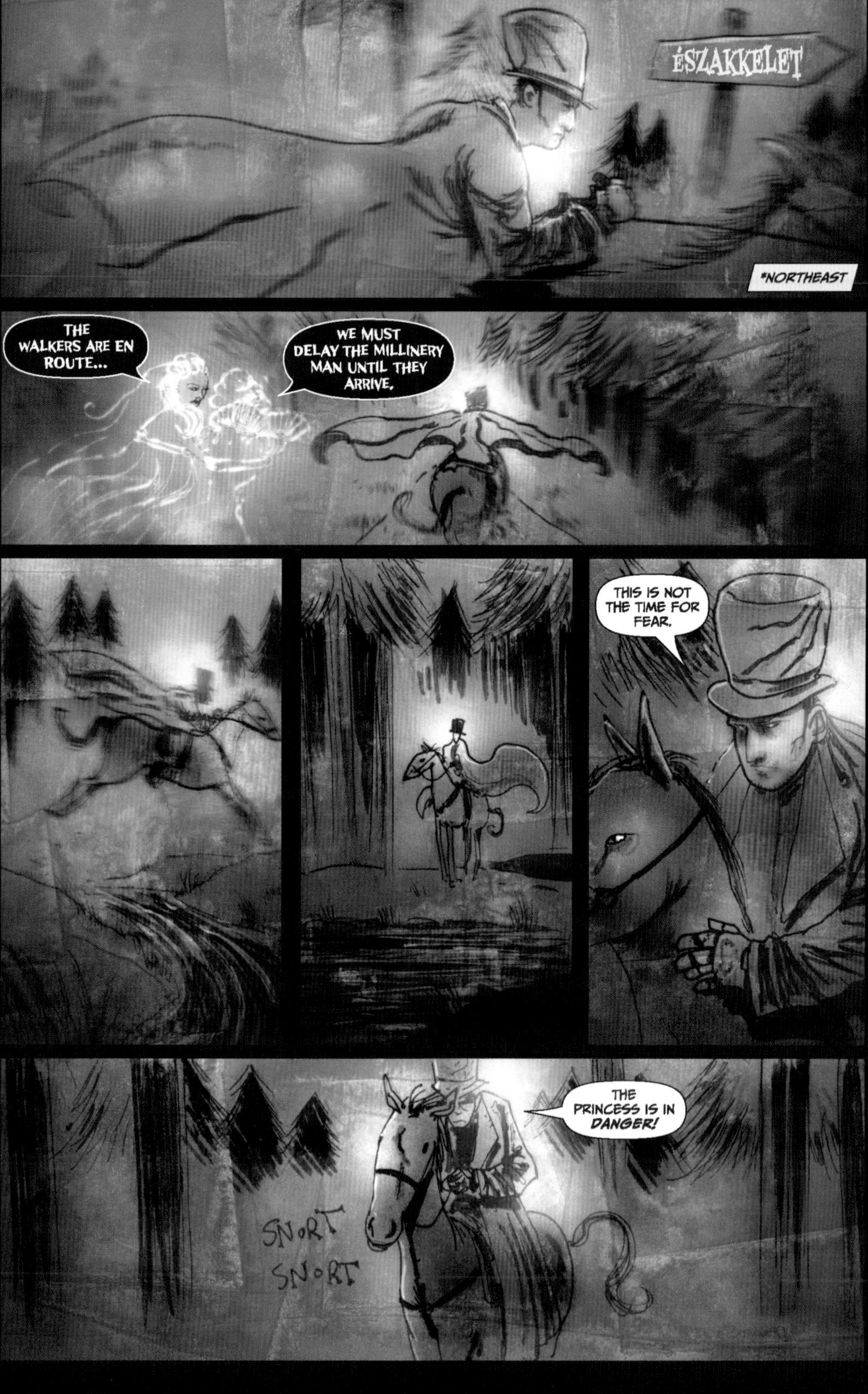
ÉSZAKKELET
*NORTHEAST
THE WALKERS ARE EN ROUTE...
WE MUST DELAY THE MILLINERY MAN UNTIL THEY ARRIVE.
THIS IS NOT THE TIME FOR FEAR.
THE PRINCESS IS IN DANGER!
SNORT
SNORT

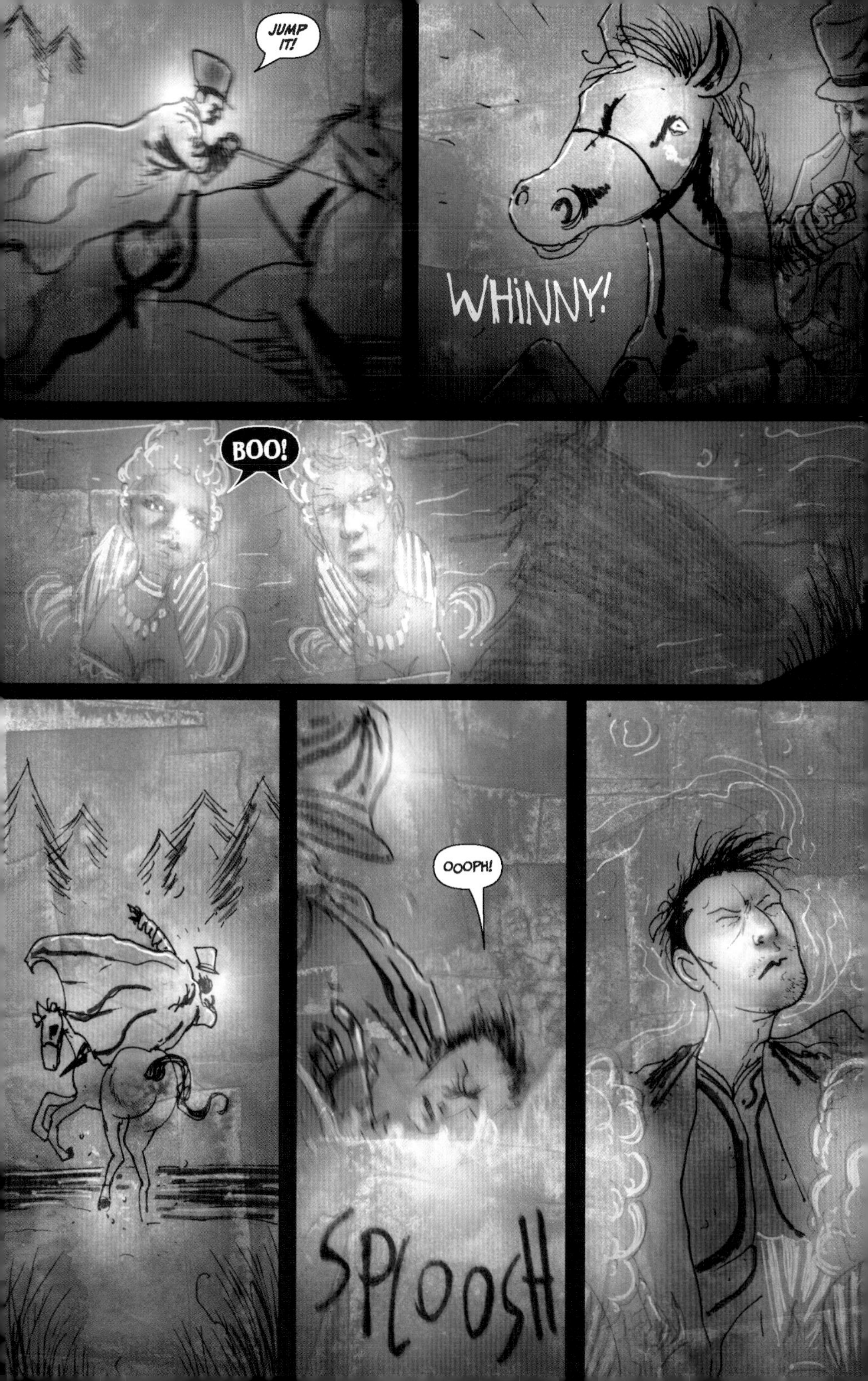
JUMP IT!
WHINNY!
BOO!
OOOPH!
SPLOOSH

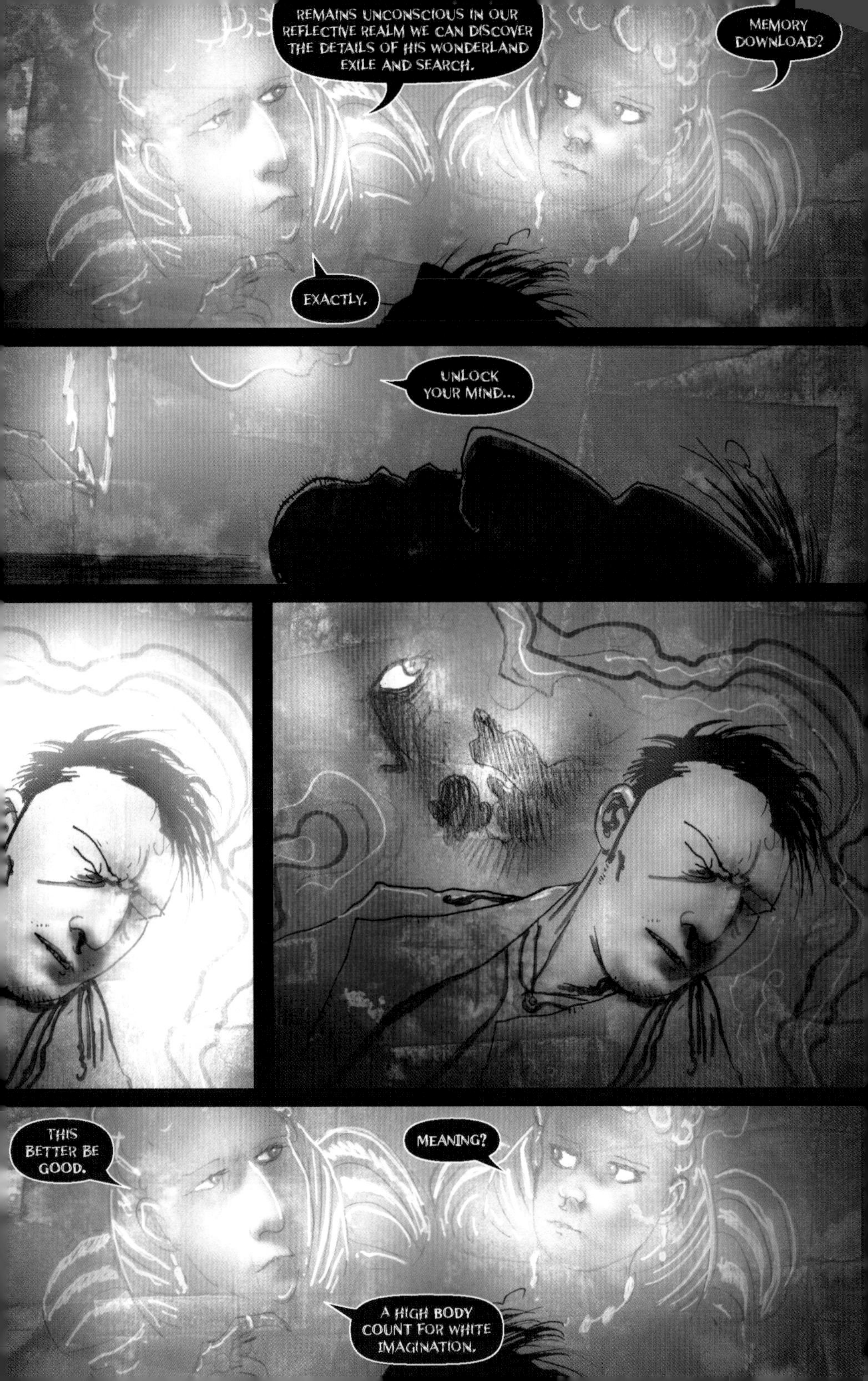
REMAINS UNCONSCIOUS IN OUR REFLECTIVE REALM WE CAN DISCOVER THE DETAILS OF HIS WONDERLAND EXILE AND SEARCH.
MEMORY DOWNLOAD?
EXACTLY.
UNLOCK YOUR MIND...
THIS BETTER BE GOOD.
MEANING?
A HIGH BODY COUNT FOR WHITE IMAGINATION.

LUMP OF SUGAR FOR YOUR TEA, MADAM? A DROP OF HONEY FOR YOUR TEA, SIR?
WE HAVE PATROL DECKS STATIONED AT EVERY PERIMETER POINT.
THE PALACE IS ON REDD ALERT. WE DON'T EXPECT ANY SURPRISES.
LADY SPADE WAS TELLING ME HOW THESE BLACK IMAGINATION SOCIETIES ARE CORRUPTING WONDERLAND'S YOUTH!
INDEED! I PRAY OUR JACK NEVER SINKS TO DRINKING JABBERWOCKY BLOOD!
BLEAHHH... WHO WOULD DRINK SUCH A REPUGNANT THING WHEN THERE IS SQUIGBERRY JUICE?

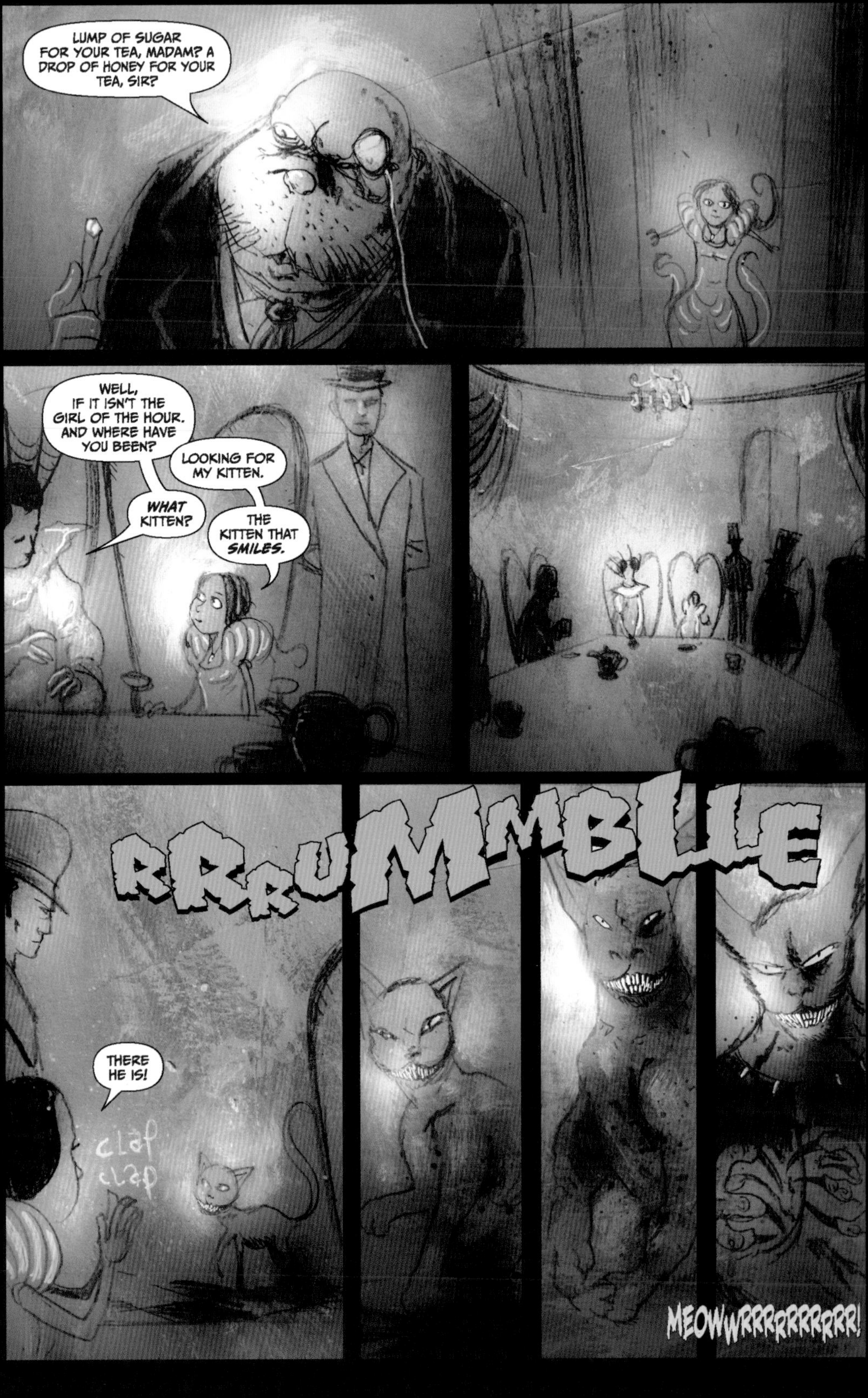
LUMP OF SUGAR FOR YOUR TEA, MADAM? A DROP OF HONEY FOR YOUR TEA, SIR?
WELL, IF IT ISN'T THE GIRL OF THE HOUR. AND WHERE HAVE YOU BEEN?
LOOKING FOR MY KITTEN.
WHAT KITTEN?
THE KITTEN THAT SMILES.
RRRUMMBLLE
THERE HE IS!
clap clap
MEOWWRRRRRRRRR!

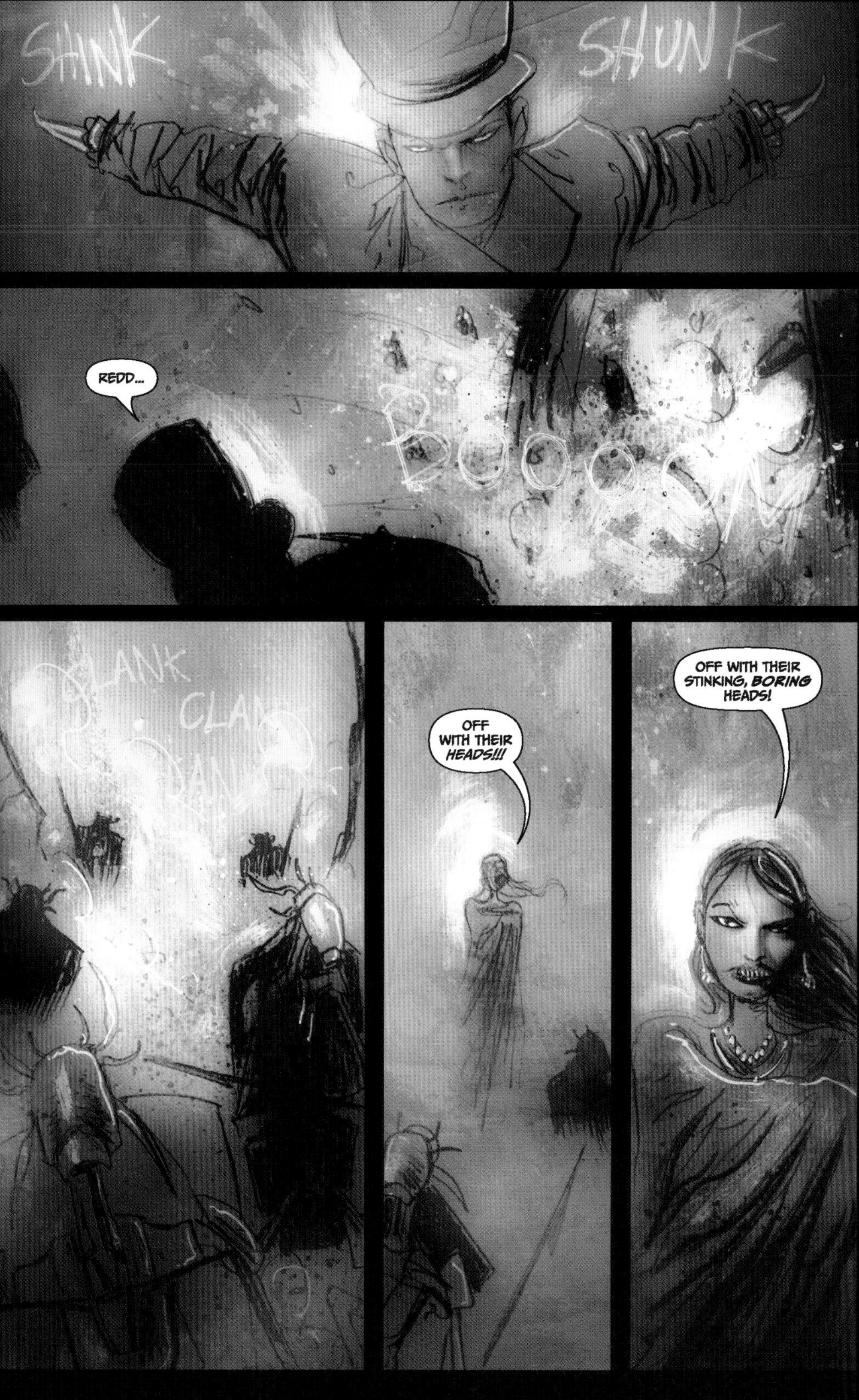
SHINK
SHUNK
REDD...
BOOOOOM
CLANK
CLAN
OFF WITH THEIR HEADS!!!
OFF WITH THEIR STINKING, BORING HEADS!

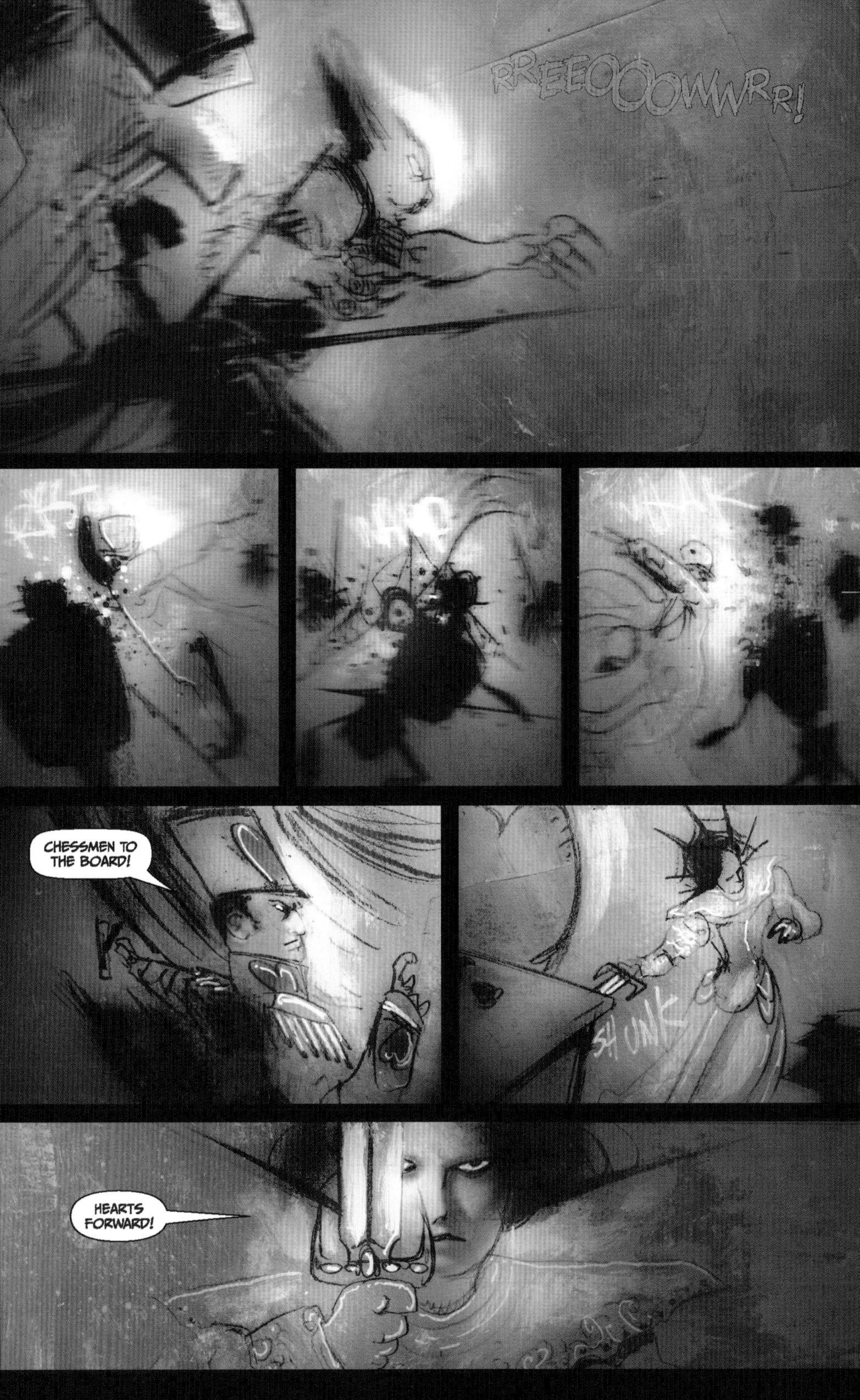
RREEOOOWWRR!
CHESSMEN TO THE BOARD!
SHUNK
HEARTS FORWARD!

CHESSMEN ATTACK!

GENERAL GÄNGER! WHERE ARE YOU?

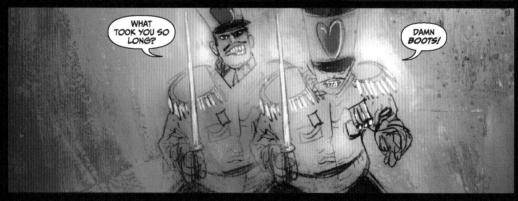

WHAT TOOK YOU SO LONG?

DAMN BOOTS!

TOO BAD YOU DON'T HAVE *NINE* LIVES LIKE ME.

BECAUSE THIS ONE IS *OVER!!*

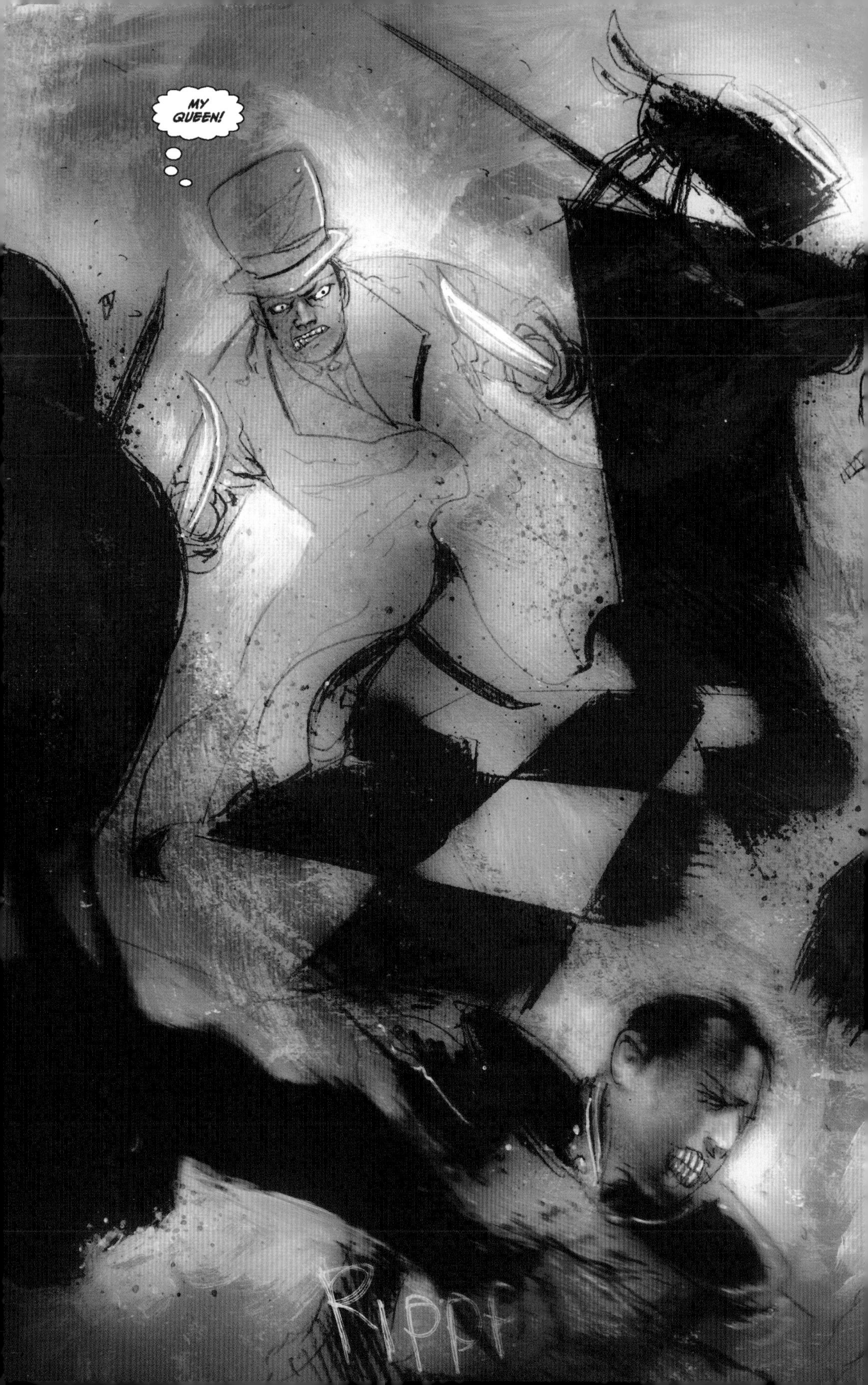
MY QUEEN!
RIPPF

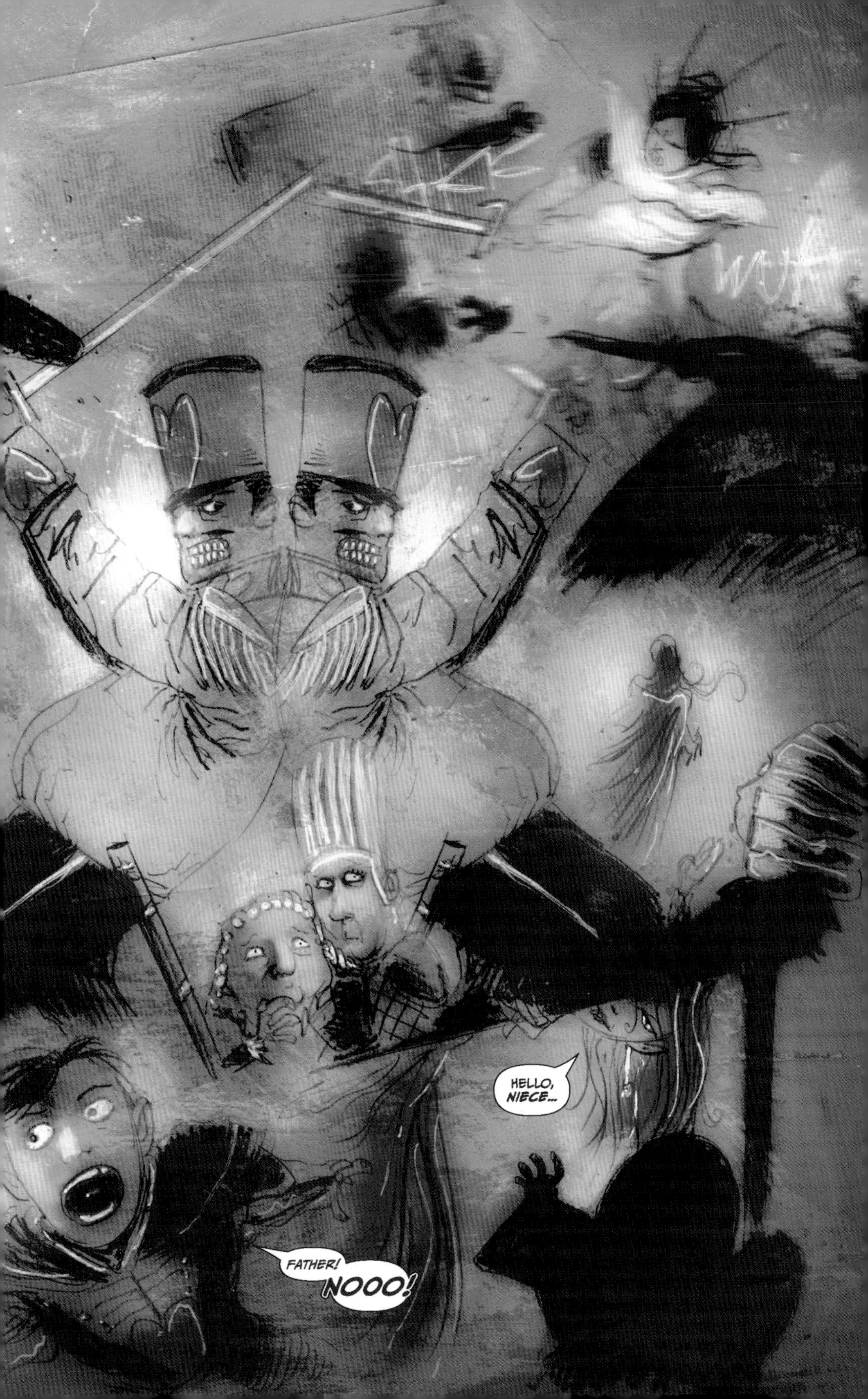
HELLO, NIECE...
FATHER! NOOO!

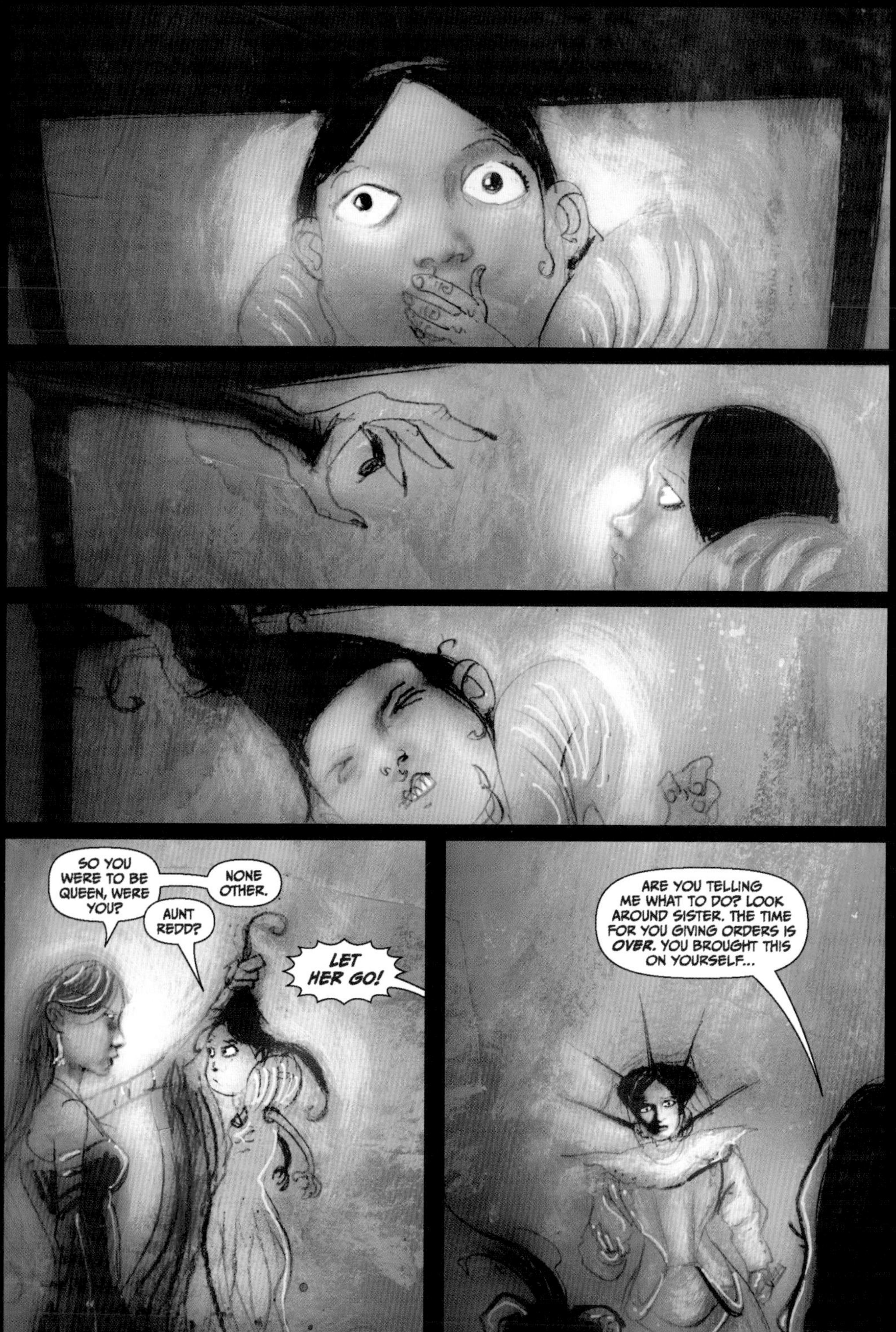
SO YOU WERE TO BE QUEEN, WERE YOU?
NONE OTHER.
AUNT REDD?
LET HER GO!
ARE YOU TELLING ME WHAT TO DO? LOOK AROUND SISTER. THE TIME FOR YOU GIVING ORDERS IS OVER. YOU BROUGHT THIS ON YOURSELF...

...QUEEN GENEVIEVE.

AND IF YOU ARE STILL WAITING FOR YOUR *KING*...

I REGRET TO INFORM YOU...

THAT HE WON'T BE RETURNING HOME...

EVER!

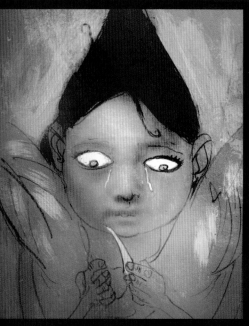

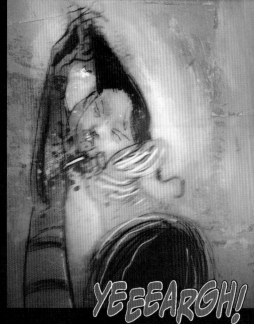

YEEEARGH!

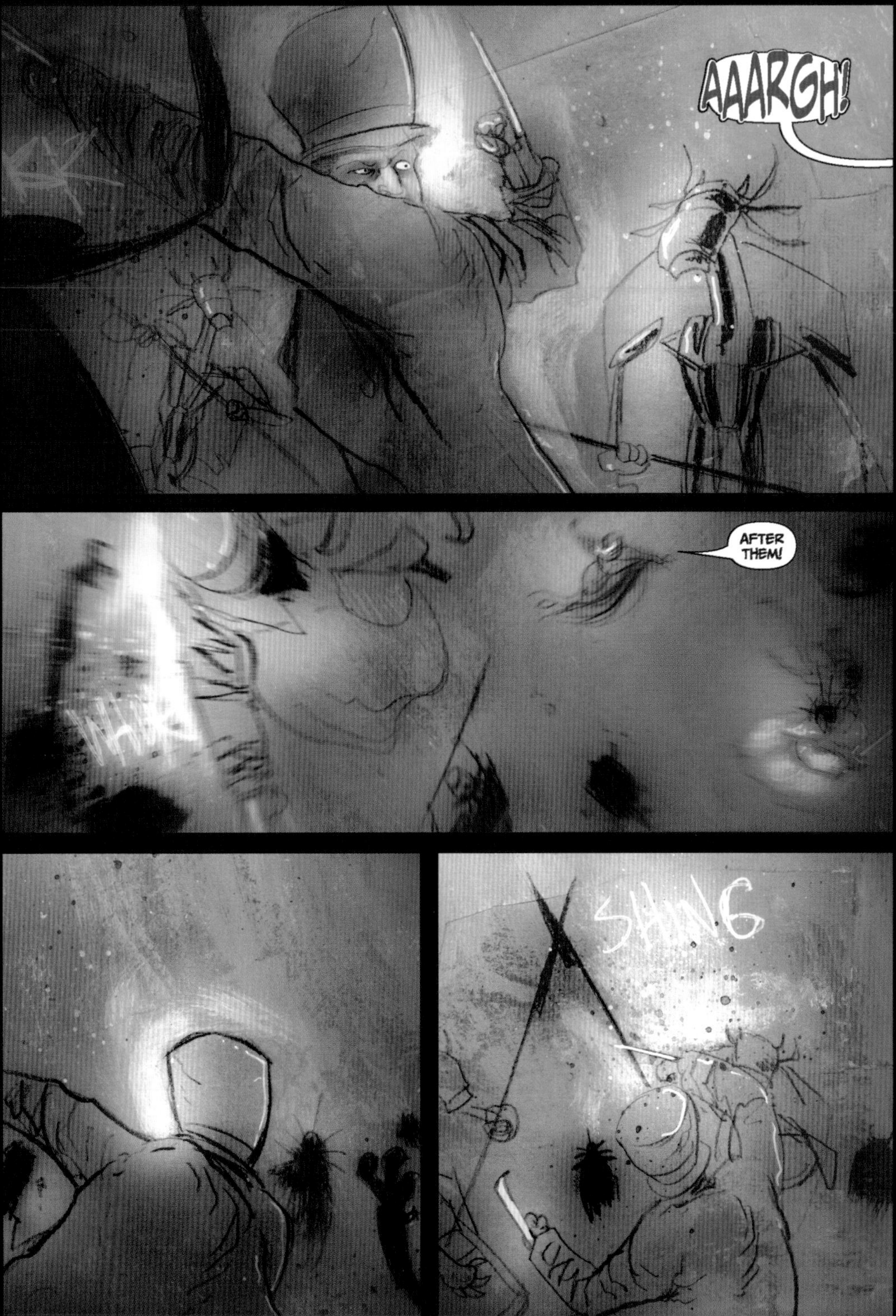
AAARGH!
AFTER THEM!
SHING

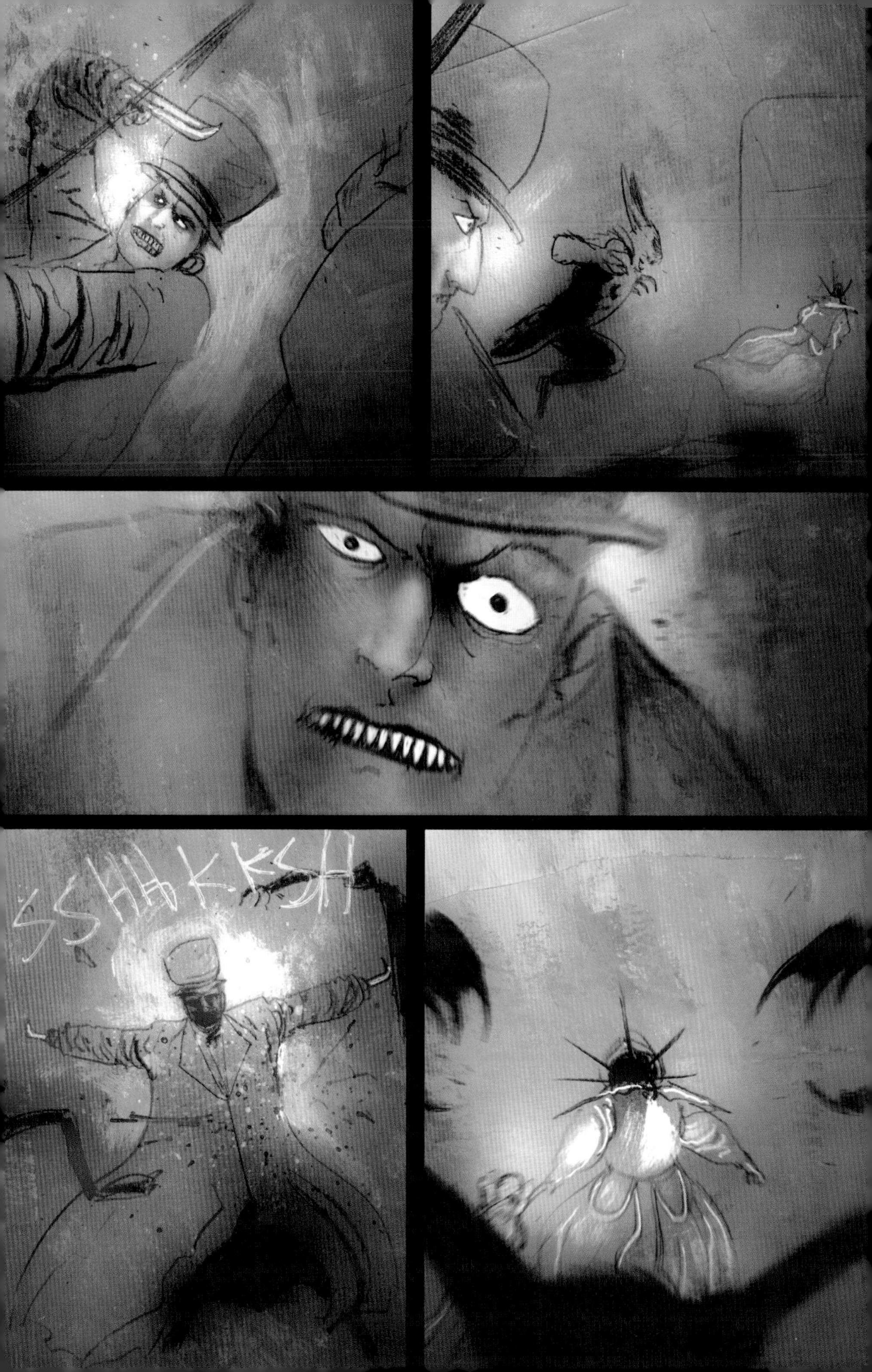
SSHHK-KSH

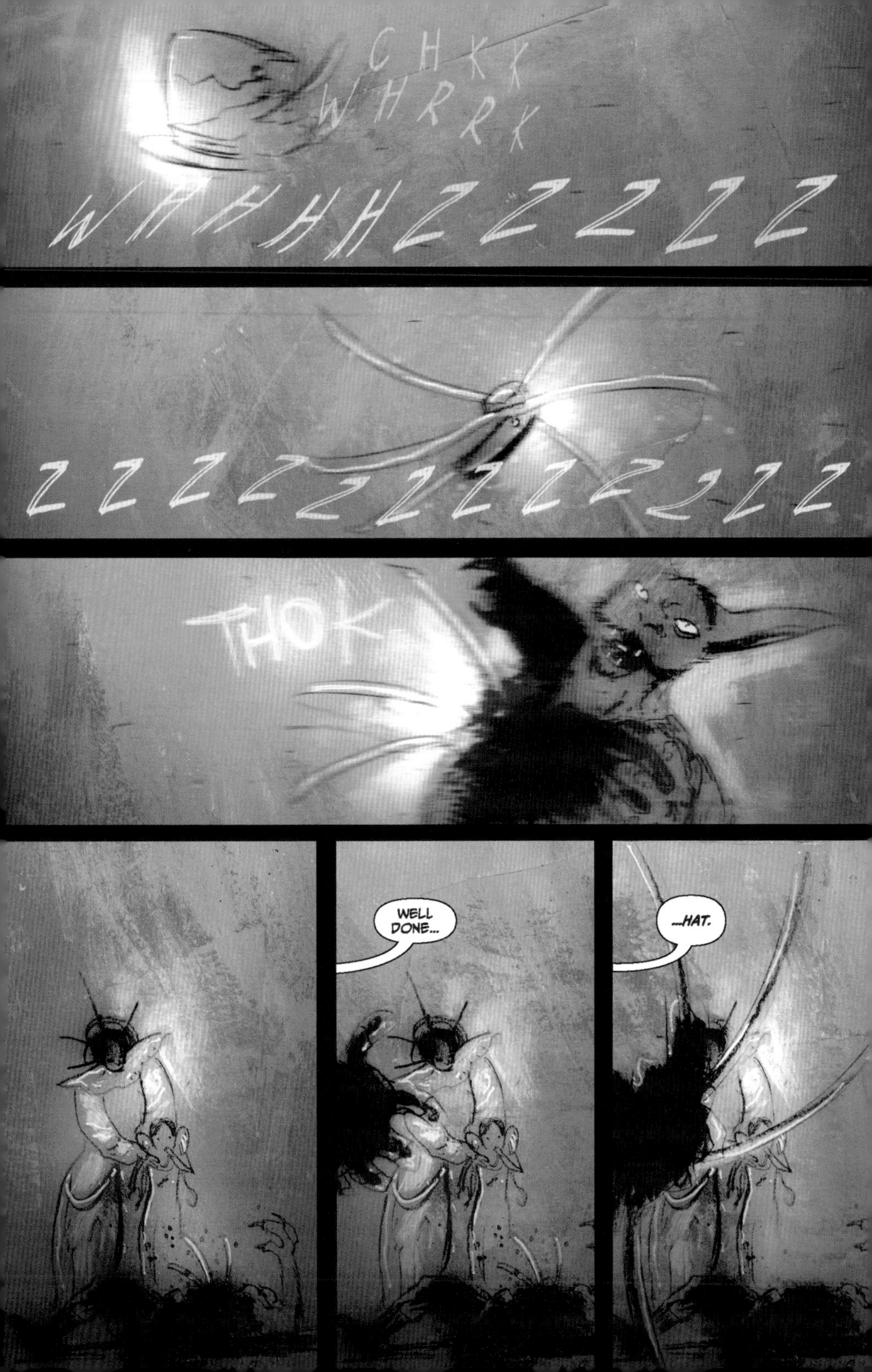
CHKK
WHRRK
WHHHHZZZZZZ
ZZZZZZZZZZZZ
THOK
WELL DONE...
...HAT.

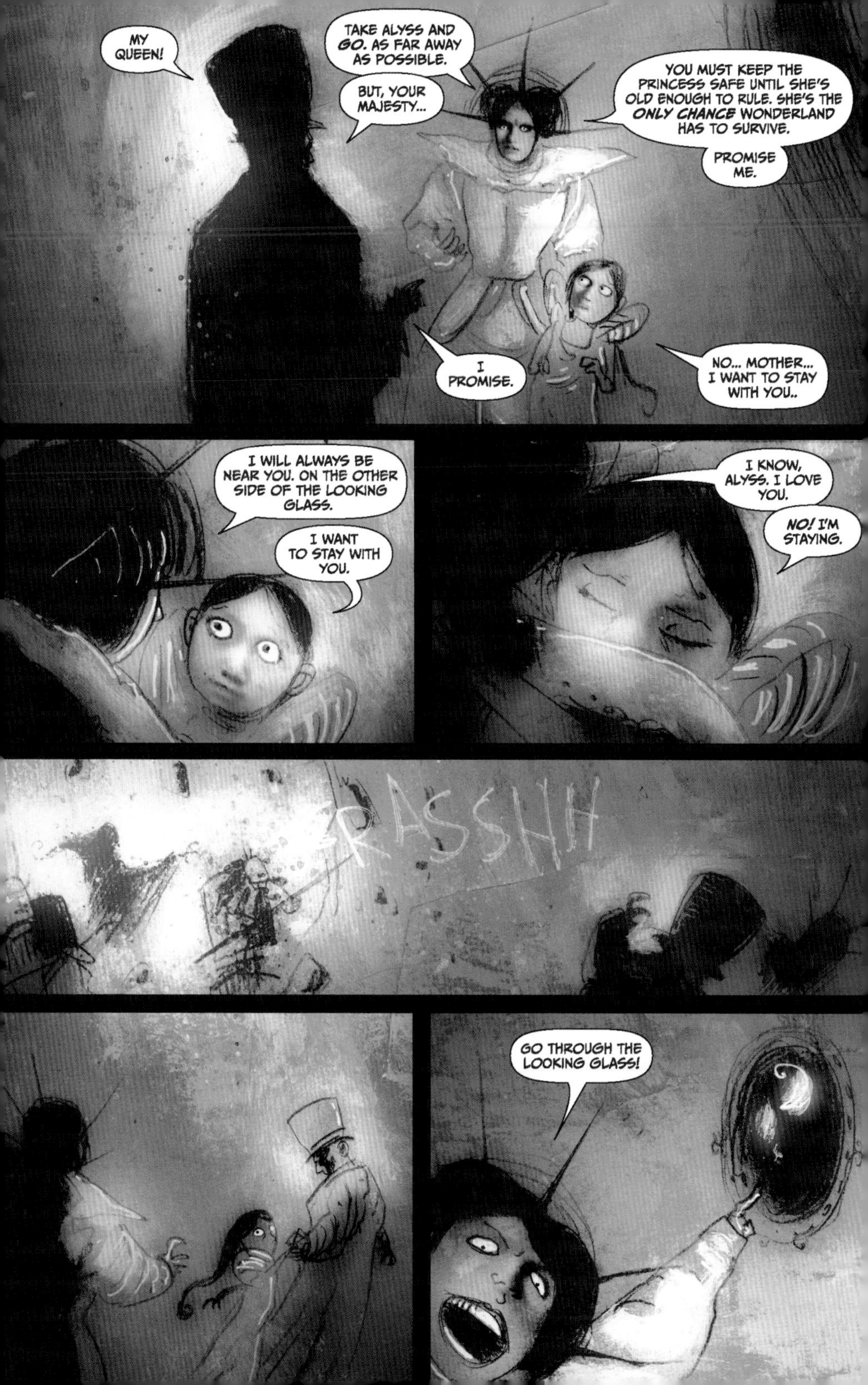
MY QUEEN!
TAKE ALYSS AND GO. AS FAR AWAY AS POSSIBLE.
BUT, YOUR MAJESTY...
YOU MUST KEEP THE PRINCESS SAFE UNTIL SHE'S OLD ENOUGH TO RULE. SHE'S THE ONLY CHANCE WONDERLAND HAS TO SURVIVE.
PROMISE ME.
I PROMISE.
NO... MOTHER... I WANT TO STAY WITH YOU..
I WILL ALWAYS BE NEAR YOU. ON THE OTHER SIDE OF THE LOOKING GLASS.
I WANT TO STAY WITH YOU.
I KNOW, ALYSS. I LOVE YOU.
NO! I'M STAYING.
RASSHH
GO THROUGH THE LOOKING GLASS!

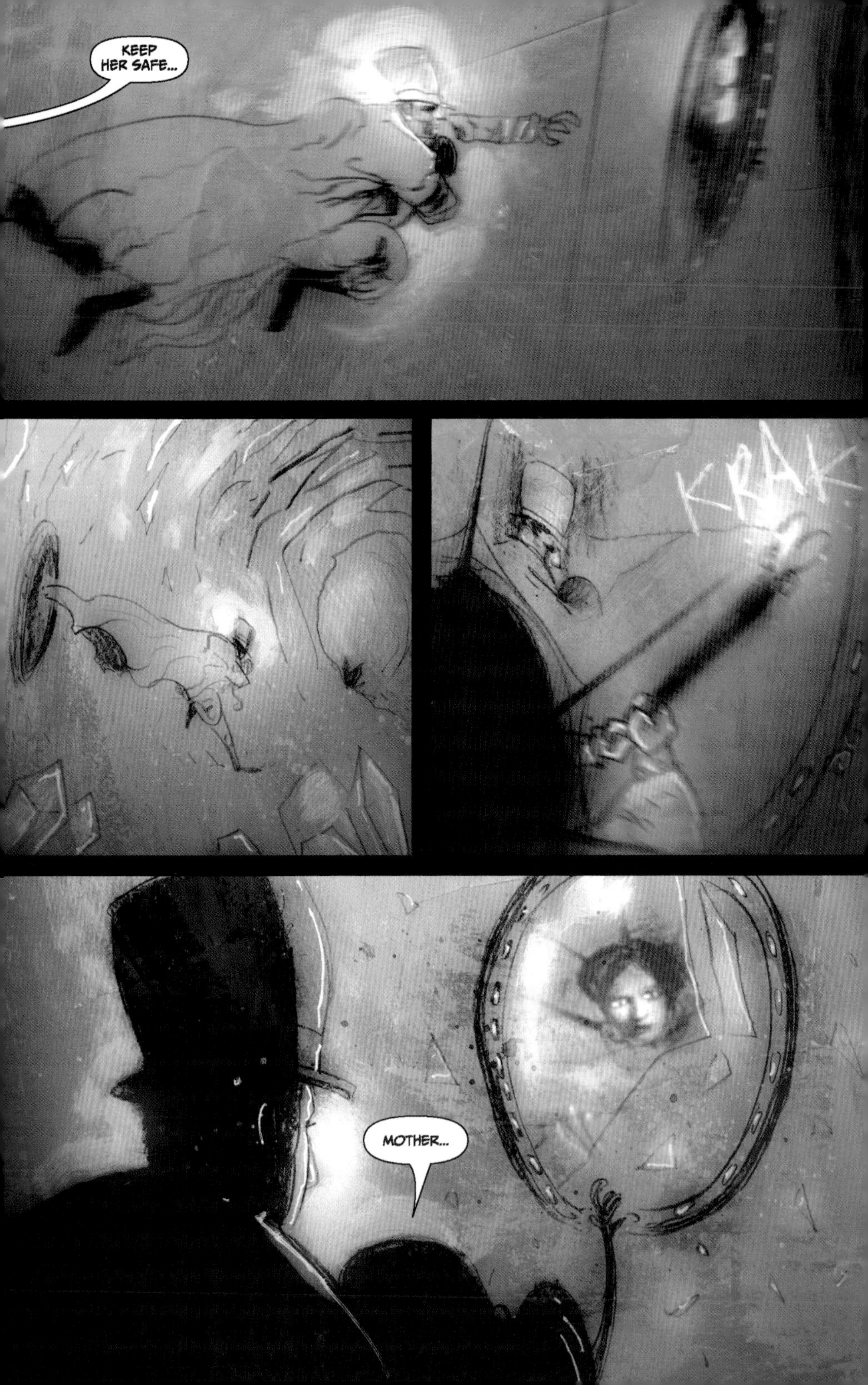

KEEP HER SAFE...
KRAK
MOTHER...

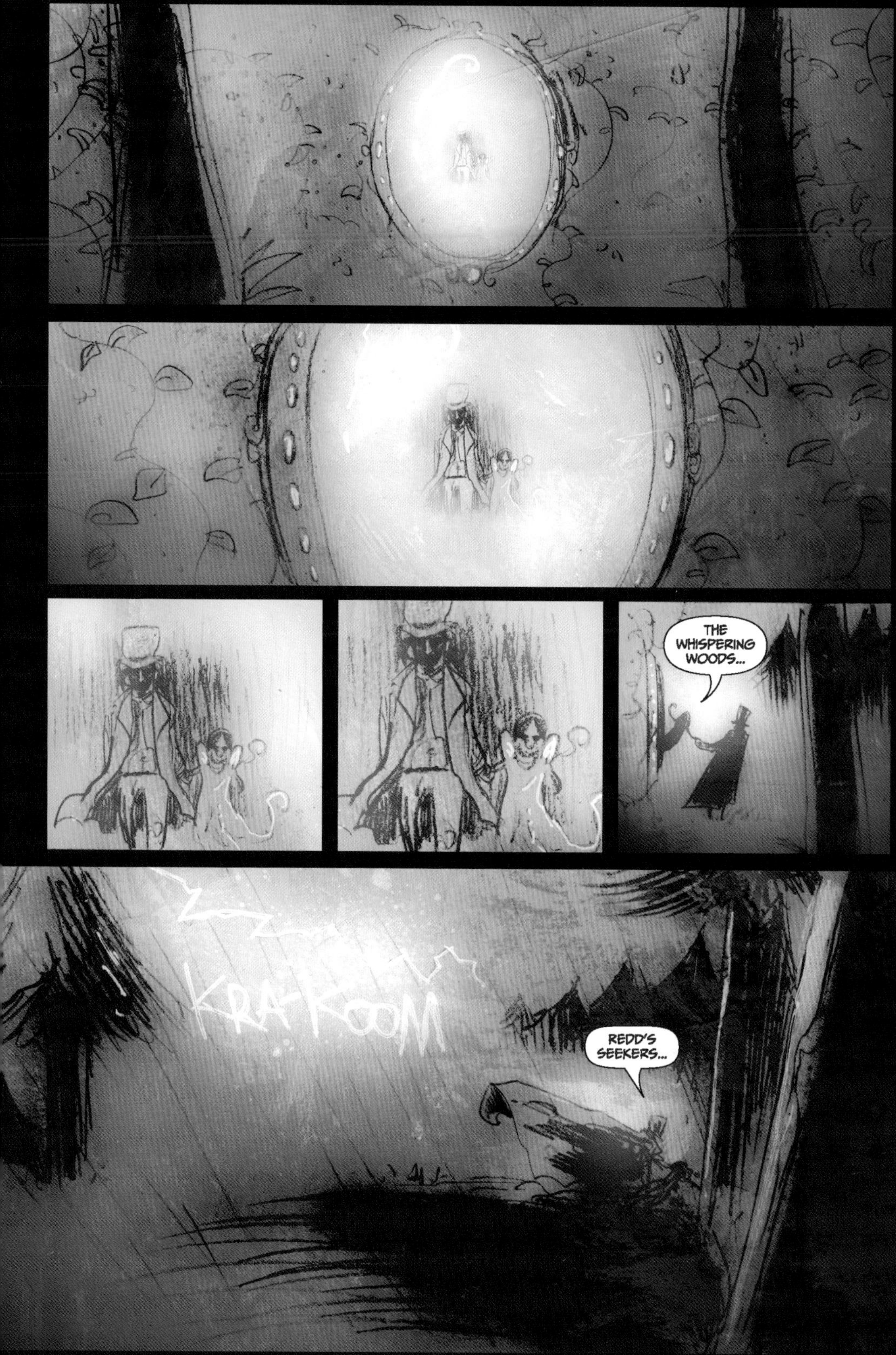
THE WHISPERING WOODS...
KRA-KOOM
REDD'S SEEKERS...

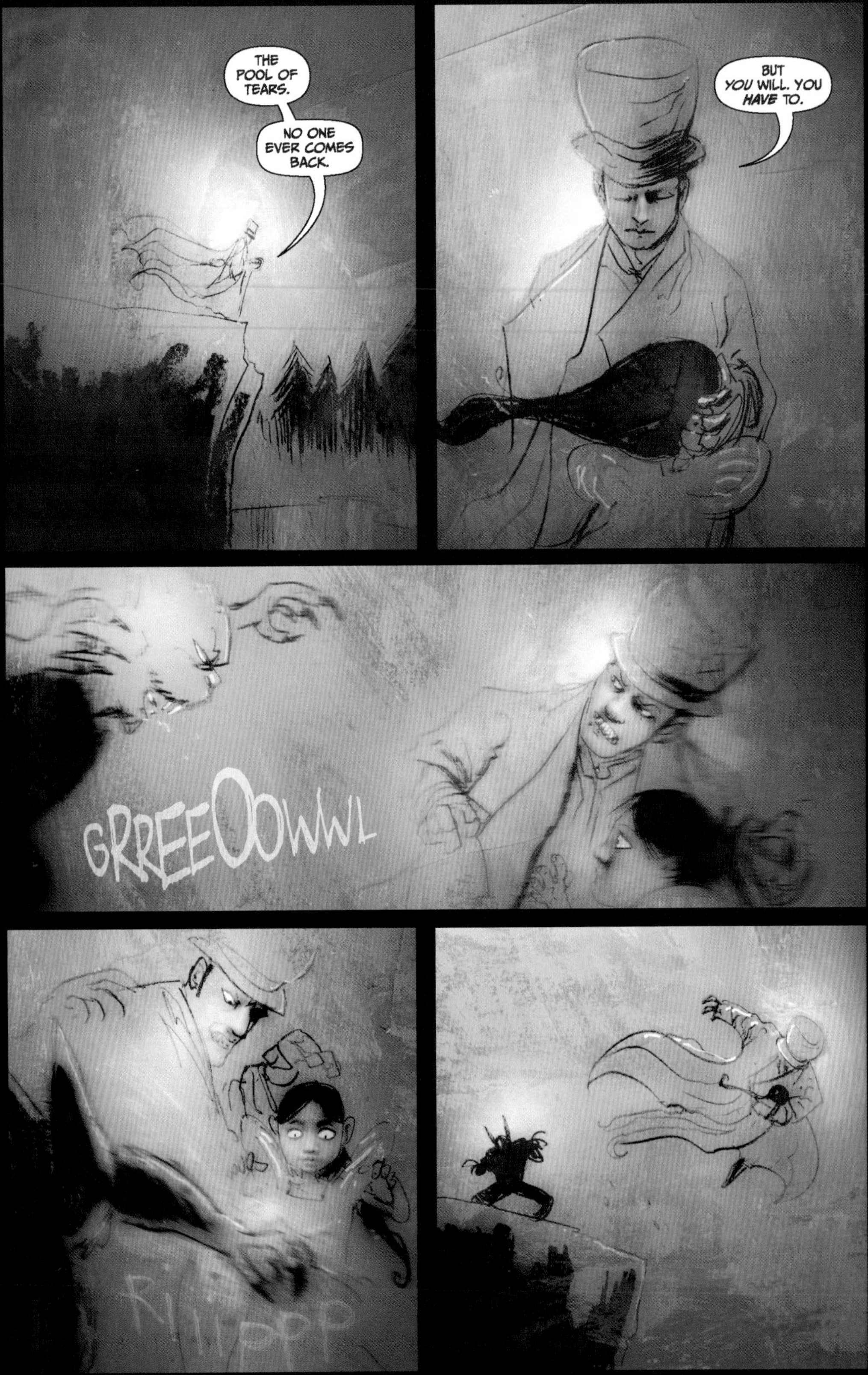
THE POOL OF TEARS.
NO ONE EVER COMES BACK.
BUT YOU WILL. YOU HAVE TO.
GRREEOOWWL
RIIIPPP

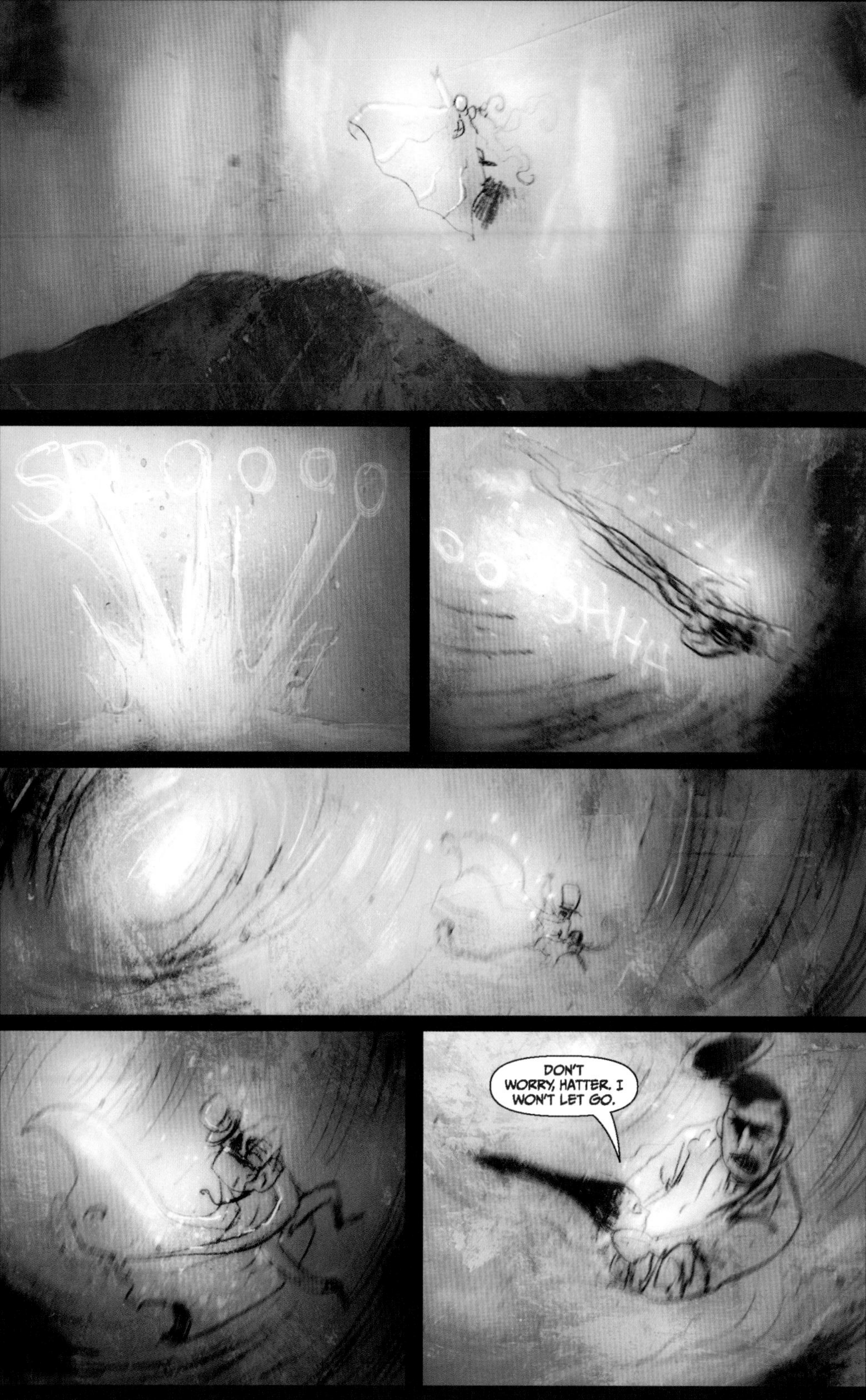
DON'T WORRY, HATTER. I WON'T LET GO.

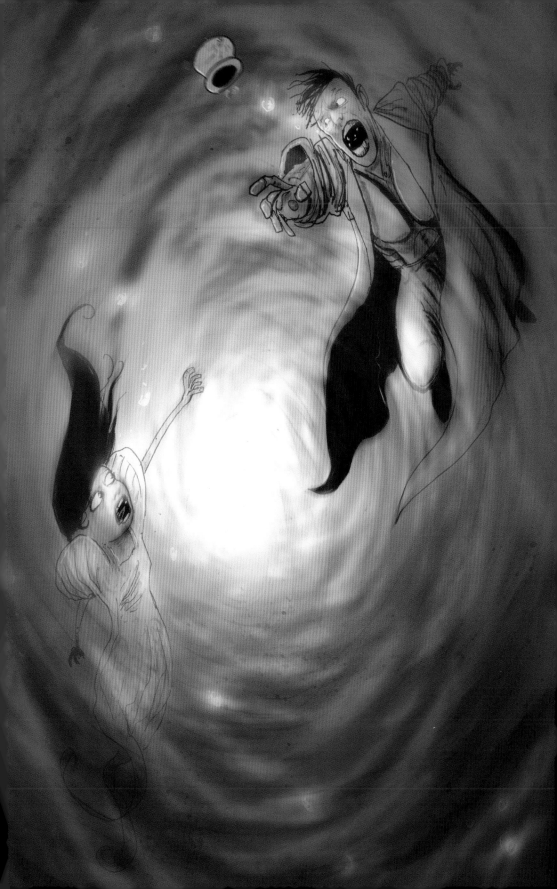

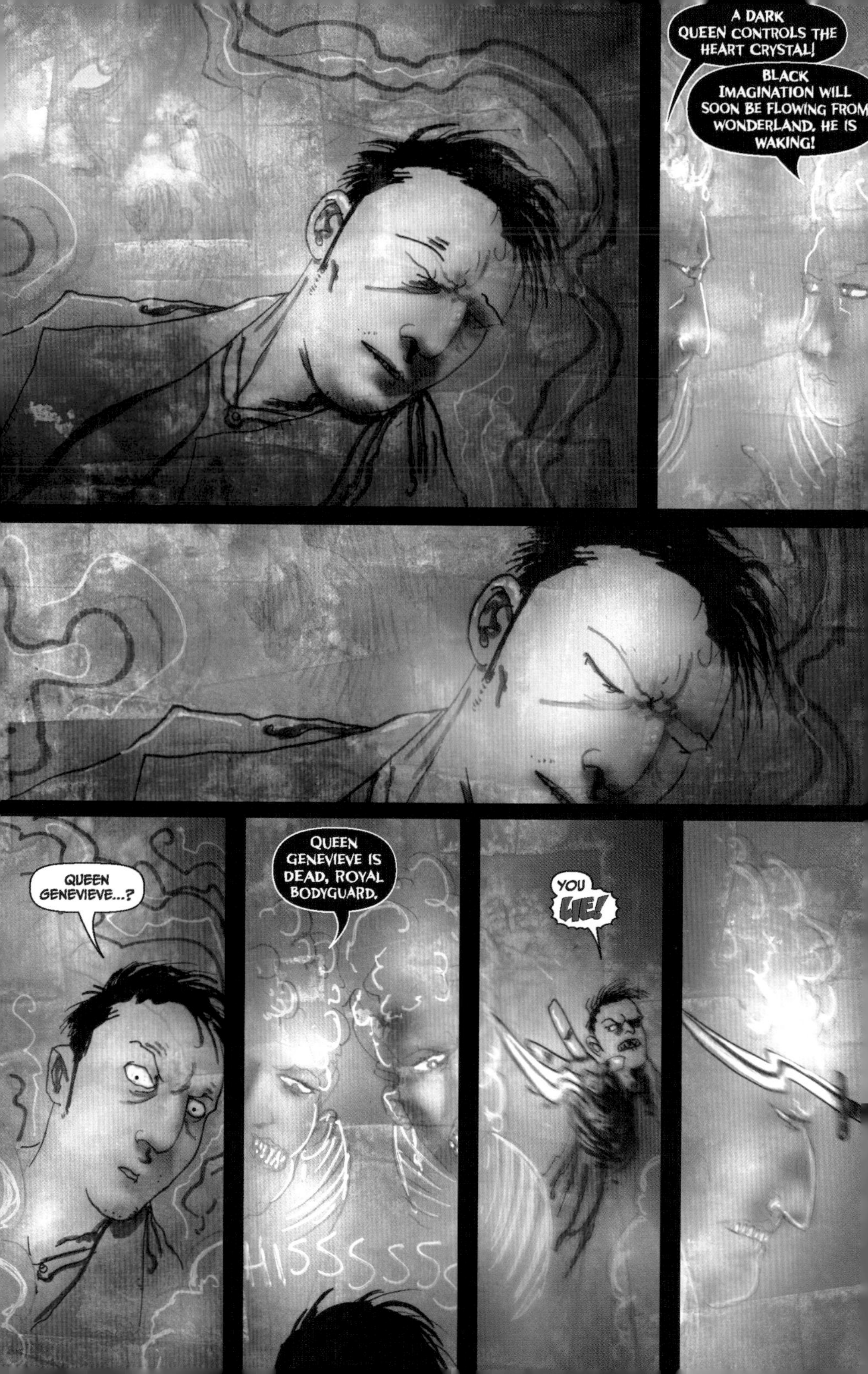
A DARK QUEEN CONTROLS THE HEART CRYSTAL!
BLACK IMAGINATION WILL SOON BE FLOWING FROM WONDERLAND. HE IS WAKING!
QUEEN GENEVIEVE...?
QUEEN GENEVIEVE IS DEAD, ROYAL BODYGUARD.
HISSSSSS
YOU LIE!

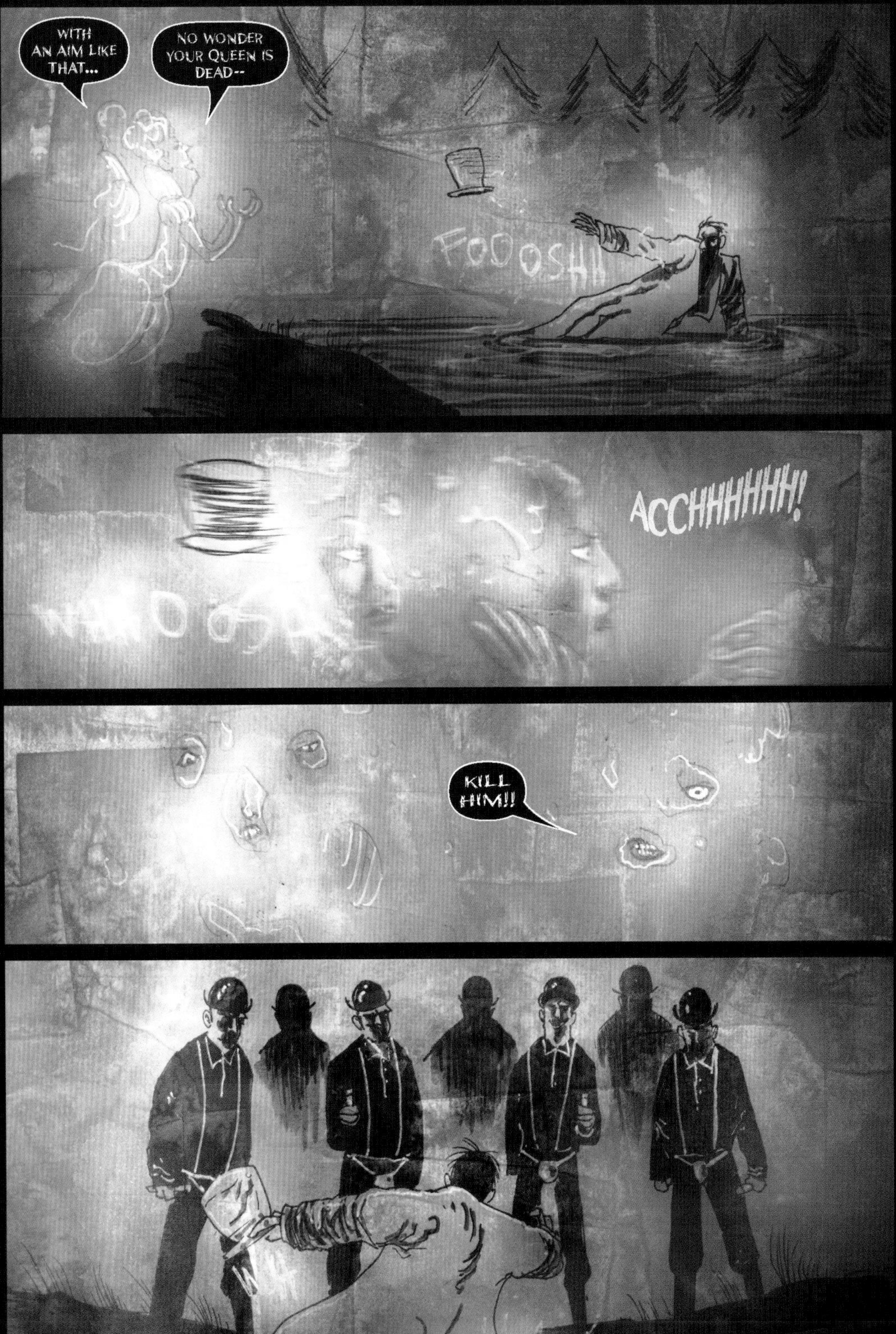
WITH AN AIM LIKE THAT...
NO WONDER YOUR QUEEN IS DEAD--
ACCHHHHHH!
KILL HIM!!

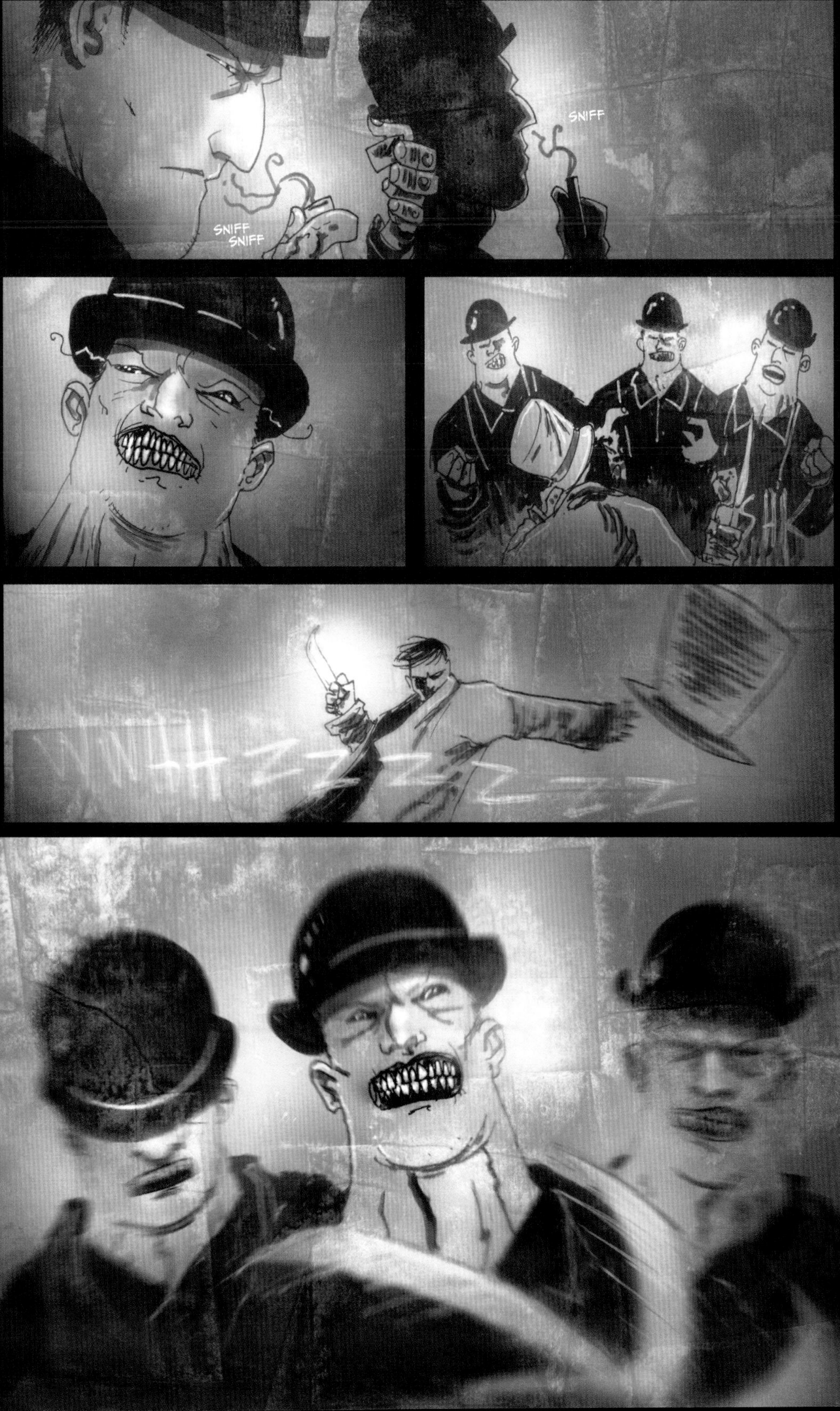
SNIFF
SNIFF
SNIFF

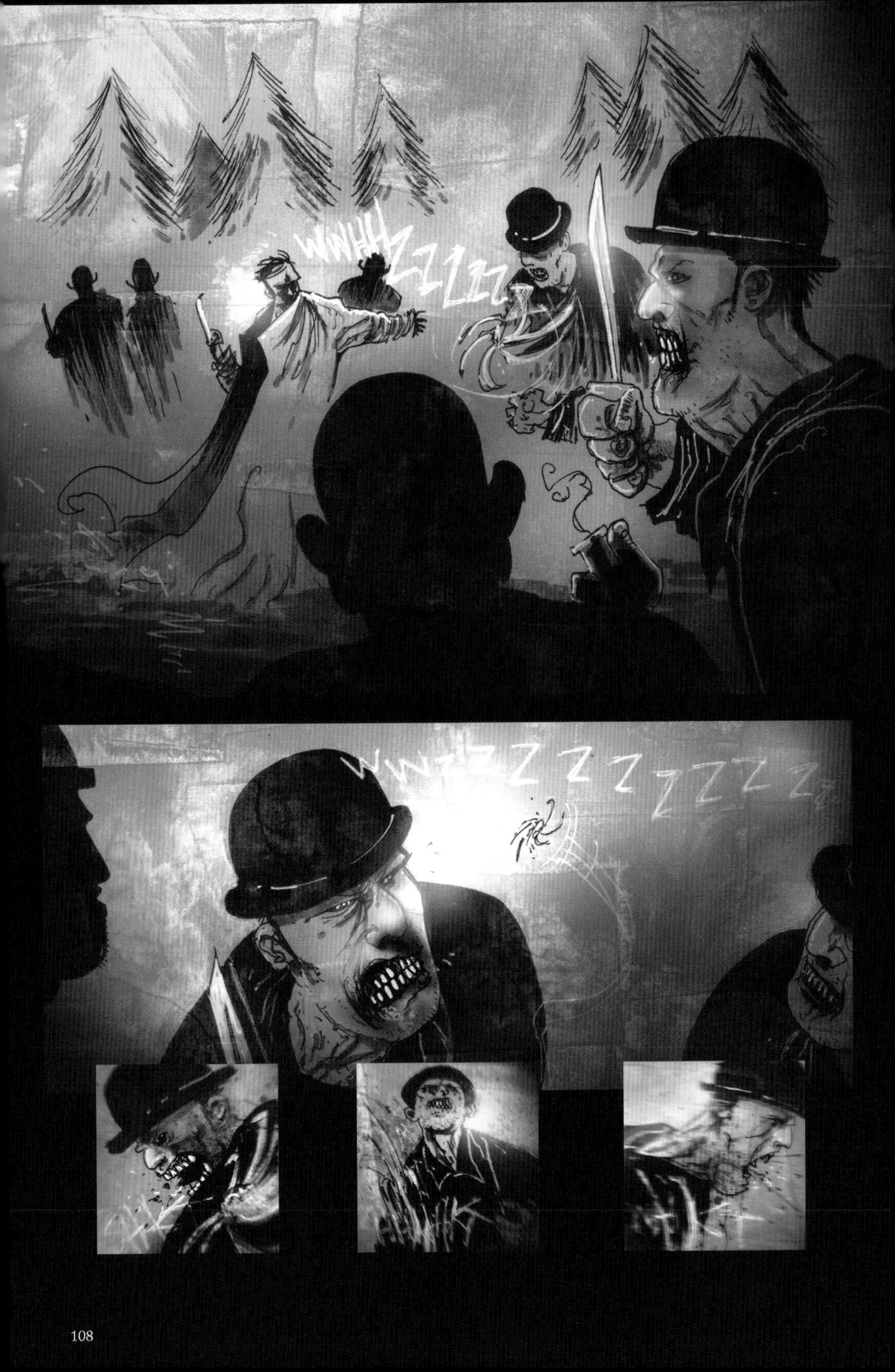
WWHHZZZZZ
WWZZZZZZZZZZZ

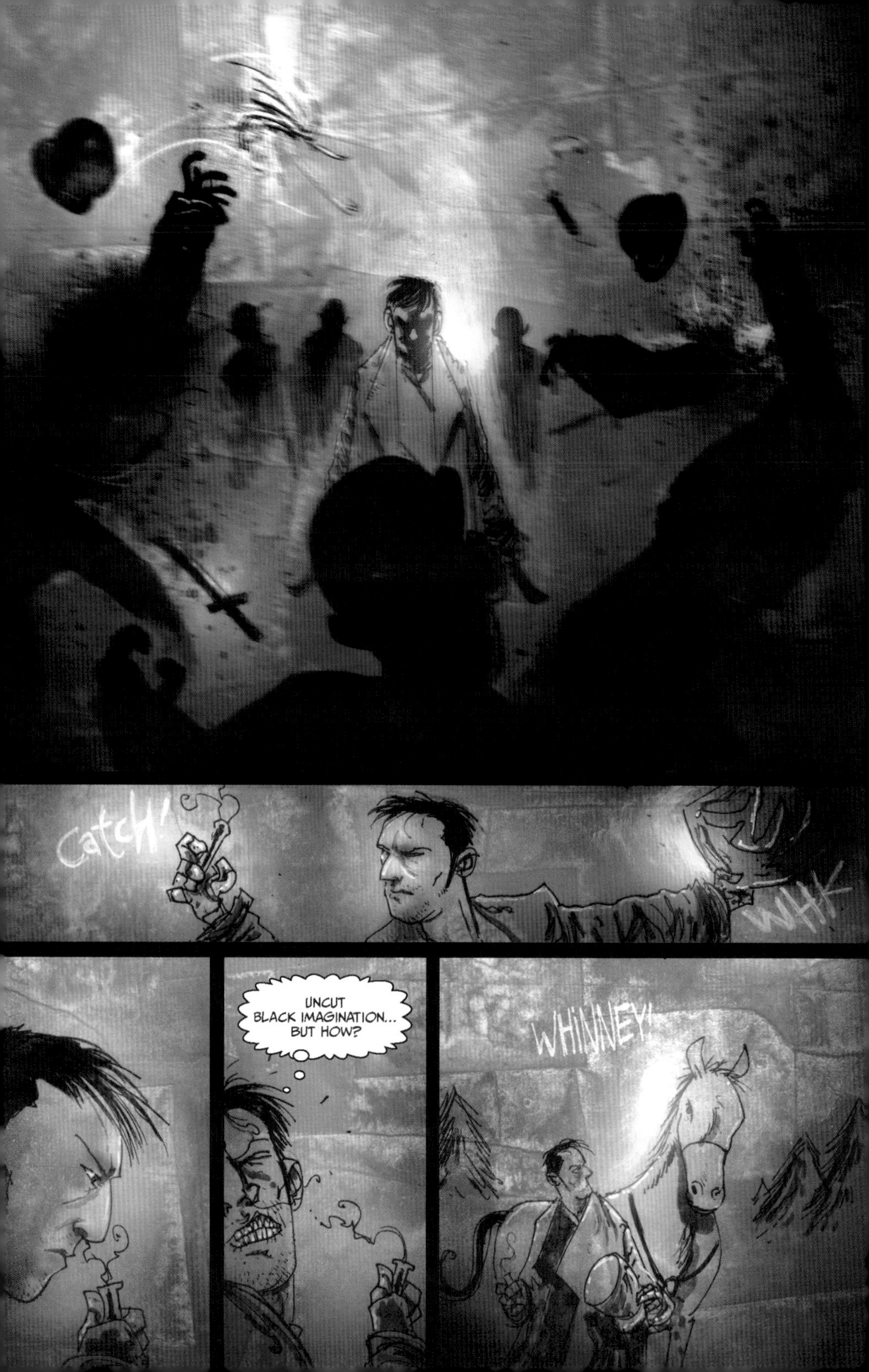
CATCH!
WHK
UNCUT
BLACK IMAGINATION...
BUT HOW?
WHINNEY!

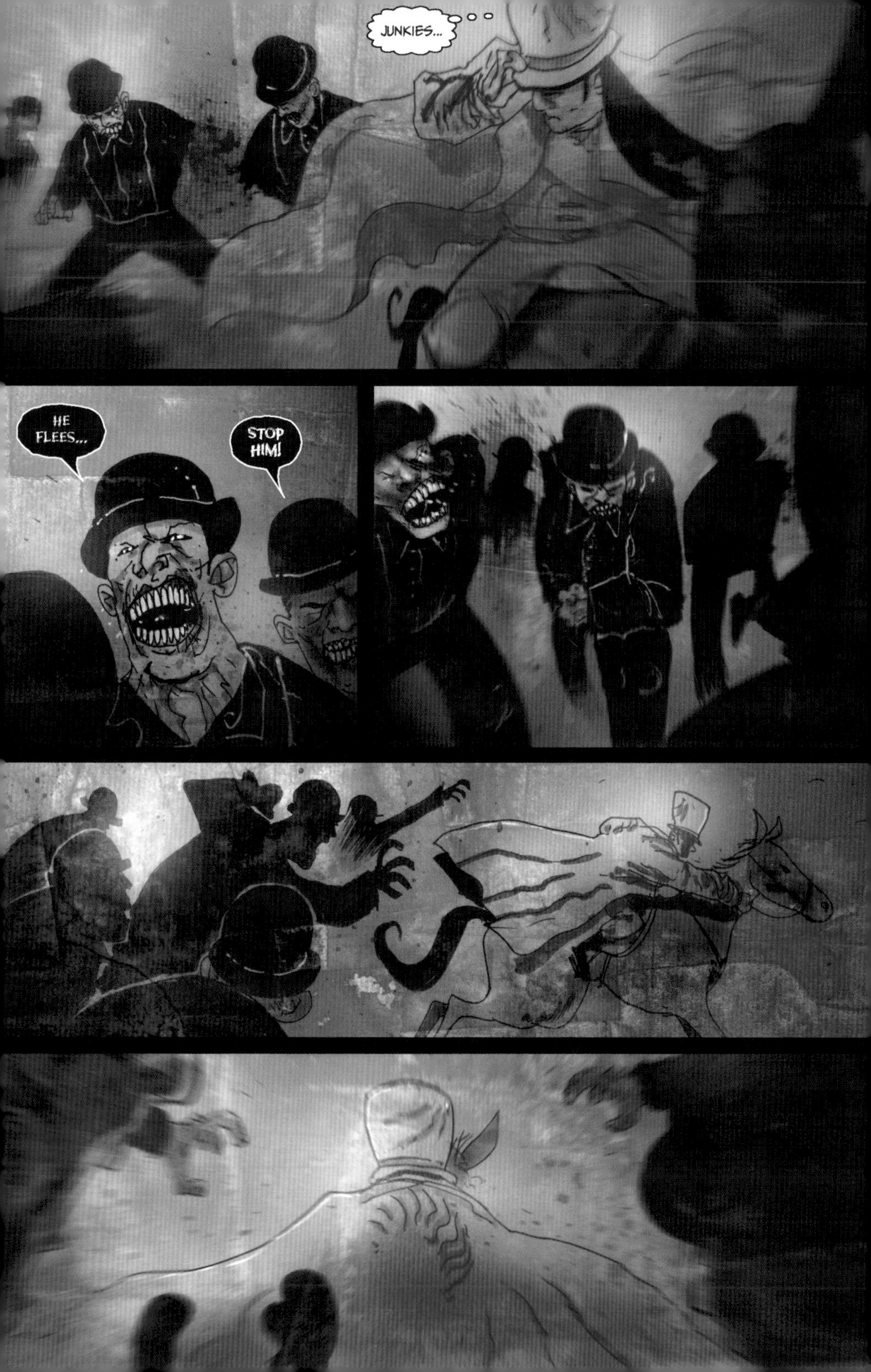
JUNKIES...
HE FLEES...
STOP HIM!

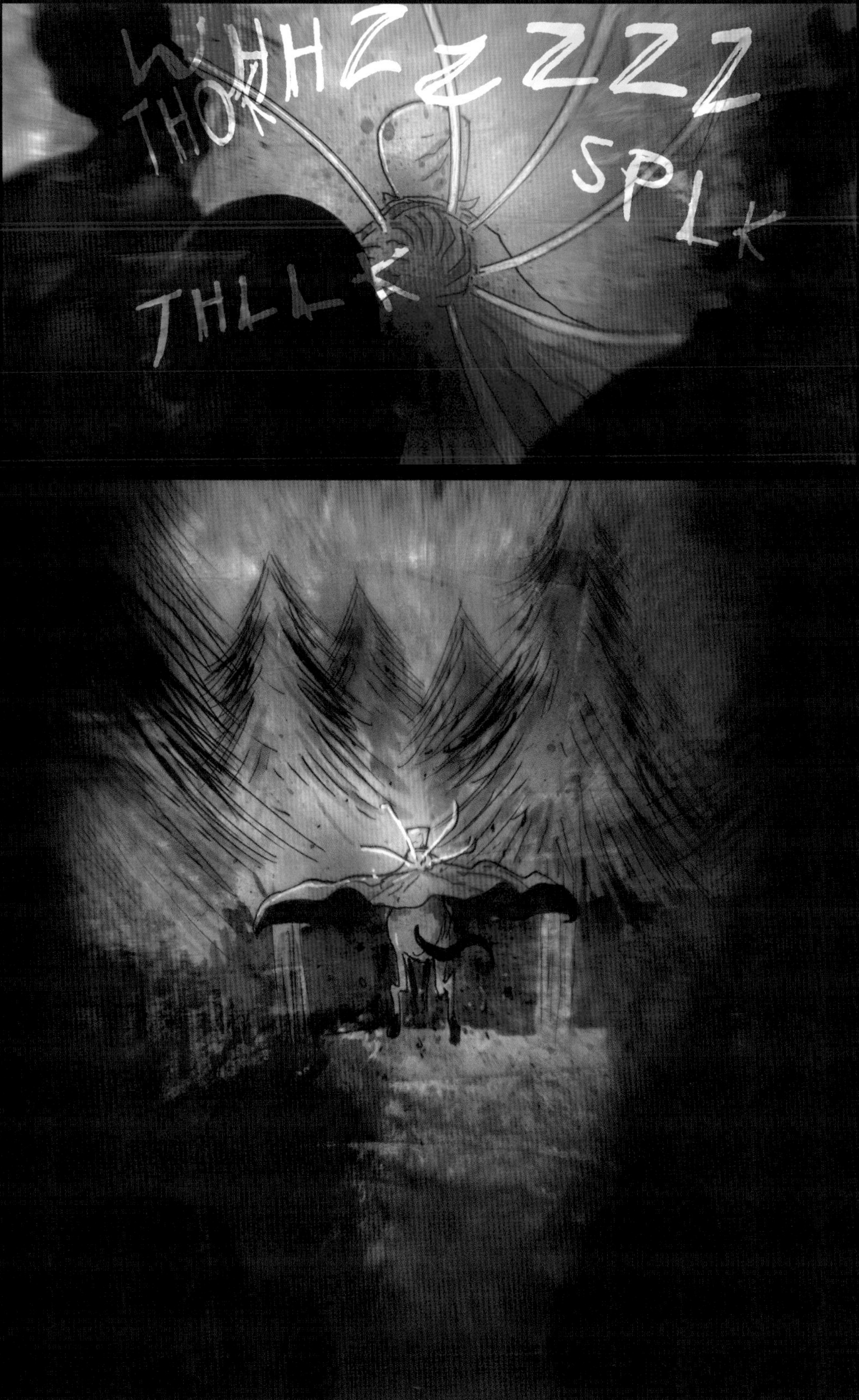
WHHZZZZZ
THOK
SPLK
THLLK

*It appears that Wonderland's gift to other worlds is
also a plague. The war of Imagination splitting
Wonderland in two is fought here with equal passion
and violence. Fool that I believed Redd to be the only
adversary in my search for Alyss when it is now obvi-
ous that those in this world who are dedicated to Black
Imagination have equal stakes in the fate of
Wonderland's future Queen.*

*As always, all hope lies in White Imagination. Just as
there are those who desire Alyss dead there are those
who would assist my search…who would join the battle…who would sacrifice everything if they only knew
the threat that faces Wonderland. For I see now that
this world's fate is closely bonded to that of my own…*

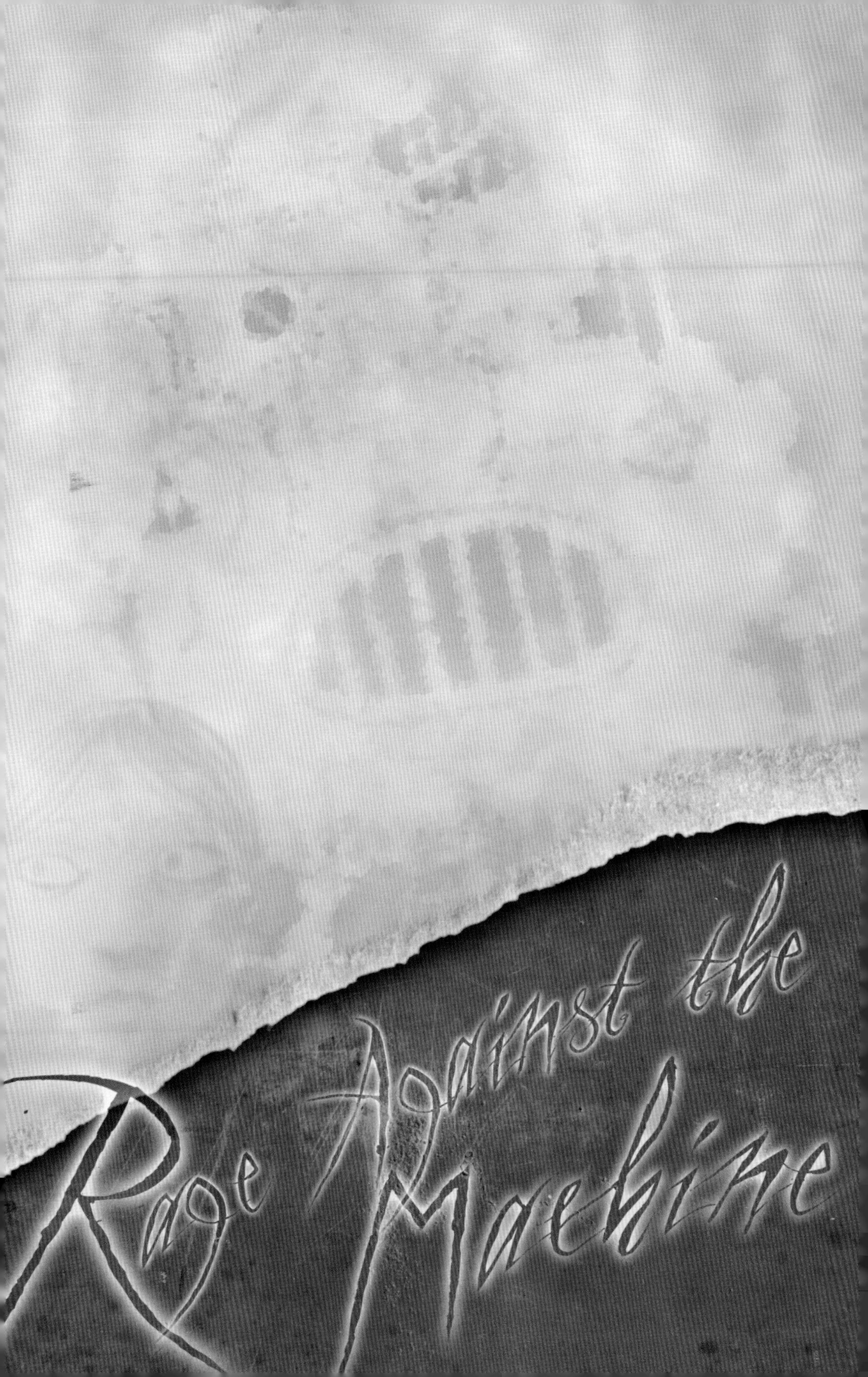
Rage Against the Machine

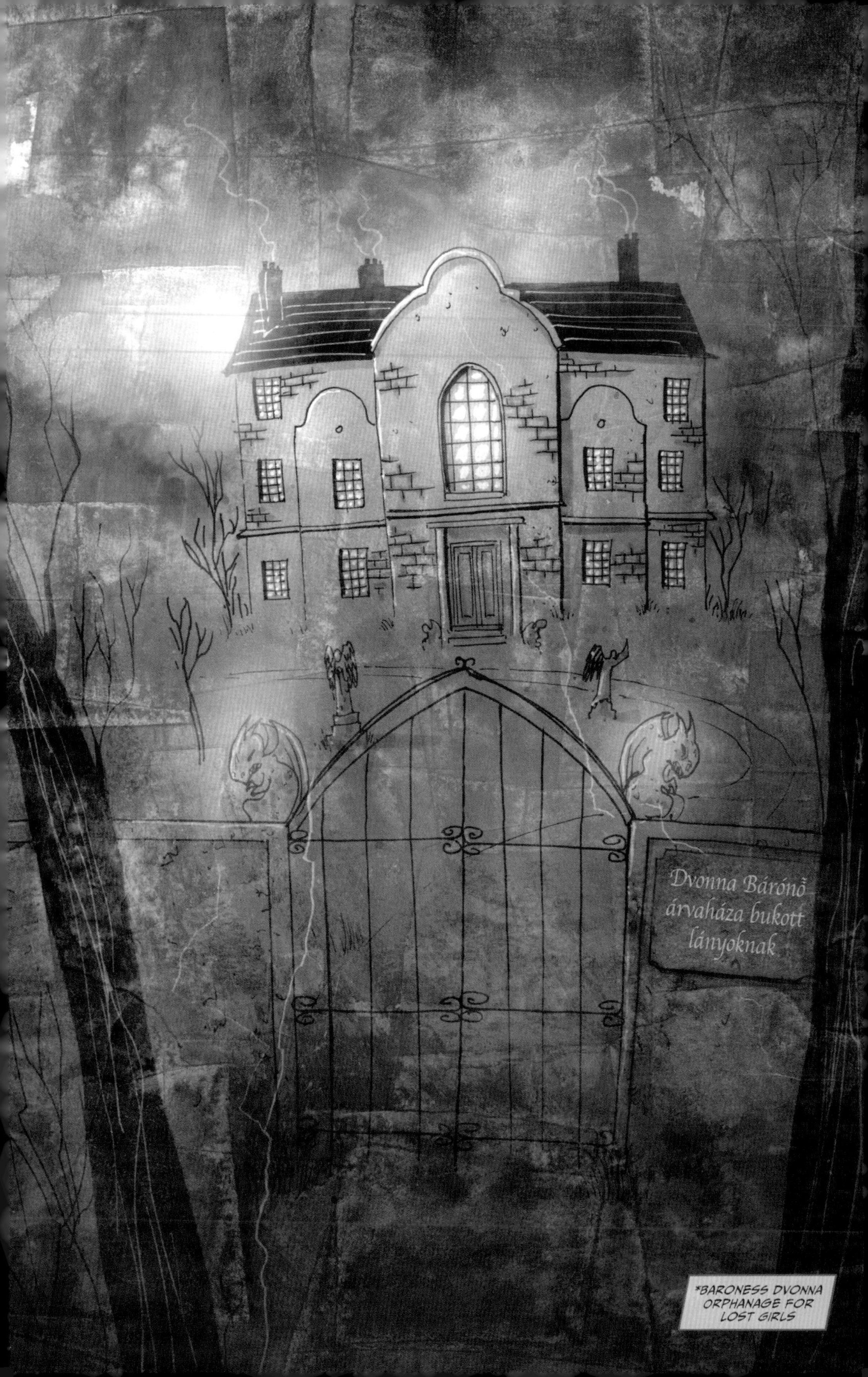
Dvonna Bárónő
árvaháza bukott
lányoknak
*BARONESS DVONNA
ORPHANAGE FOR
LOST GIRLS

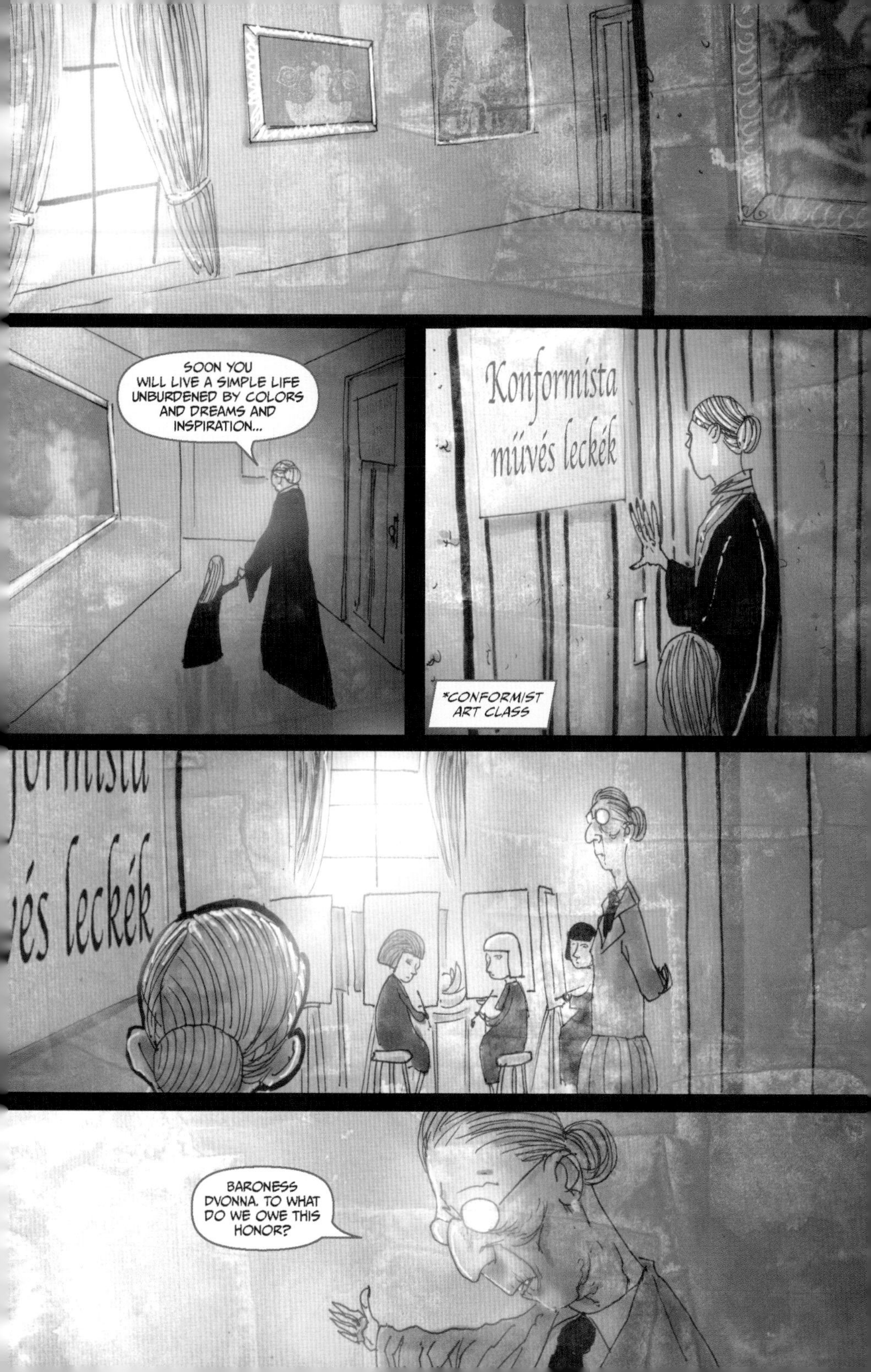

SOON YOU WILL LIVE A SIMPLE LIFE UNBURDENED BY COLORS AND DREAMS AND INSPIRATION...
Konformista művés leckék
*CONFORMIST ART CLASS
BARONESS DVONNA. TO WHAT DO WE OWE THIS HONOR?

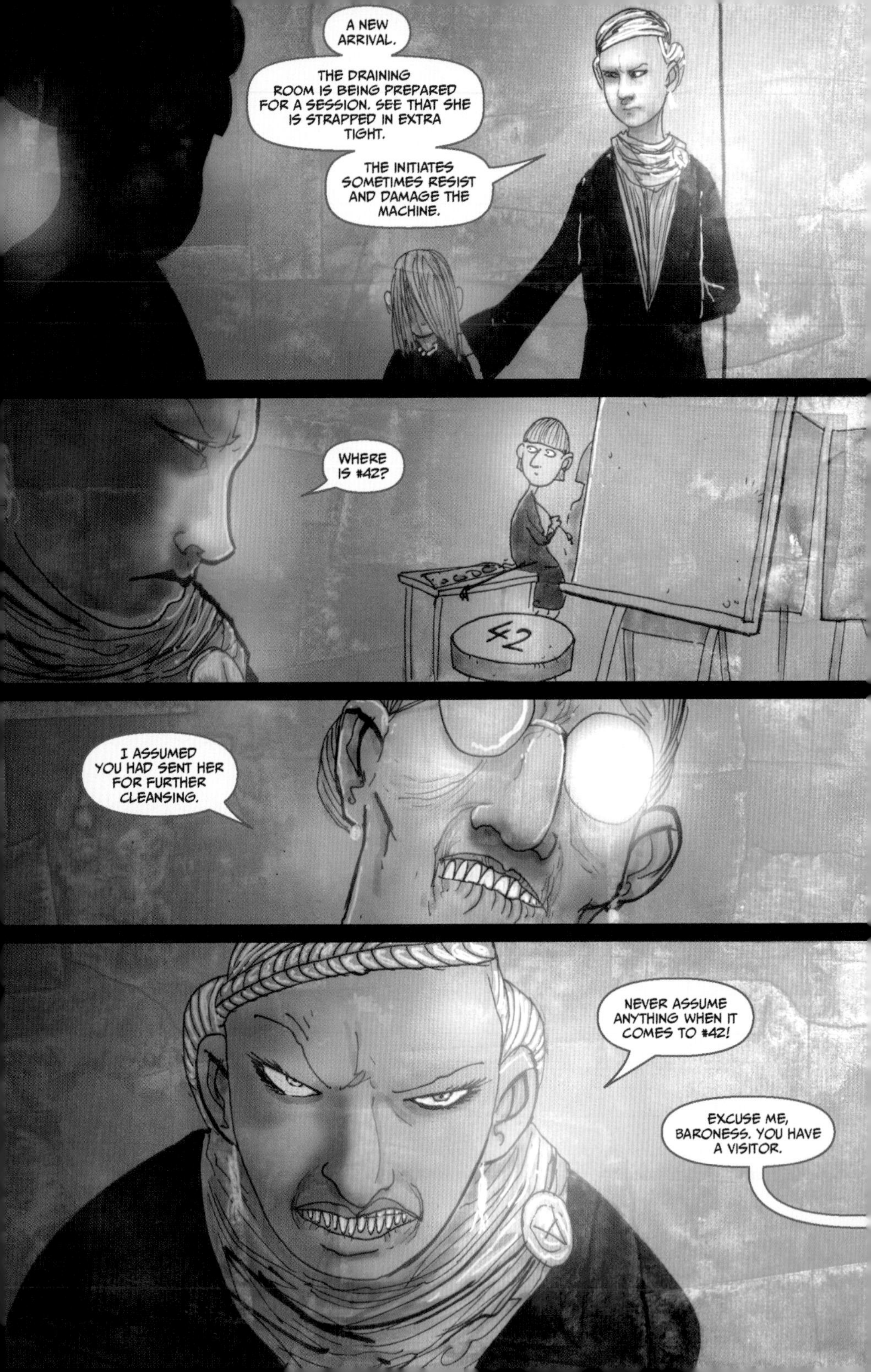
A NEW ARRIVAL.
THE DRAINING ROOM IS BEING PREPARED FOR A SESSION. SEE THAT SHE IS STRAPPED IN EXTRA TIGHT.
THE INITIATES SOMETIMES RESIST AND DAMAGE THE MACHINE.
WHERE IS #42?
42
I ASSUMED YOU HAD SENT HER FOR FURTHER CLEANSING.
NEVER ASSUME ANYTHING WHEN IT COMES TO #42!
EXCUSE ME, BARONESS. YOU HAVE A VISITOR.

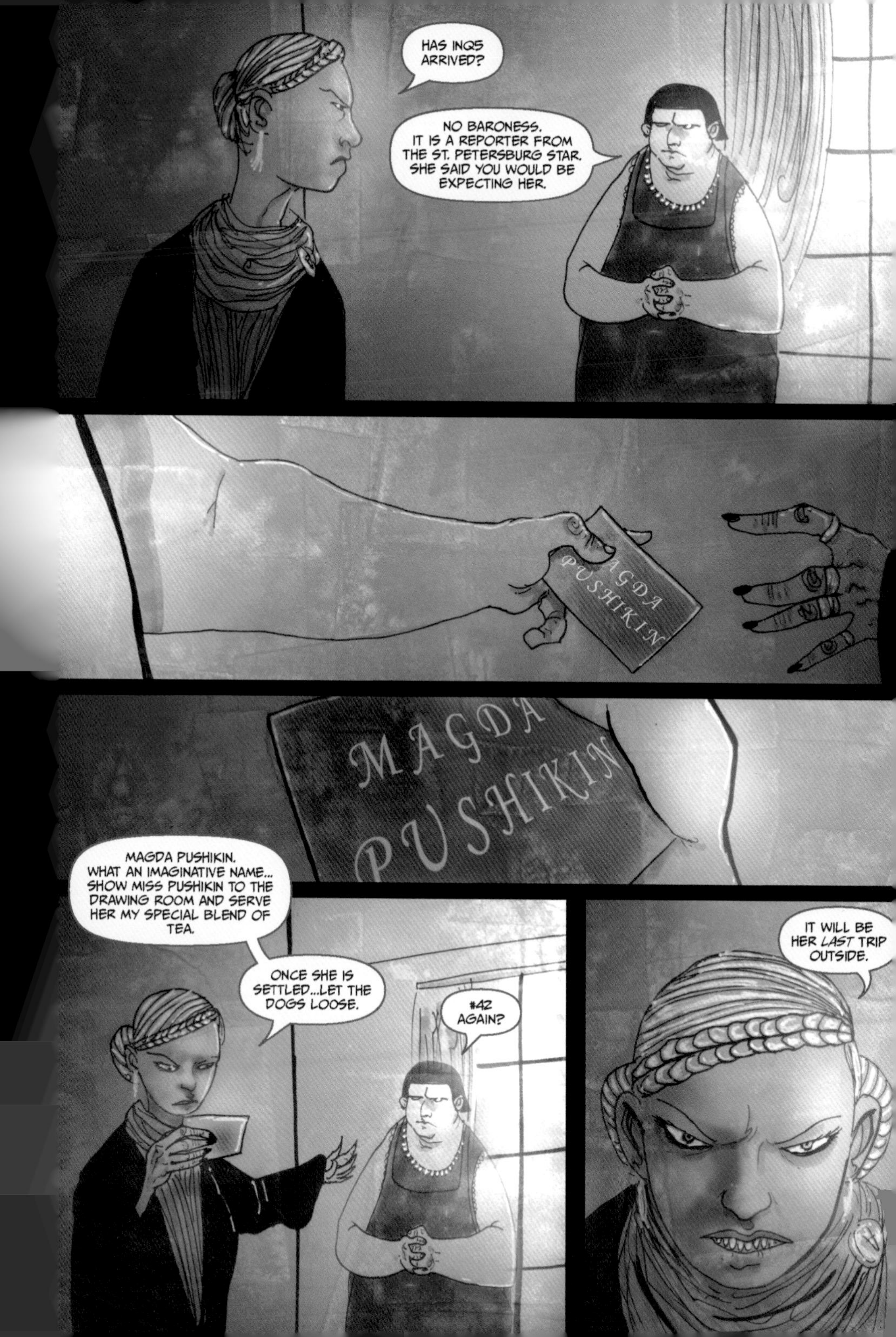
HAS INQ5 ARRIVED?
NO BARONESS. IT IS A REPORTER FROM THE ST. PETERSBURG STAR. SHE SAID YOU WOULD BE EXPECTING HER.
MAGDA PUSHIKIN
MAGDA PUSHIKIN
MAGDA PUSHIKIN. WHAT AN IMAGINATIVE NAME... SHOW MISS PUSHIKIN TO THE DRAWING ROOM AND SERVE HER MY SPECIAL BLEND OF TEA.
ONCE SHE IS SETTLED...LET THE DOGS LOOSE.
#42 AGAIN?
IT WILL BE HER *LAST* TRIP OUTSIDE.

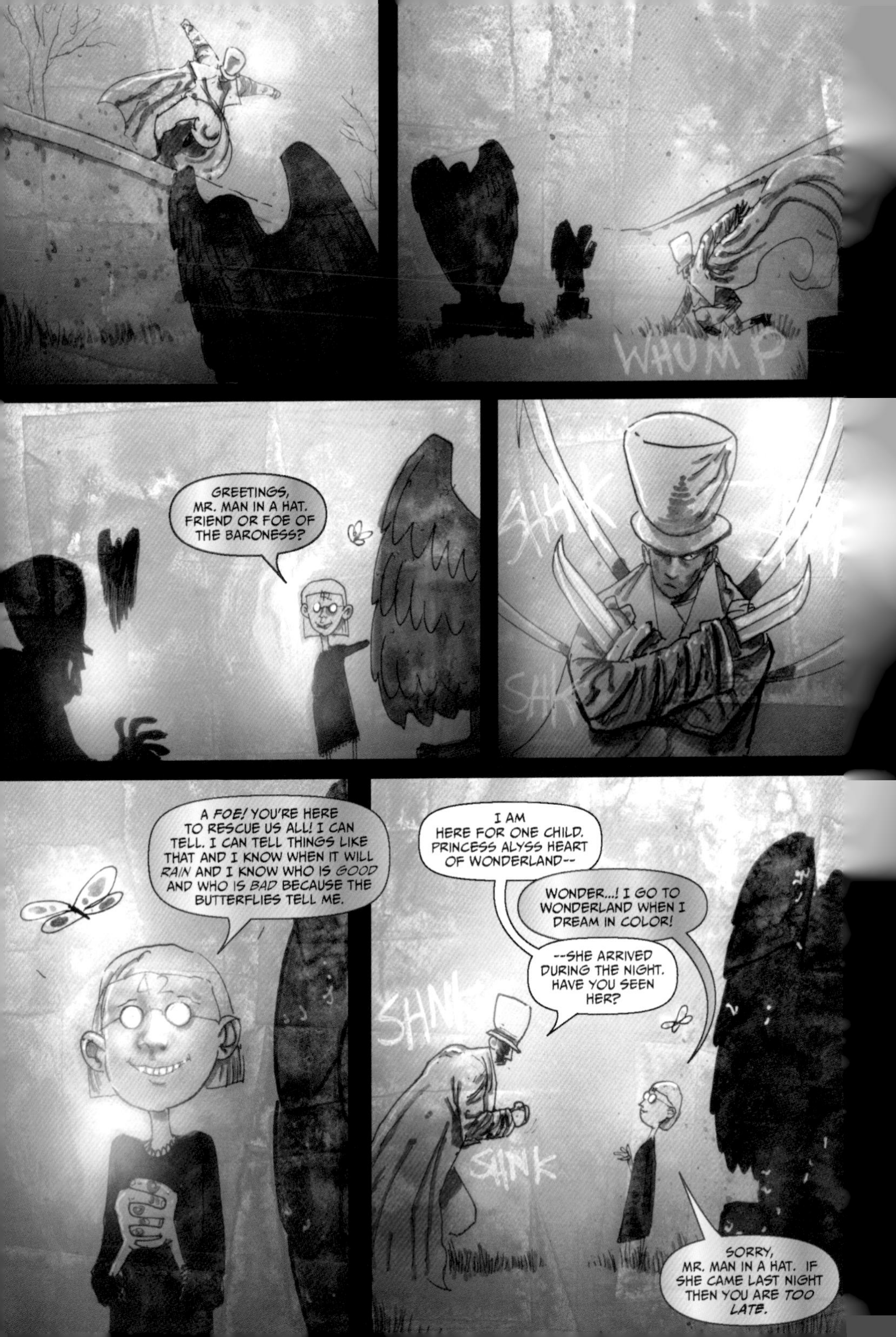
WHUMP
GREETINGS, MR. MAN IN A HAT. FRIEND OR FOE OF THE BARONESS?
SHNK
SHNK
A FOE! YOU'RE HERE TO RESCUE US ALL! I CAN TELL. I CAN TELL THINGS LIKE THAT AND I KNOW WHEN IT WILL RAIN AND I KNOW WHO IS GOOD AND WHO IS BAD BECAUSE THE BUTTERFLIES TELL ME.
I AM HERE FOR ONE CHILD. PRINCESS ALYSS HEART OF WONDERLAND--
WONDER...! I GO TO WONDERLAND WHEN I DREAM IN COLOR!
--SHE ARRIVED DURING THE NIGHT. HAVE YOU SEEN HER?
SHNK
SHNK
SORRY, MR. MAN IN A HAT. IF SHE CAME LAST NIGHT THEN YOU ARE TOO LATE.

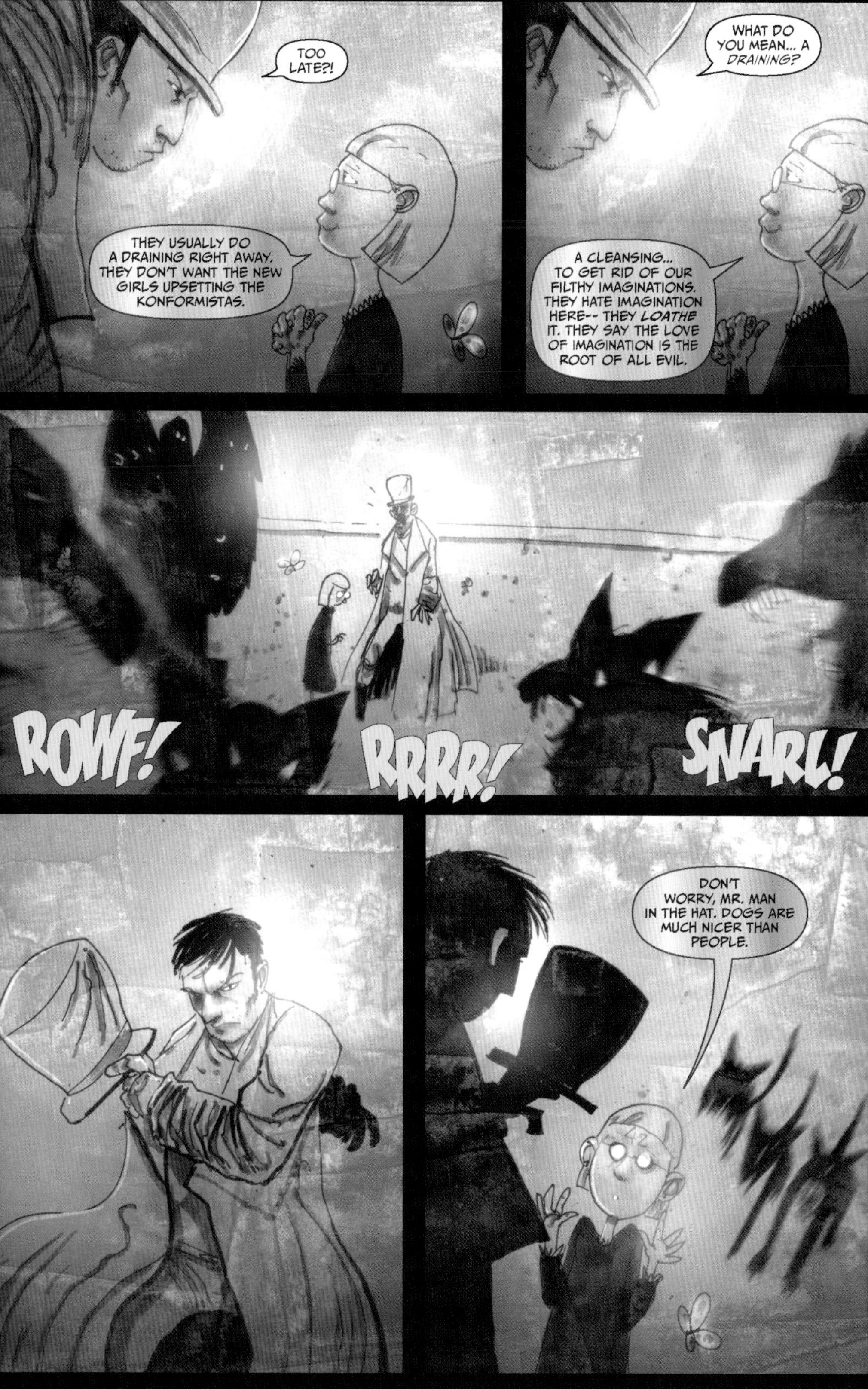
TOO LATE?!
THEY USUALLY DO A DRAINING RIGHT AWAY. THEY DON'T WANT THE NEW GIRLS UPSETTING THE KONFORMISTAS.
WHAT DO YOU MEAN... A *DRAINING?*
A CLEANSING... TO GET RID OF OUR FILTHY IMAGINATIONS. THEY HATE IMAGINATION HERE-- THEY *LOATHE* IT. THEY SAY THE LOVE OF IMAGINATION IS THE ROOT OF ALL EVIL.
ROWF!
RRRR!
SNARL!
DON'T WORRY, MR. MAN IN THE HAT. DOGS ARE MUCH NICER THAN PEOPLE.

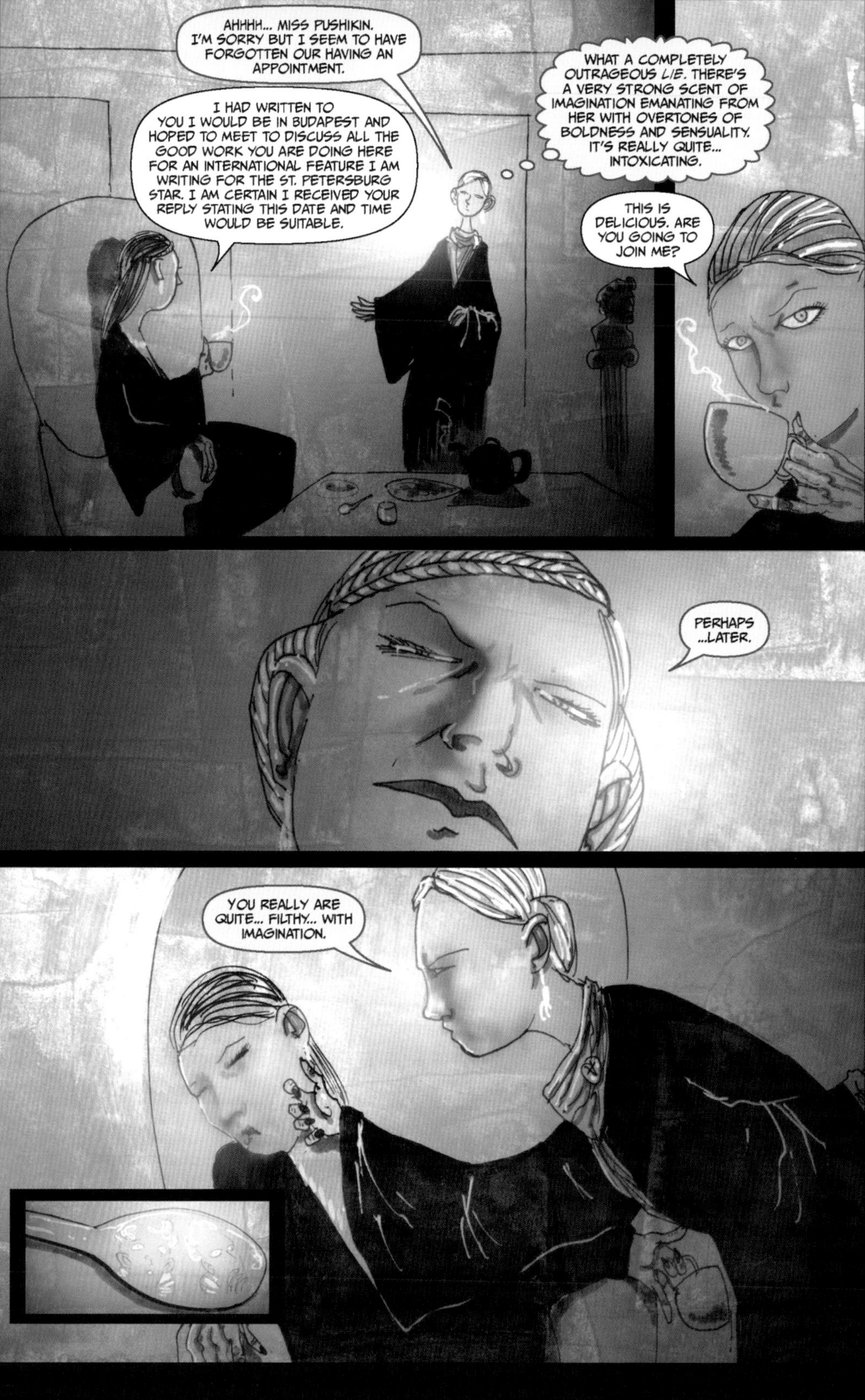
AHHHH... MISS PUSHIKIN. I'M SORRY BUT I SEEM TO HAVE FORGOTTEN OUR HAVING AN APPOINTMENT.
I HAD WRITTEN TO YOU I WOULD BE IN BUDAPEST AND HOPED TO MEET TO DISCUSS ALL THE GOOD WORK YOU ARE DOING HERE FOR AN INTERNATIONAL FEATURE I AM WRITING FOR THE ST. PETERSBURG STAR. I AM CERTAIN I RECEIVED YOUR REPLY STATING THIS DATE AND TIME WOULD BE SUITABLE.
WHAT A COMPLETELY OUTRAGEOUS LIE. THERE'S A VERY STRONG SCENT OF IMAGINATION EMANATING FROM HER WITH OVERTONES OF BOLDNESS AND SENSUALITY. IT'S REALLY QUITE... INTOXICATING.
THIS IS DELICIOUS. ARE YOU GOING TO JOIN ME?
PERHAPS ...LATER.
YOU REALLY ARE QUITE... FILTHY... WITH IMAGINATION.

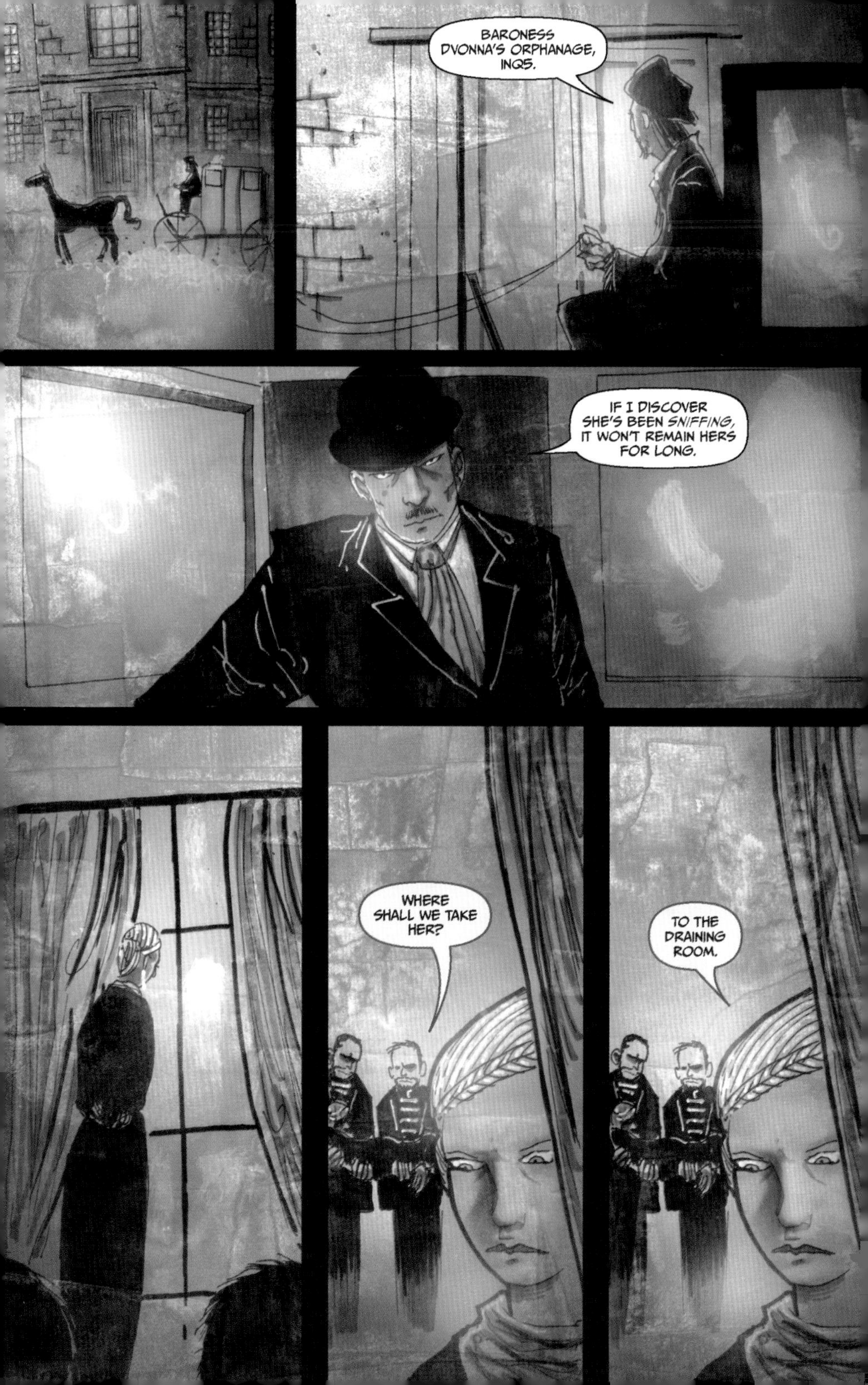
BARONESS DVONNA'S ORPHANAGE, INQ5.
IF I DISCOVER SHE'S BEEN SNIFFING, IT WON'T REMAIN HERS FOR LONG.
WHERE SHALL WE TAKE HER?
TO THE DRAINING ROOM.

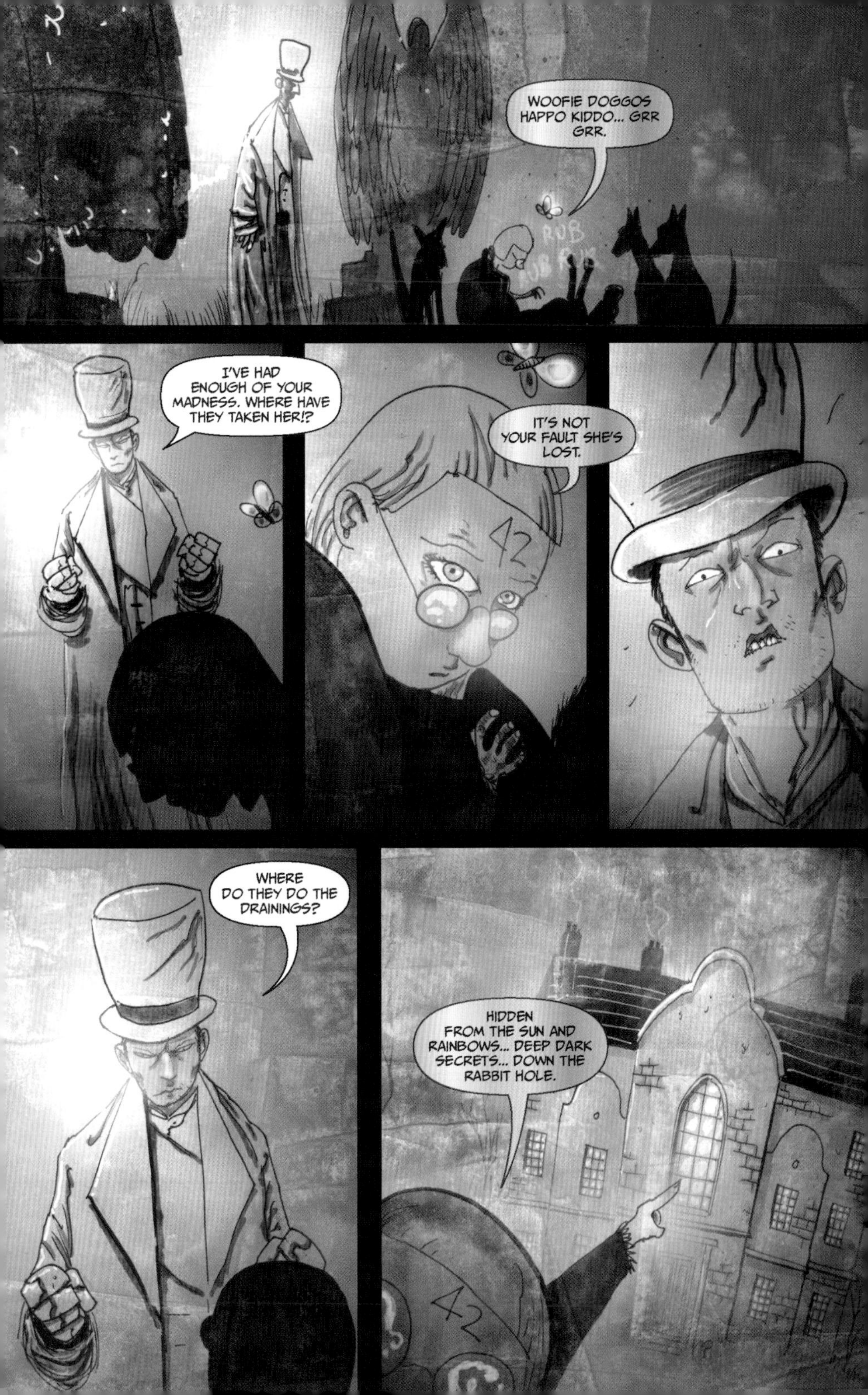
WOOFIE DOGGOS HAPPO KIDDO... GRR GRR.
RUB RUB RUB
I'VE HAD ENOUGH OF YOUR MADNESS. WHERE HAVE THEY TAKEN HER!?
IT'S NOT YOUR FAULT SHE'S LOST.
WHERE DO THEY DO THE DRAININGS?
HIDDEN FROM THE SUN AND RAINBOWS... DEEP DARK SECRETS... DOWN THE RABBIT HOLE.

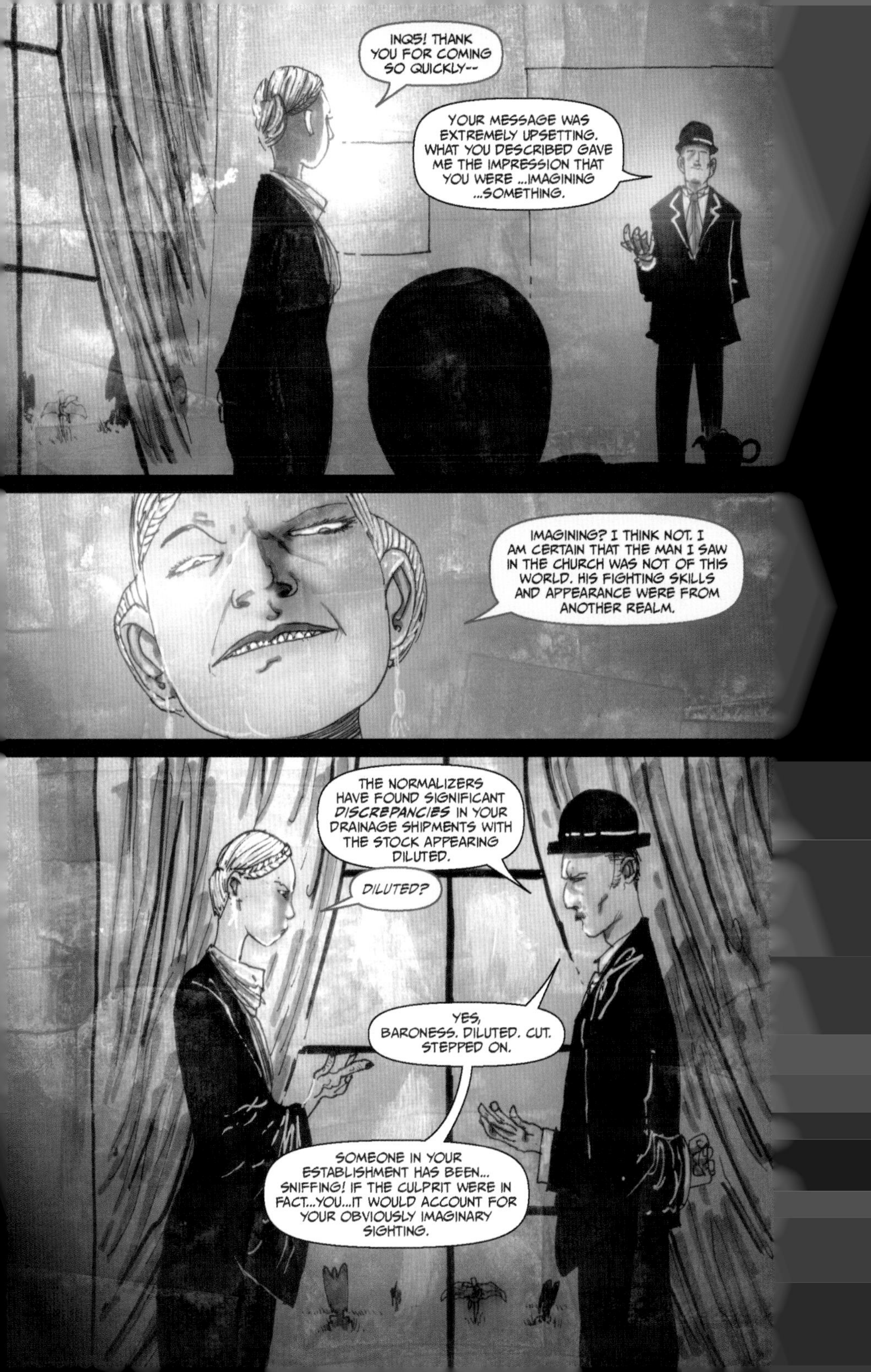
INQ5! THANK YOU FOR COMING SO QUICKLY--
YOUR MESSAGE WAS EXTREMELY UPSETTING. WHAT YOU DESCRIBED GAVE ME THE IMPRESSION THAT YOU WERE ...IMAGINING ...SOMETHING.
IMAGINING? I THINK NOT. I AM CERTAIN THAT THE MAN I SAW IN THE CHURCH WAS NOT OF THIS WORLD. HIS FIGHTING SKILLS AND APPEARANCE WERE FROM ANOTHER REALM.
THE NORMALIZERS HAVE FOUND SIGNIFICANT *DISCREPANCIES* IN YOUR DRAINAGE SHIPMENTS WITH THE STOCK APPEARING DILUTED.
DILUTED?
YES, BARONESS. DILUTED. CUT. STEPPED ON.
SOMEONE IN YOUR ESTABLISHMENT HAS BEEN... SNIFFING! IF THE CULPRIT WERE IN FACT...YOU...IT WOULD ACCOUNT FOR YOUR OBVIOUSLY IMAGINARY SIGHTING.

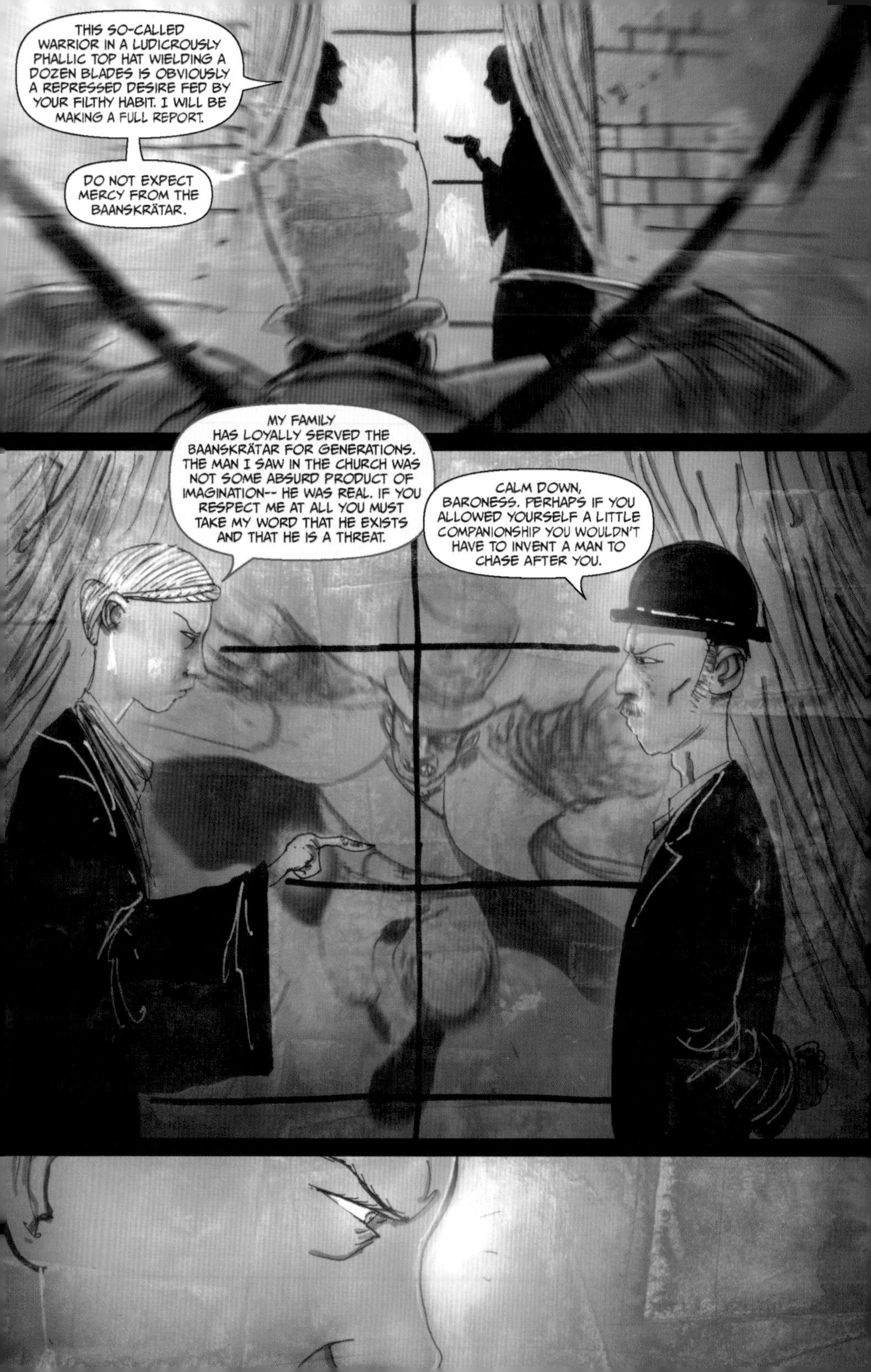
THIS SO-CALLED WARRIOR IN A LUDICROUSLY PHALLIC TOP HAT WIELDING A DOZEN BLADES IS OBVIOUSLY A REPRESSED DESIRE FED BY YOUR FILTHY HABIT. I WILL BE MAKING A FULL REPORT.
DO NOT EXPECT MERCY FROM THE BAANSKRÄTAR.
MY FAMILY HAS LOYALLY SERVED THE BAANSKRÄTAR FOR GENERATIONS. THE MAN I SAW IN THE CHURCH WAS NOT SOME ABSURD PRODUCT OF IMAGINATION-- HE WAS REAL. IF YOU RESPECT ME AT ALL YOU MUST TAKE MY WORD THAT HE EXISTS AND THAT HE IS A THREAT.
CALM DOWN, BARONESS. PERHAPS IF YOU ALLOWED YOURSELF A LITTLE COMPANIONSHIP YOU WOULDN'T HAVE TO INVENT A MAN TO CHASE AFTER YOU.

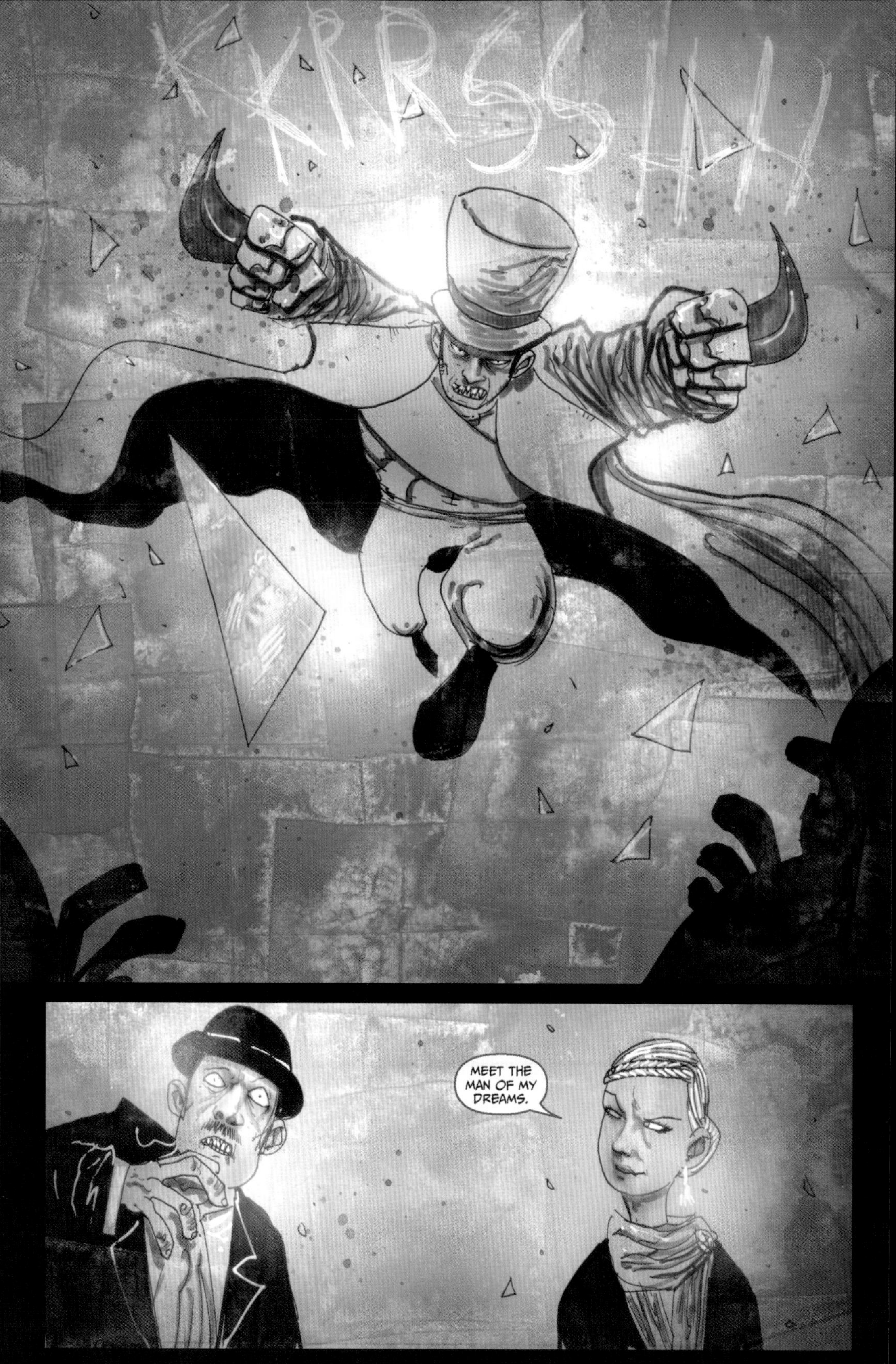
KKRRSSHH
MEET THE MAN OF MY DREAMS.

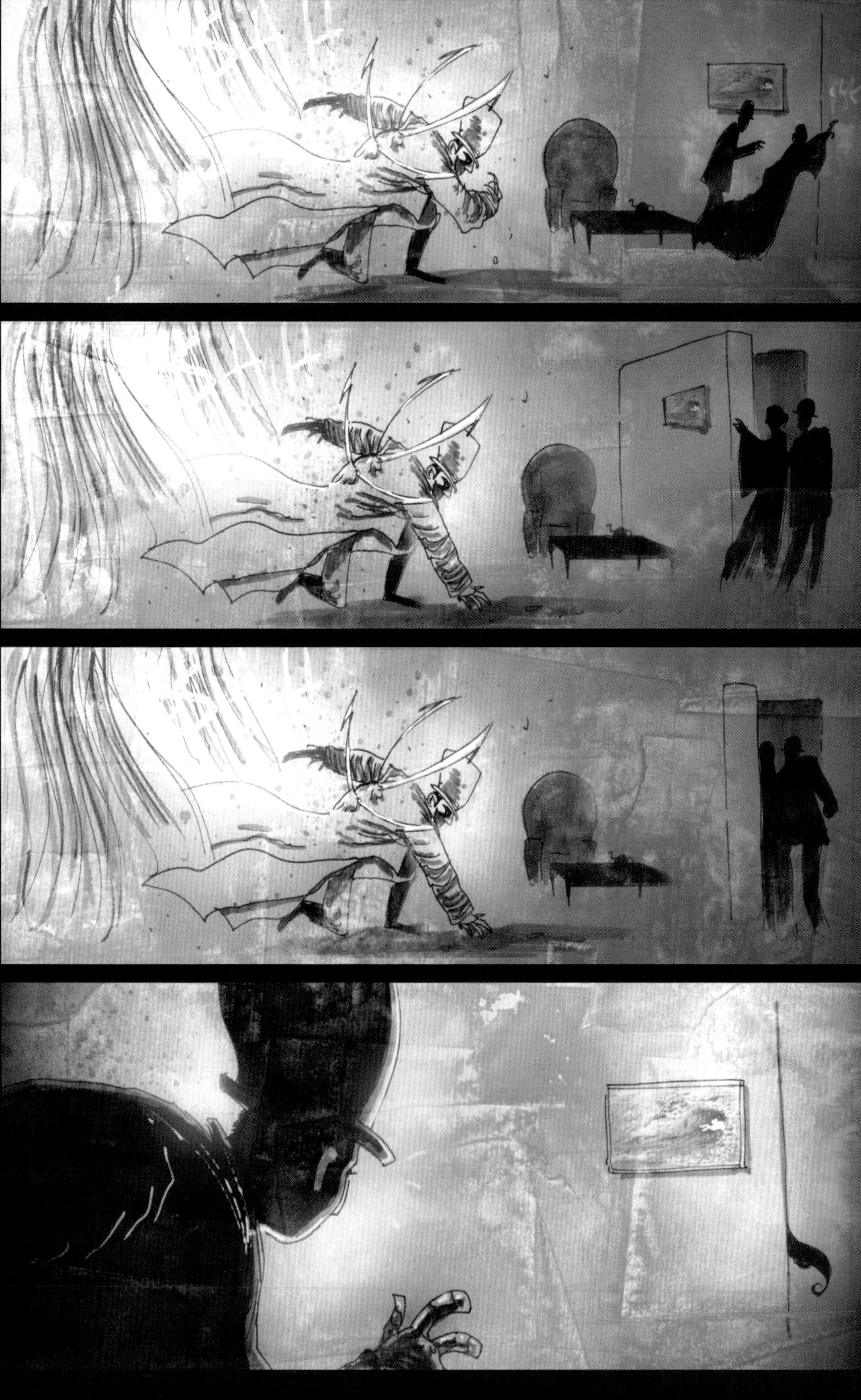

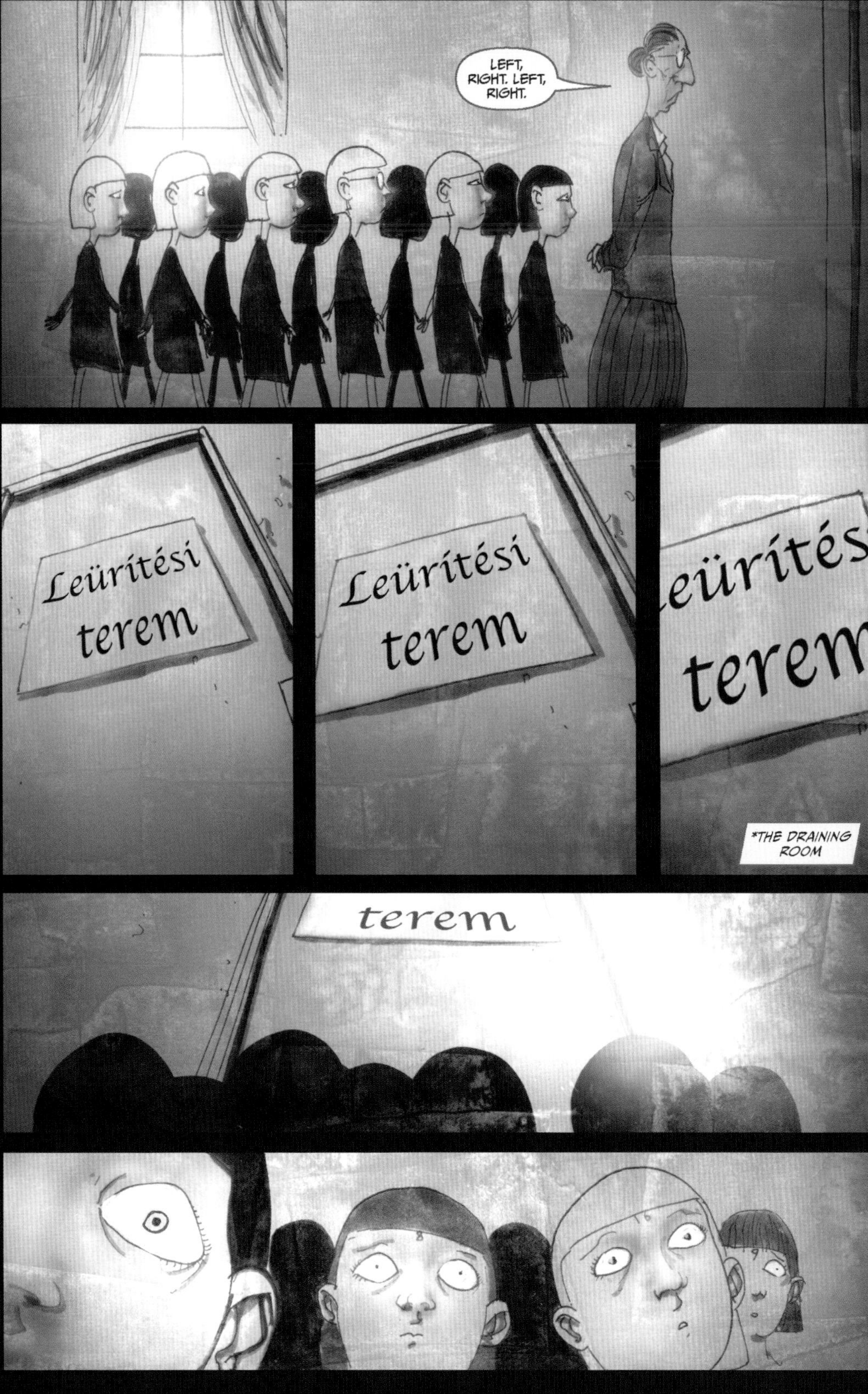
LEFT, RIGHT. LEFT, RIGHT.
Leürítési terem
Leürítési terem
eürítés terem
*THE DRAINING ROOM
terem

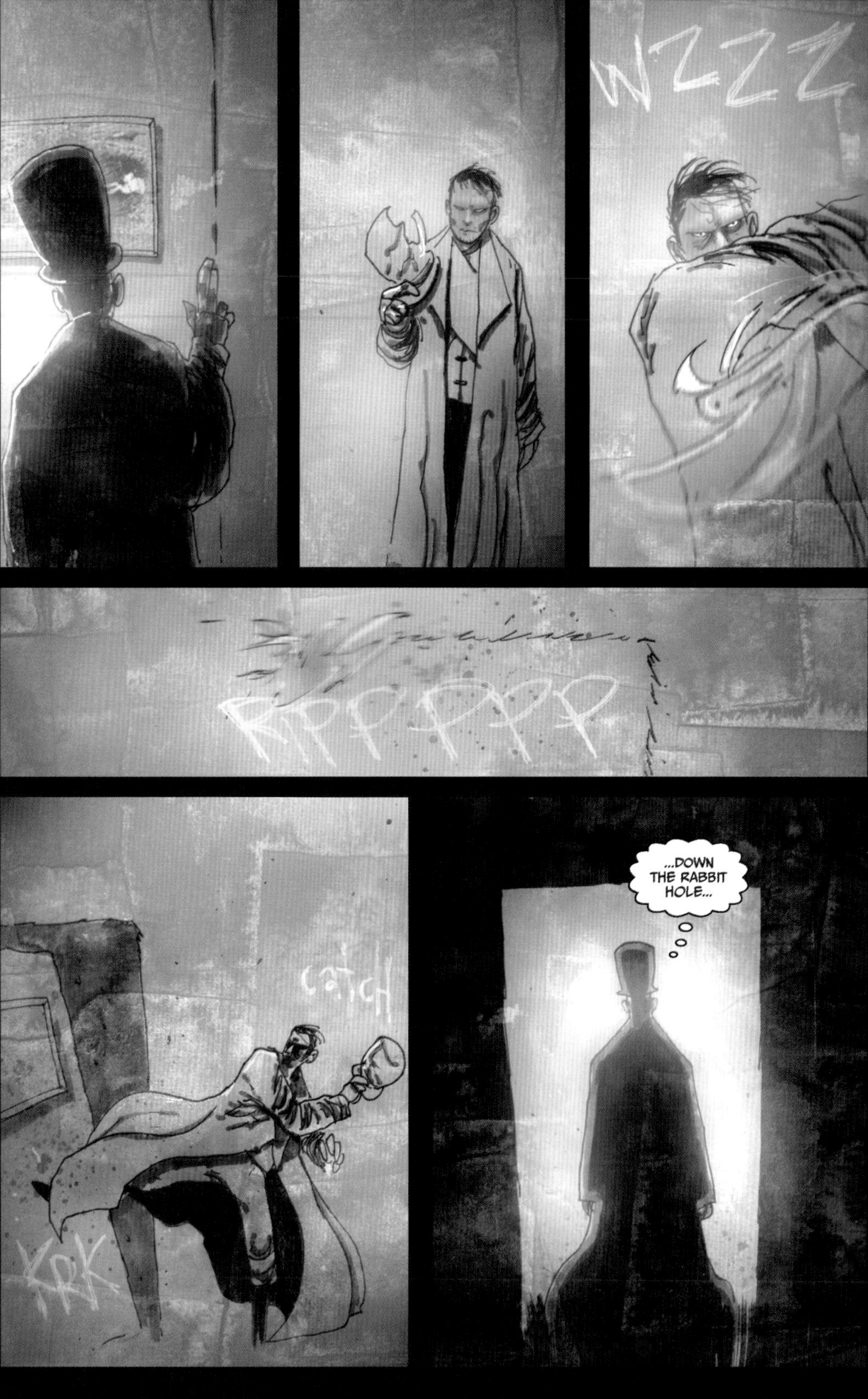
WZZZ
RPPPPP
catch
KRK
...DOWN THE RABBIT HOLE...

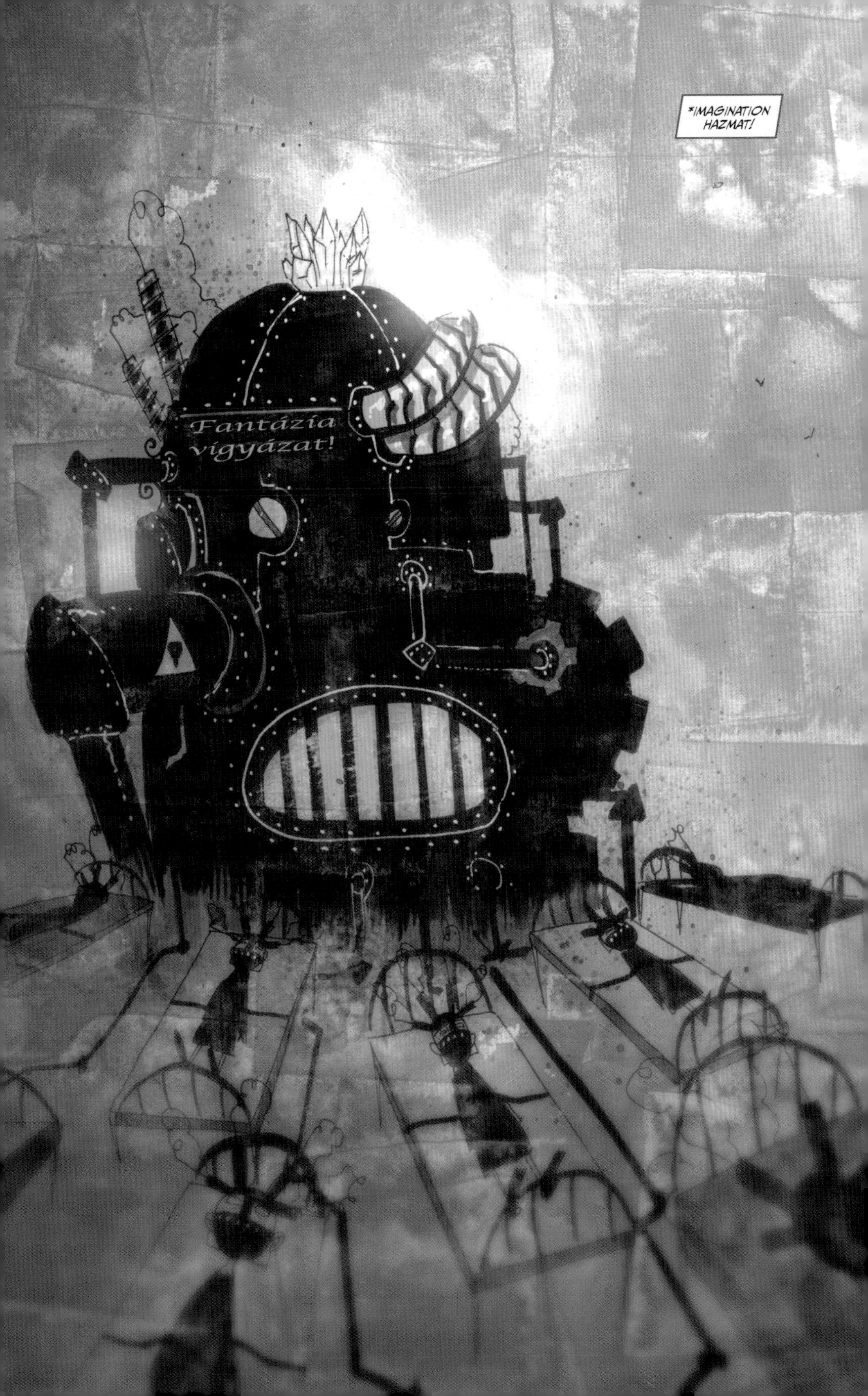
*IMAGINATION HAZMAT!
Fantázia vigyázat!

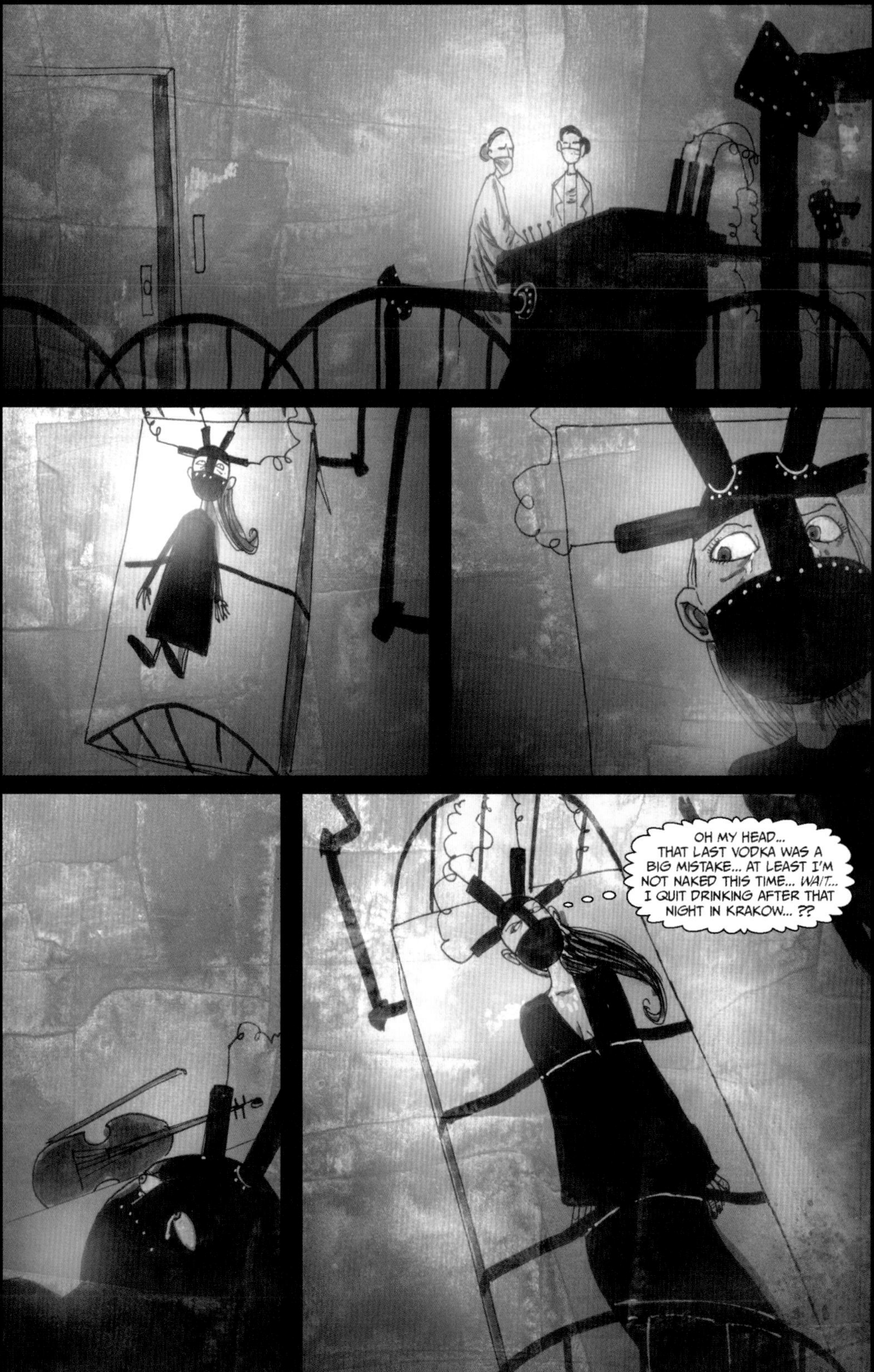
OH MY HEAD... THAT LAST VODKA WAS A BIG MISTAKE... AT LEAST I'M NOT NAKED THIS TIME... *WAIT...* I QUIT DRINKING AFTER THAT NIGHT IN KRAKOW... ??

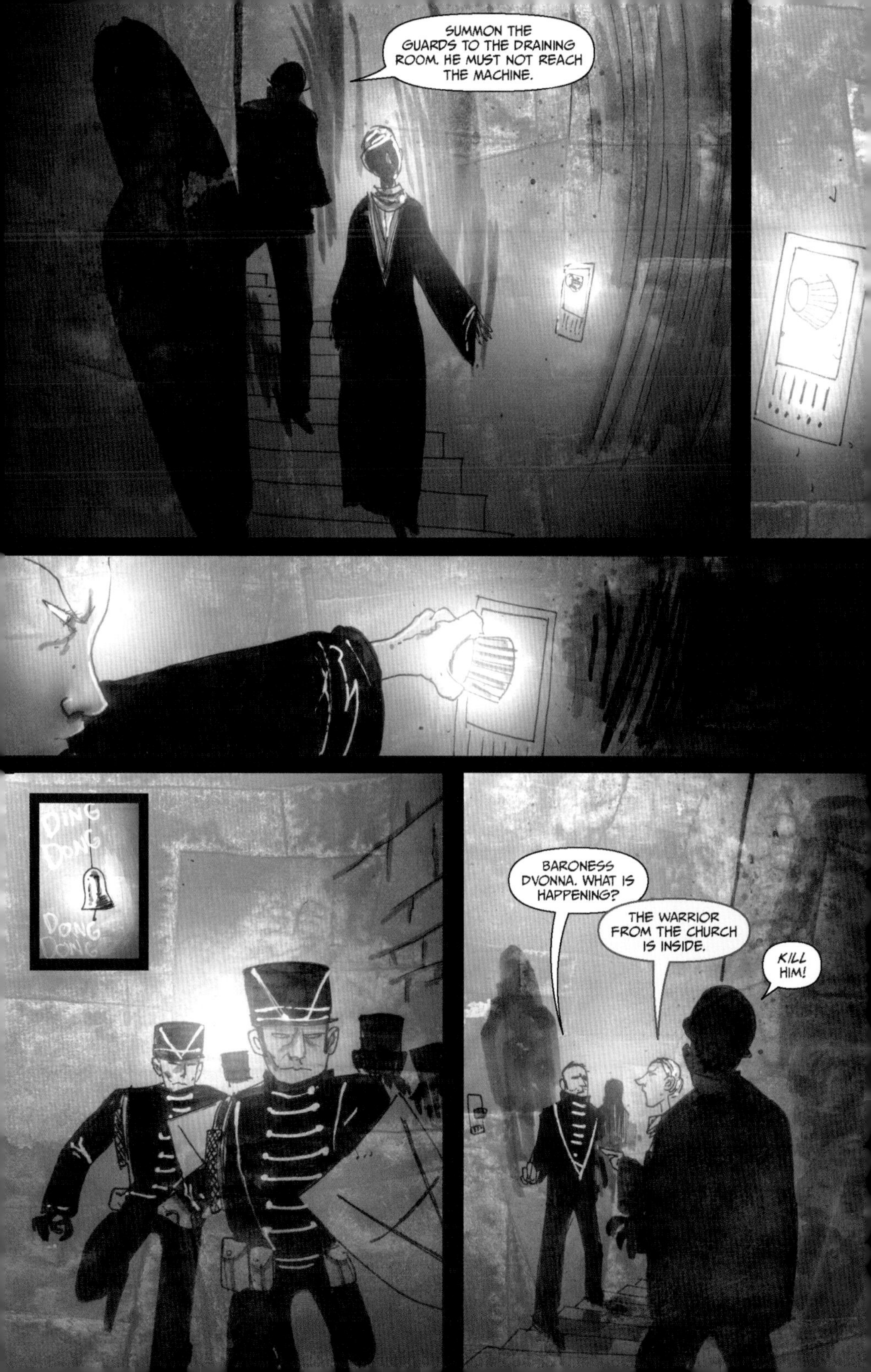
SUMMON THE GUARDS TO THE DRAINING ROOM. HE MUST NOT REACH THE MACHINE.
DING DONG
DONG DONG
BARONESS DVONNA. WHAT IS HAPPENING?
THE WARRIOR FROM THE CHURCH IS INSIDE.
KILL HIM!

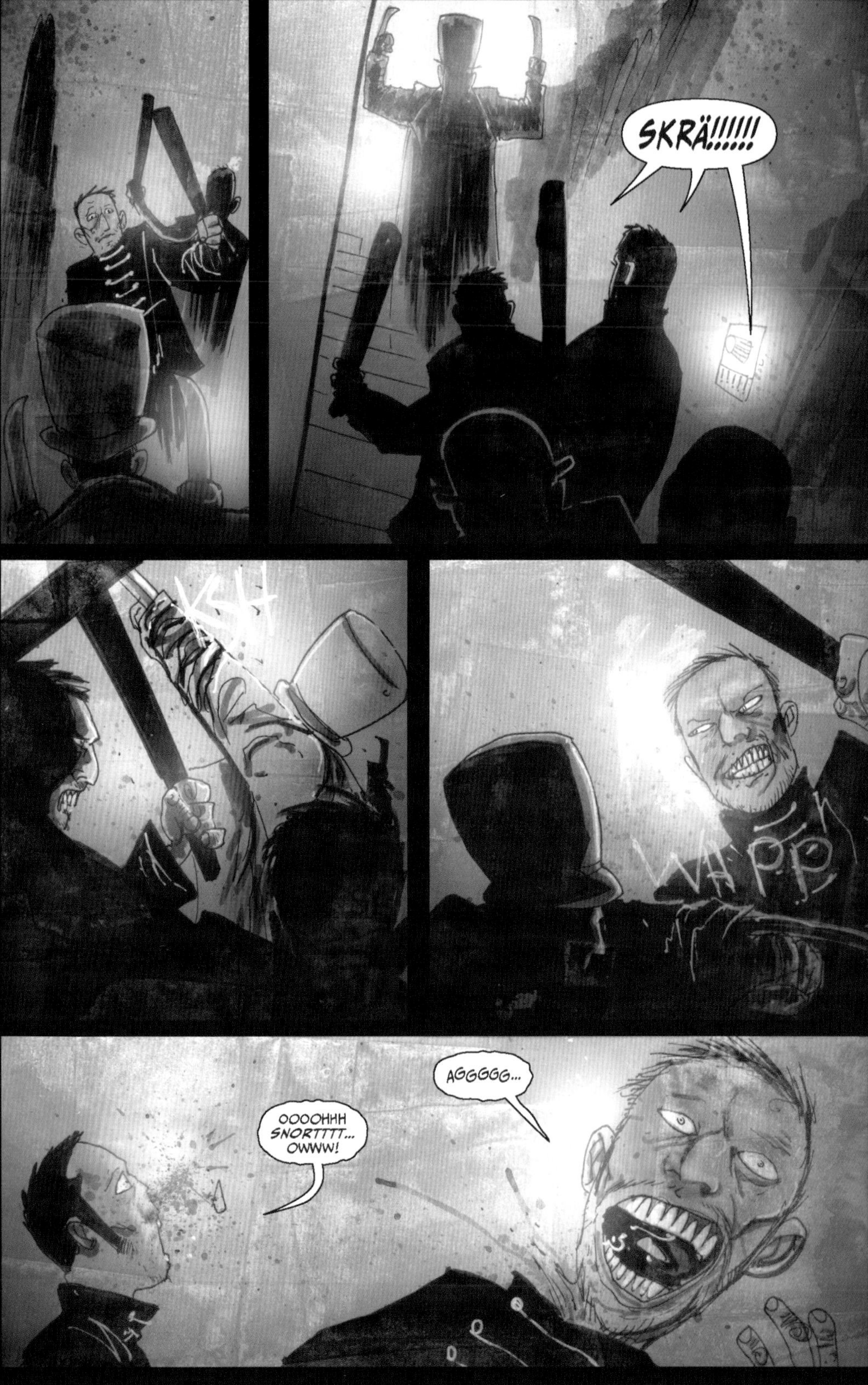
SKRÄ!!!!!!
AGGGGG...
OOOOHHH SNORTTTT... OWWW!

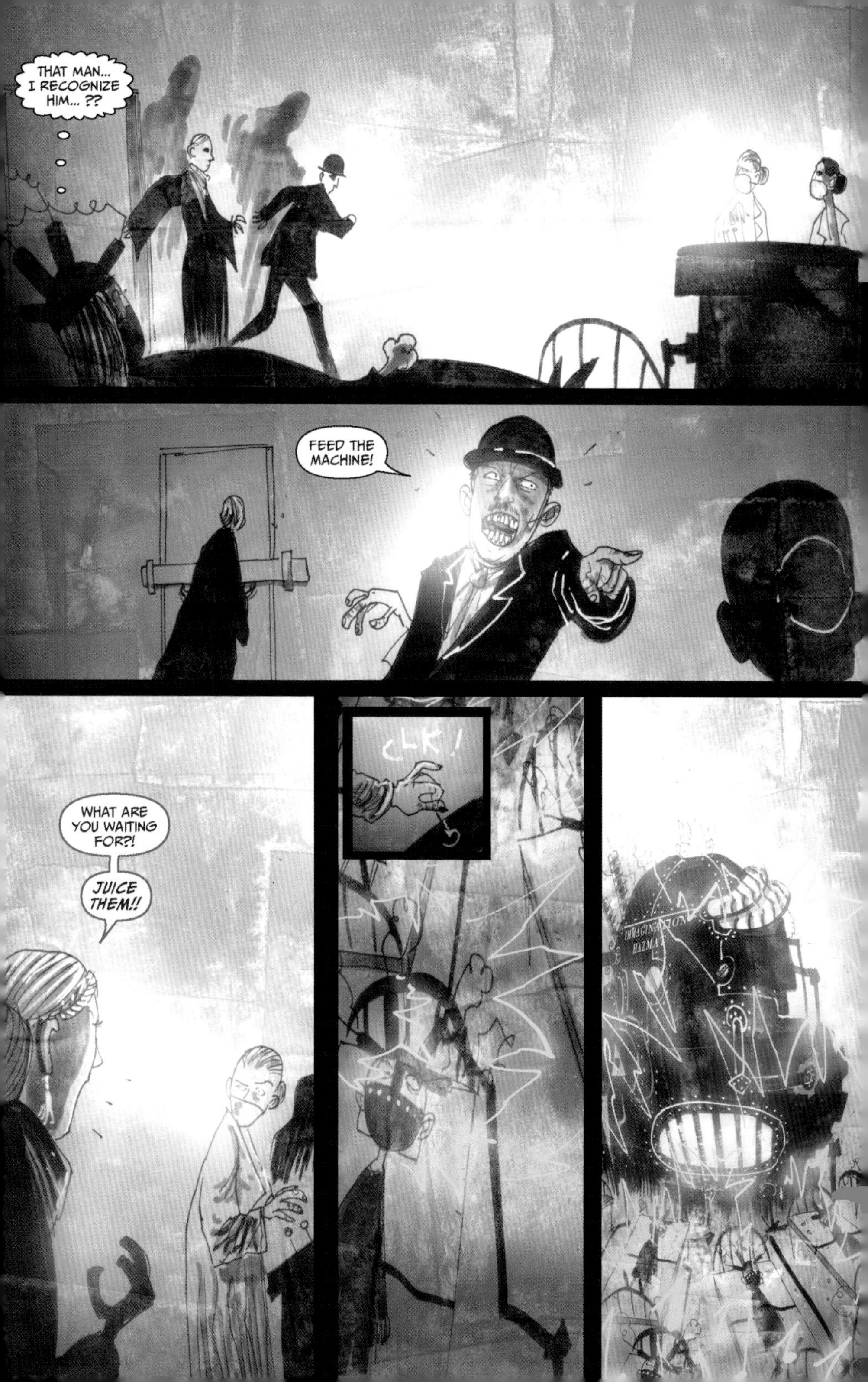
THAT MAN... I RECOGNIZE HIM... ??
FEED THE MACHINE!
WHAT ARE YOU WAITING FOR?!
JUICE THEM!!
CLK!

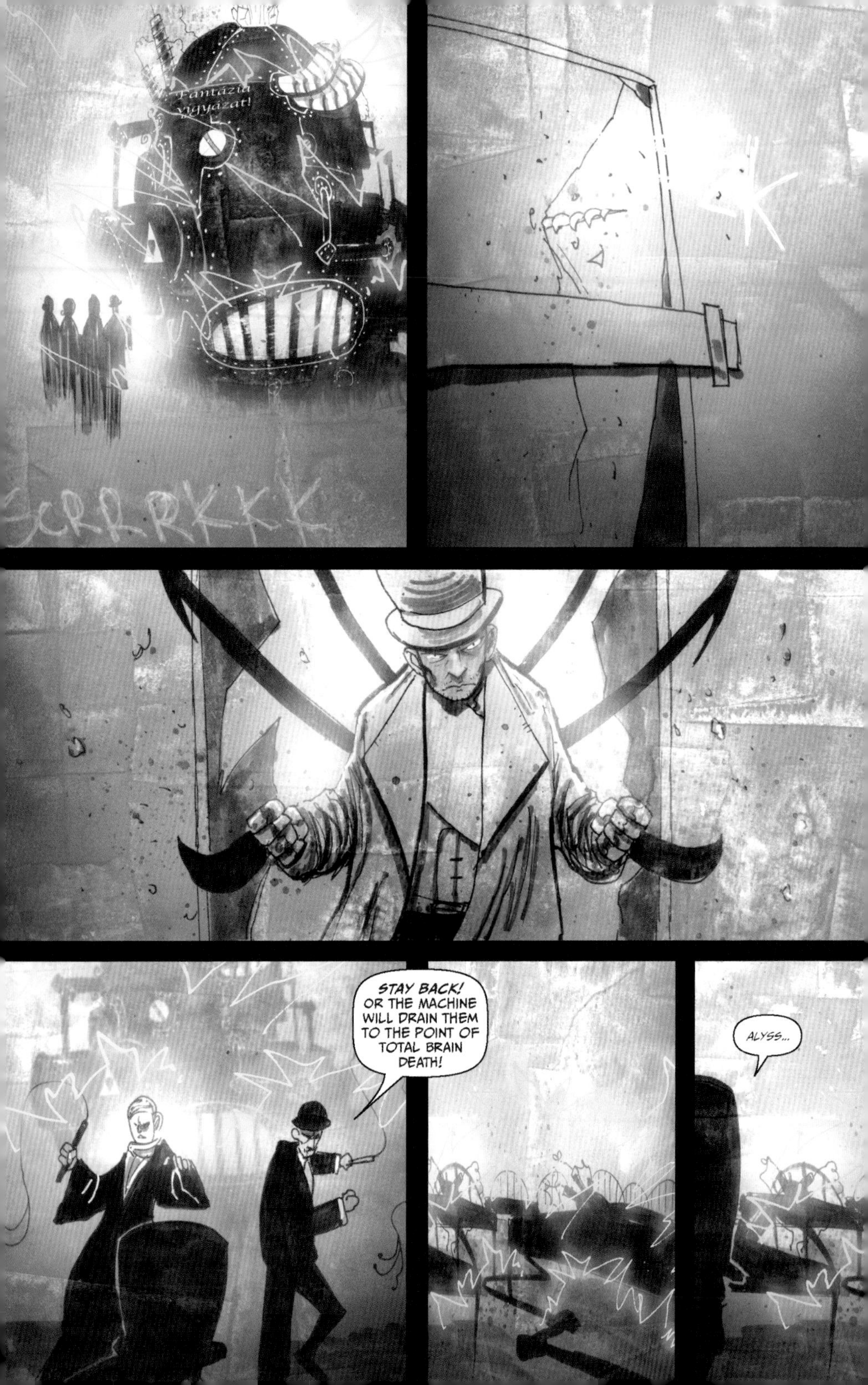
Fantázia vigyázat!
SCRRRKKK
STAY BACK! OR THE MACHINE WILL DRAIN THEM TO THE POINT OF TOTAL BRAIN DEATH!
ALYSS...

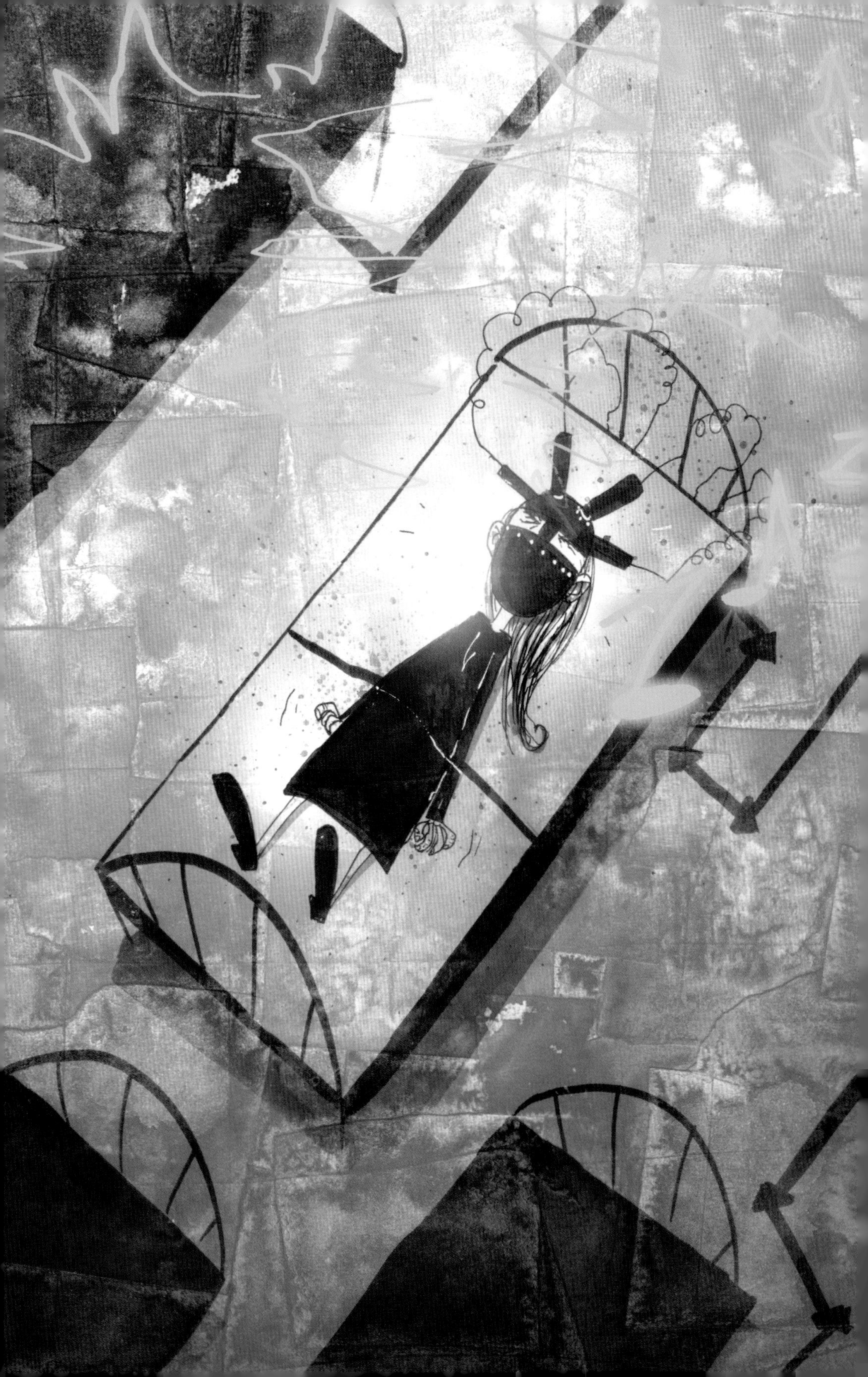

YAAGGH!

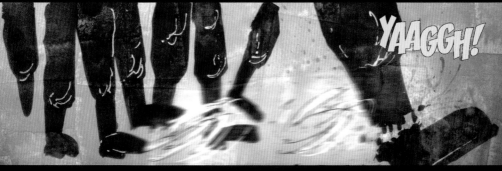

URRK! YAAH!

FULL THROTTLE!!!

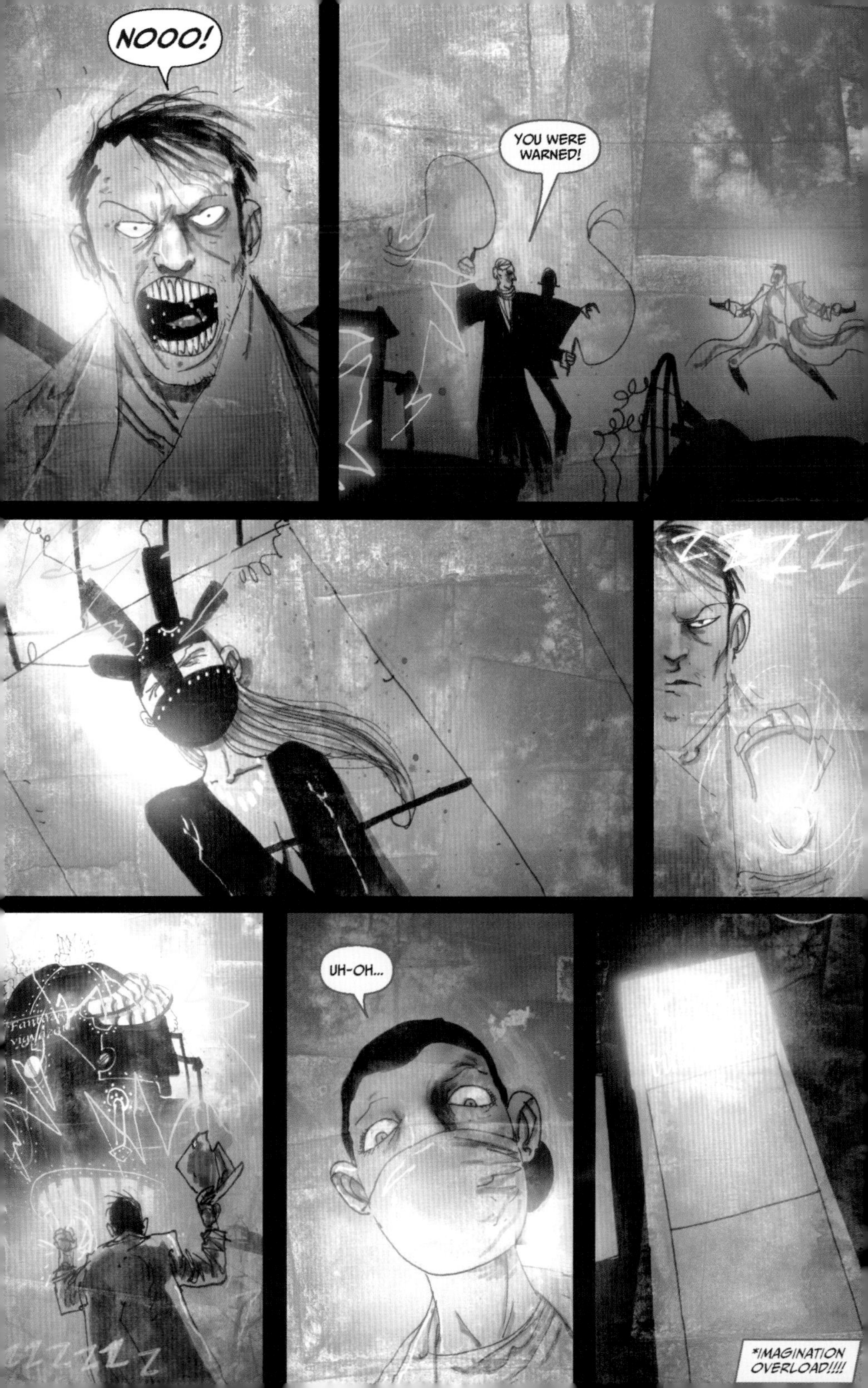
NOOO!
YOU WERE WARNED!
UH-OH...
*IMAGINATION OVERLOAD!!!!

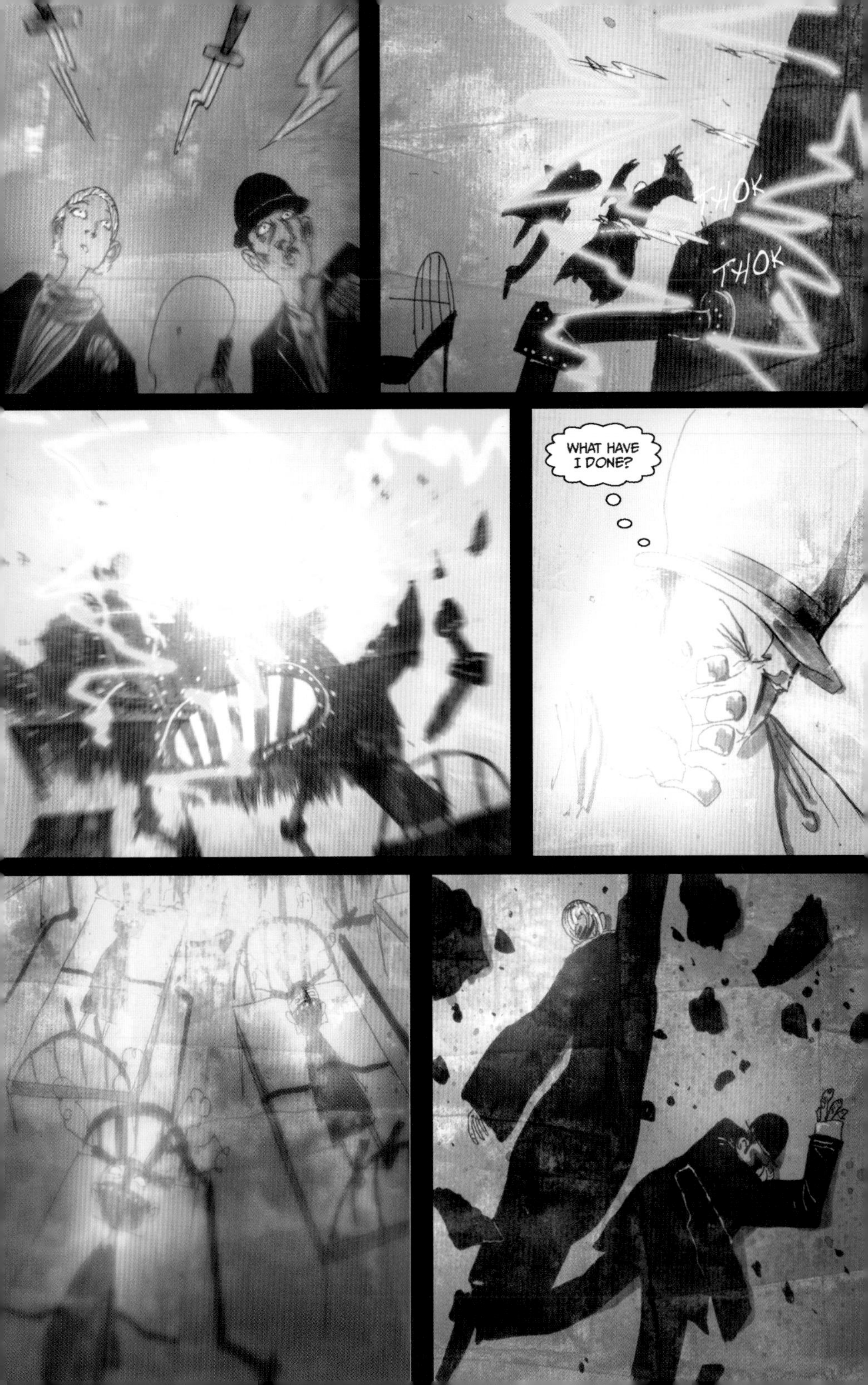
THOK
THOK
WHAT HAVE I DONE?

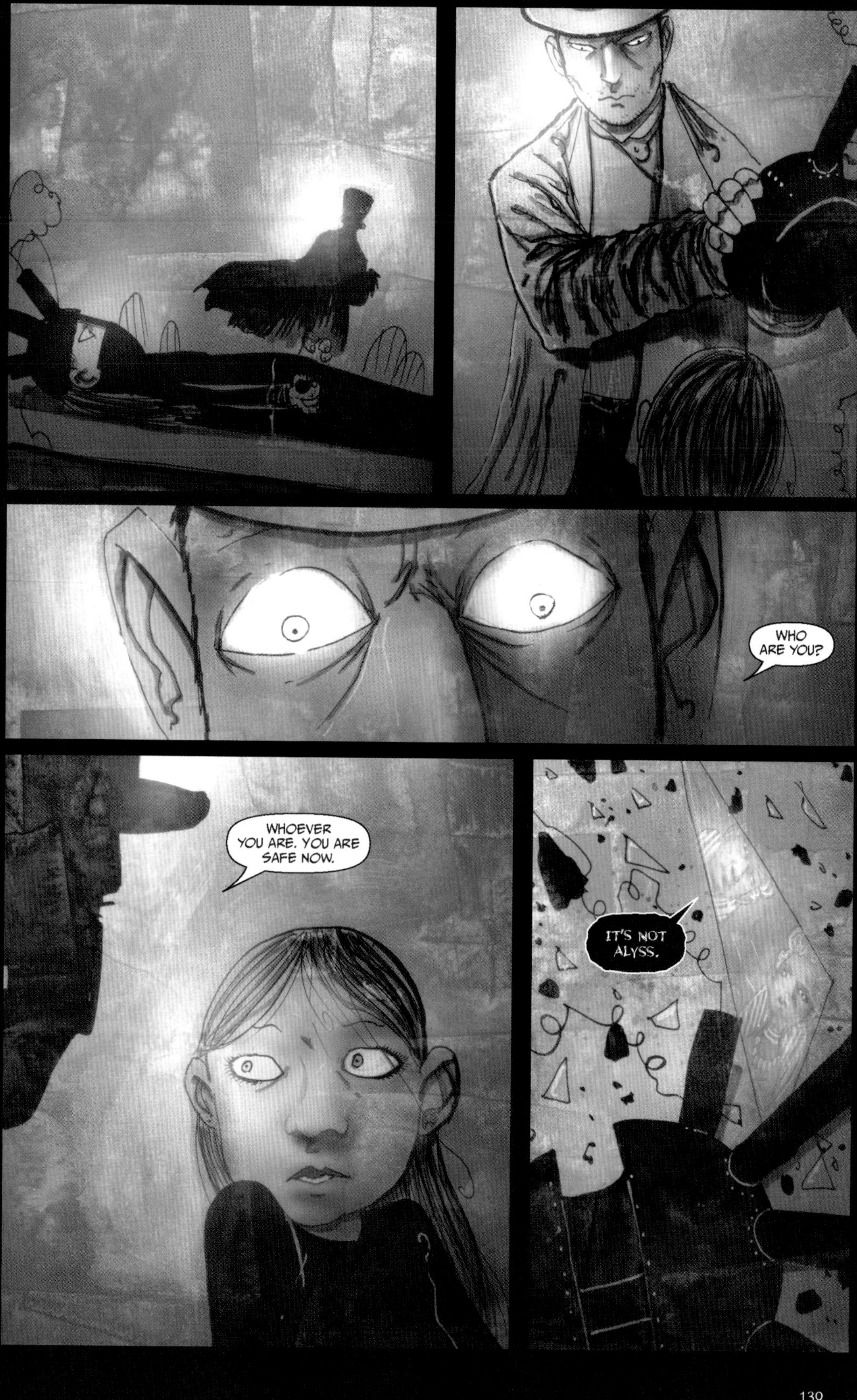
WHO ARE YOU?
WHOEVER YOU ARE. YOU ARE SAFE NOW.
IT'S NOT ALYSS.

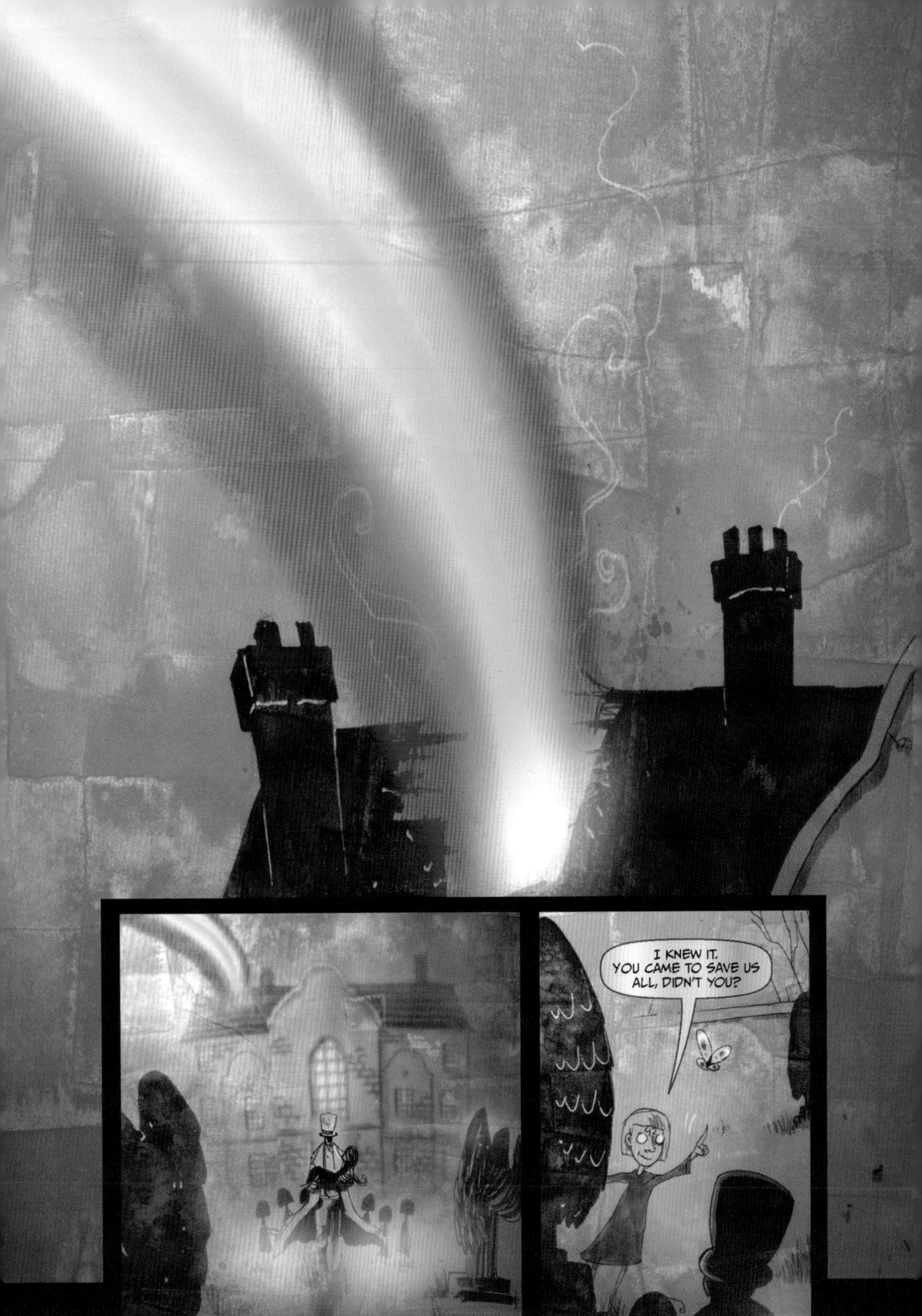
I KNEW IT. YOU CAME TO SAVE US ALL, DIDN'T YOU?

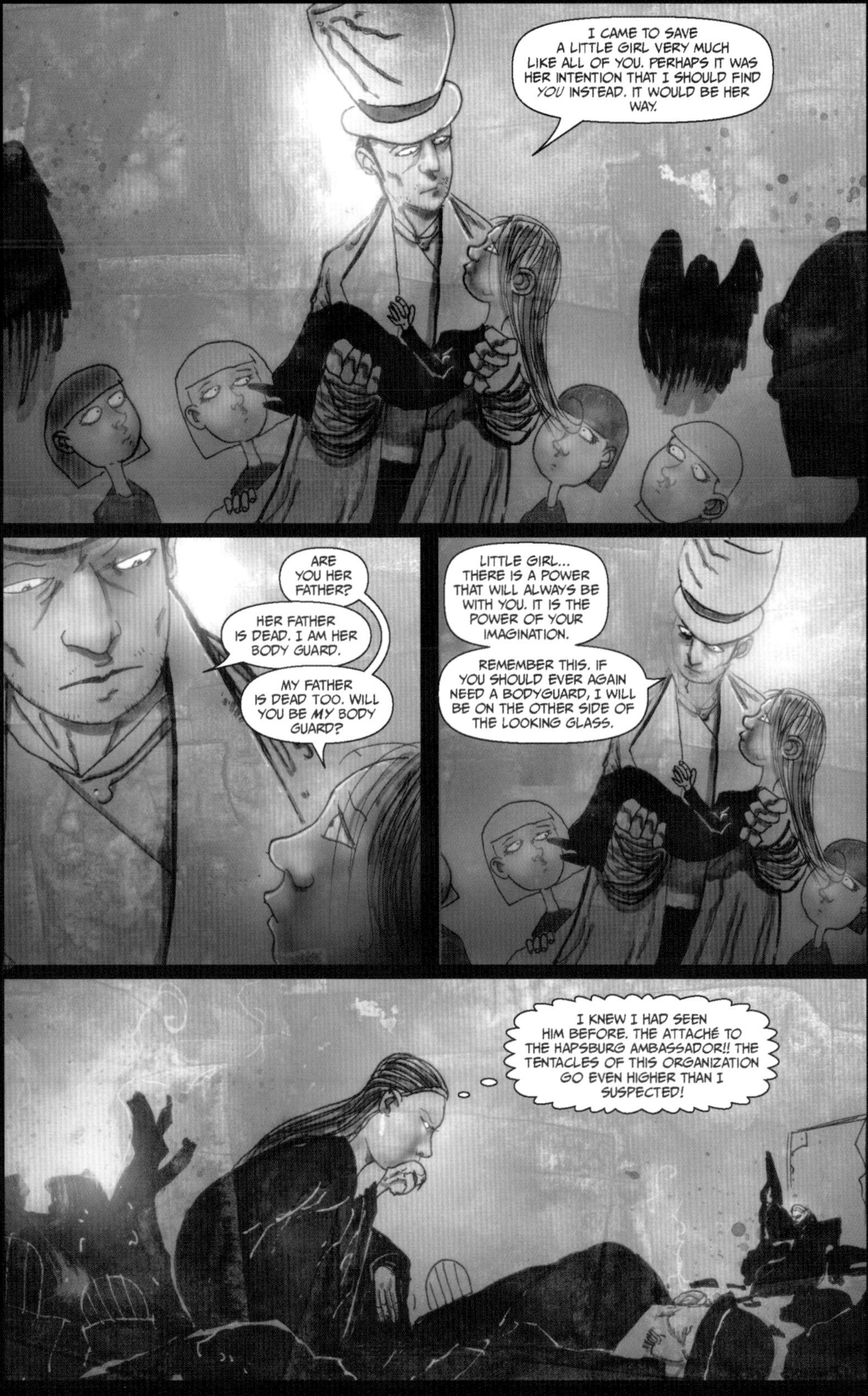
I CAME TO SAVE A LITTLE GIRL VERY MUCH LIKE ALL OF YOU. PERHAPS IT WAS HER INTENTION THAT I SHOULD FIND YOU INSTEAD. IT WOULD BE HER WAY.
ARE YOU HER FATHER?
HER FATHER IS DEAD. I AM HER BODY GUARD.
MY FATHER IS DEAD TOO. WILL YOU BE MY BODY GUARD?
LITTLE GIRL... THERE IS A POWER THAT WILL ALWAYS BE WITH YOU. IT IS THE POWER OF YOUR IMAGINATION.
REMEMBER THIS. IF YOU SHOULD EVER AGAIN NEED A BODYGUARD, I WILL BE ON THE OTHER SIDE OF THE LOOKING GLASS.
I KNEW I HAD SEEN HIM BEFORE. THE ATTACHÉ TO THE HAPSBURG AMBASSADOR!! THE TENTACLES OF THIS ORGANIZATION GO EVEN HIGHER THAN I SUSPECTED!

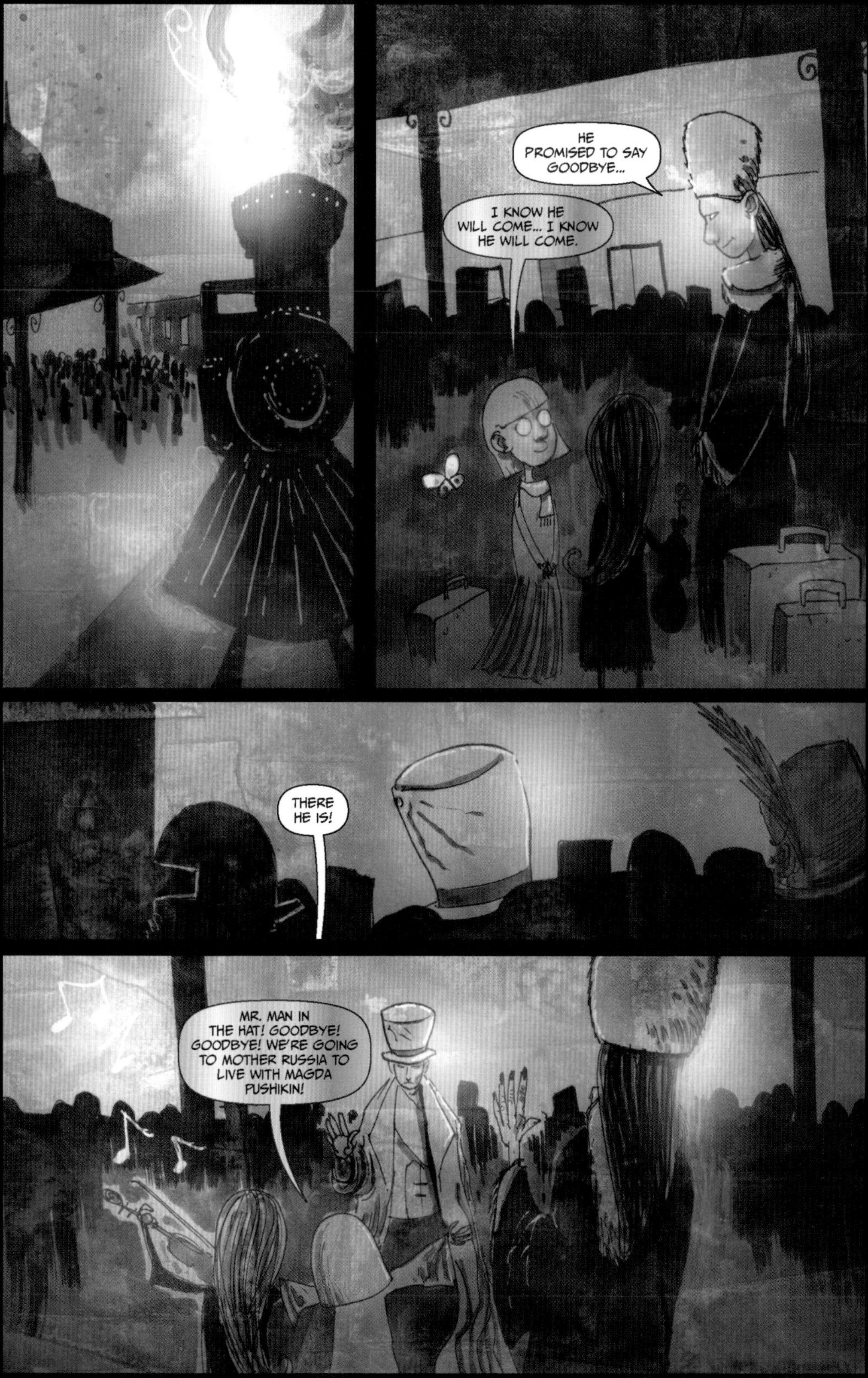
HE PROMISED TO SAY GOODBYE...
I KNOW HE WILL COME... I KNOW HE WILL COME.
THERE HE IS!
MR. MAN IN THE HAT! GOODBYE! GOODBYE! WE'RE GOING TO MOTHER RUSSIA TO LIVE WITH MAGDA PUSHIKIN!

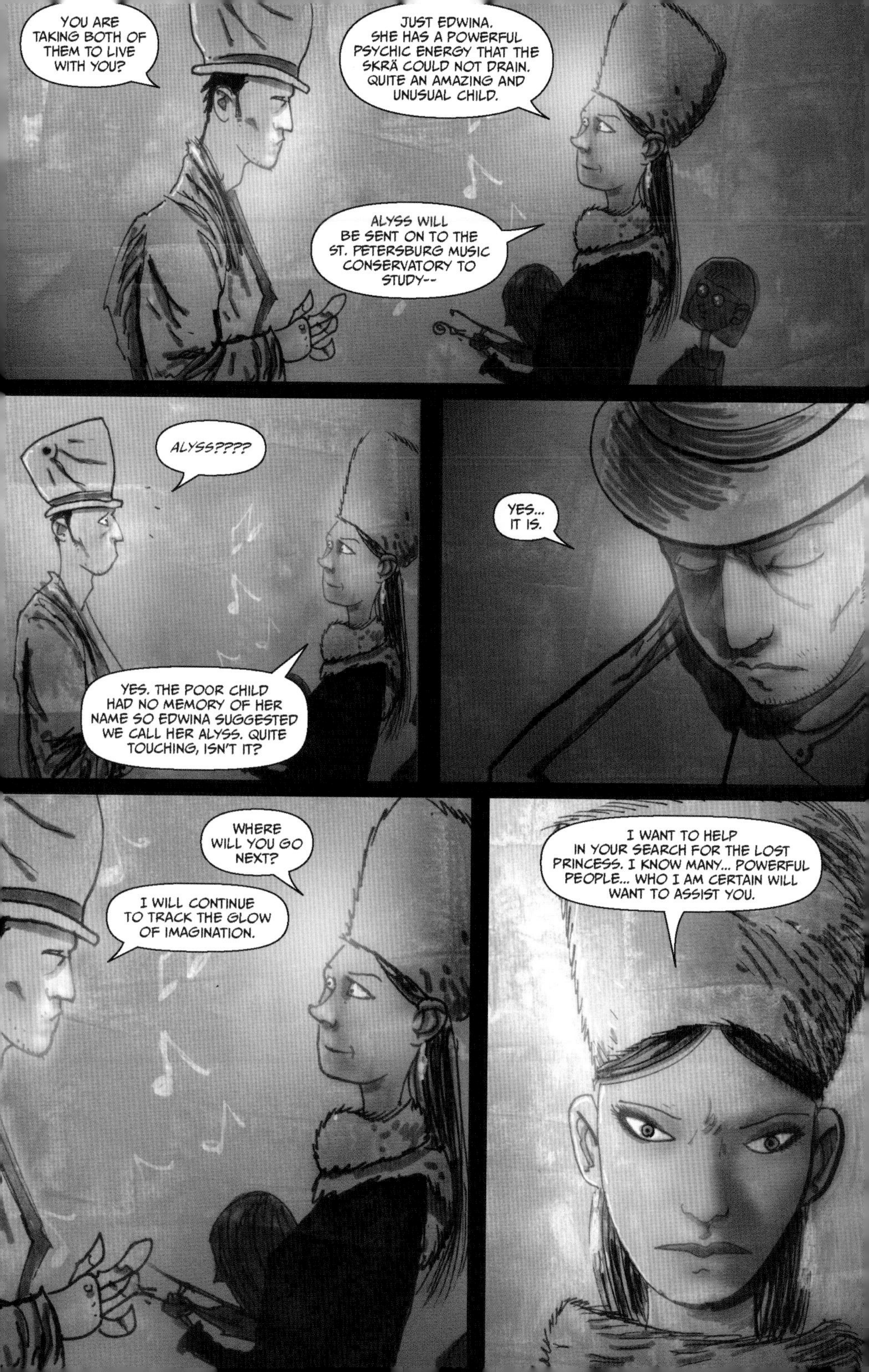
YOU ARE TAKING BOTH OF THEM TO LIVE WITH YOU?
JUST EDWINA. SHE HAS A POWERFUL PSYCHIC ENERGY THAT THE SKRÄ COULD NOT DRAIN. QUITE AN AMAZING AND UNUSUAL CHILD.
ALYSS WILL BE SENT ON TO THE ST. PETERSBURG MUSIC CONSERVATORY TO STUDY--
ALYSS????
YES. THE POOR CHILD HAD NO MEMORY OF HER NAME SO EDWINA SUGGESTED WE CALL HER ALYSS. QUITE TOUCHING, ISN'T IT?
YES... IT IS.
WHERE WILL YOU GO NEXT?
I WILL CONTINUE TO TRACK THE GLOW OF IMAGINATION.
I WANT TO HELP IN YOUR SEARCH FOR THE LOST PRINCESS. I KNOW MANY... POWERFUL PEOPLE... WHO I AM CERTAIN WILL WANT TO ASSIST YOU.

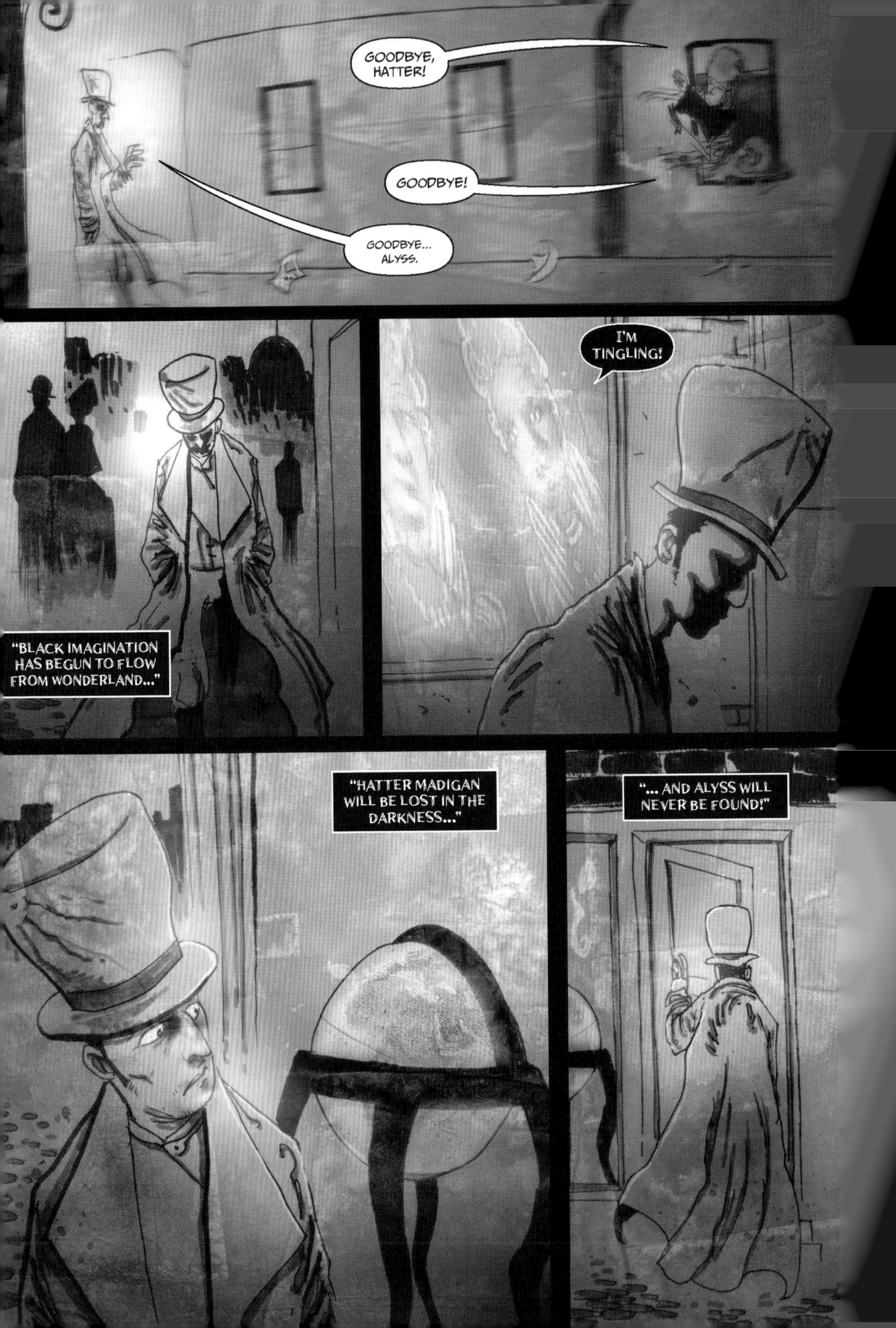
GOODBYE, HATTER!
GOODBYE!
GOODBYE... ALYSS.
"BLACK IMAGINATION HAS BEGUN TO FLOW FROM WONDERLAND..."
I'M TINGLING!
"HATTER MADIGAN WILL BE LOST IN THE DARKNESS..."
"... AND ALYSS WILL NEVER BE FOUND!"

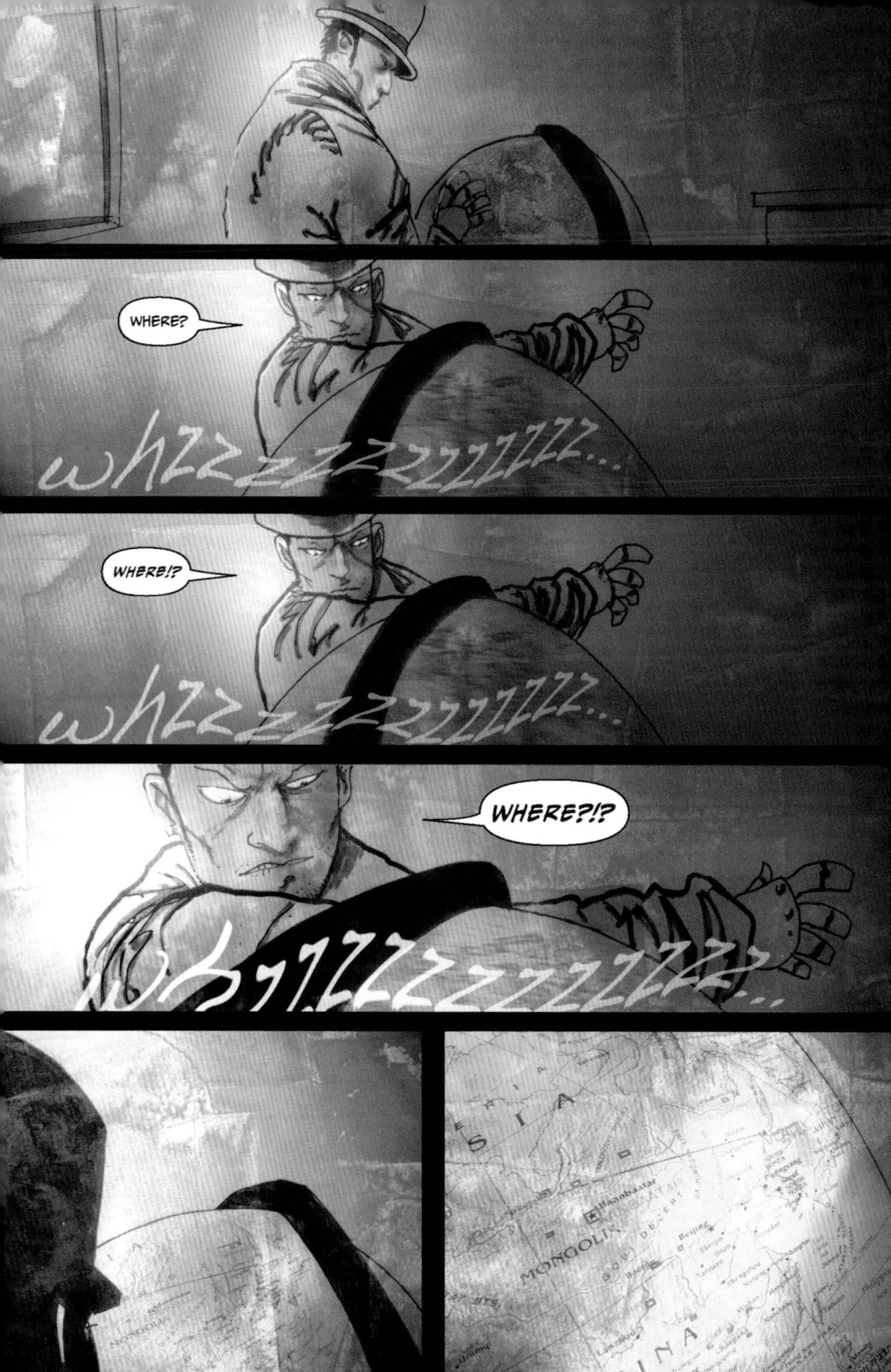
WHERE?
whzzzzzzzzzz...
WHERE!?
whzzzzzzzzzz...
WHERE?!?
whzzzzzzzzzzzz...
MONGOLIA
CHINA
ASIA
Ulaanbaatar
GOBI DESERT
Beijing

Probing Questions

"The World is a book, and those who do not travel

Hatter's signature weapon, the Hat, is a martial enigma wrapped in a haberdashery riddle! Why is the hat so personal to Hatter? It also appears to exhibit quite a sophisticated Artificial Intelligence. How can this be explained?

—Harold Sakata, The Big Island

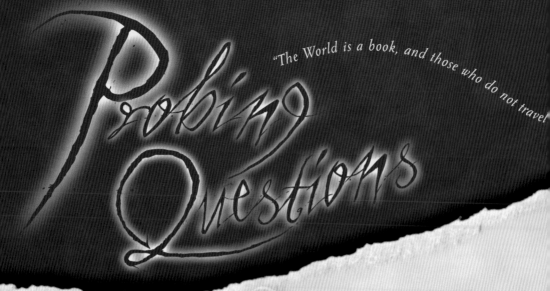

Since the launching of our HATTER M comic book series queries and kudos have arrived from around the world as readers contacted the Institute en masse to enthusiastically join with us in deepening Hatter's search and adventure. Probing questions, 19th century photographs, historical sightings, family anecdotes, lost knives and other stunning ephemera arrived from every corner of the globe as our growing number of readers contacted us with further evidence of Hatter's time spent traveling the earth.

We have assembled the following questions and answers to both respond to our readers and share the latest, fascinating revelations with any and all who are interested in knowing more about the mysterious top hatted visitor from Wonderland.

We called upon our panel of experts to roundtable the latest inquiries and developments in a series of Looking Glass Wars Deep Travel Symposiums. We have chosen the term Deep Travel as representative of the paranormal activity we are investigating and have recently submitted this definition to Webster's:

Deep Travel
vb. noun adv. adj (2006)
A state of travel surpassing accepted geographical and mental boundaries to go 'beyond' what is deemed possible as in "Whoa. Where the hell am I?"

We have received a great deal of correspondence from martial headwear fans such as your self. Wonderland texts, eyewitness accounts and Millinery records have thus far provided the bulk of our information though we do have high hopes for a field research team in the Himalayas currently searching for a Hat supposedly belonging to another member of the Wonderland Millinery that may have been lost during a fierce battle sometime in 1862 and preserved in ice. But all suppositions aside, this is what we do know.

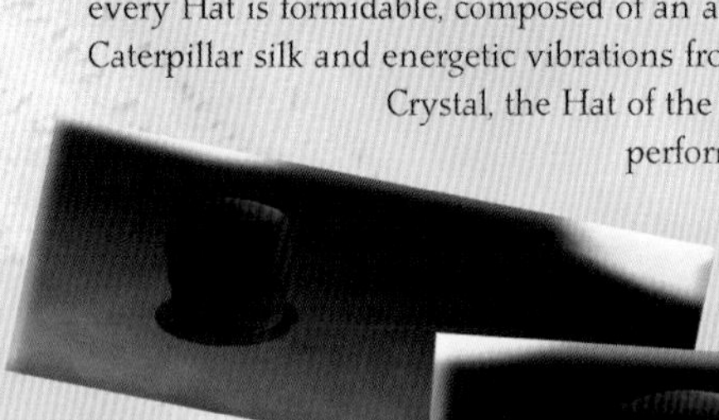

Each graduating member of the Wonderland Millinery is presented with a Hat created from materials found only in the realm of wonder. The Hat and its blades are what determine the rank and power of each individual Hatter. While every Hat is formidable, composed of an amalgamation of Caterpillar silk and energetic vibrations from the Heart Crystal, the Hat of the Millinery's top performing bladesman

read only a page." —St. Augustin

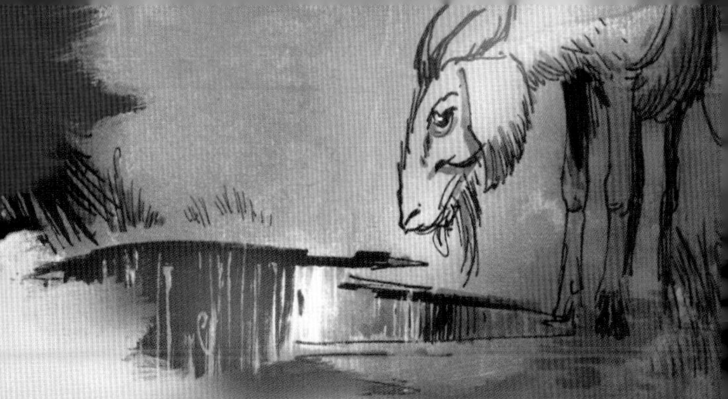

chosen to be the Queen's personal Royal Bodyguard, surpasses all others. In a devotional ceremony, blending scepter and Hat, an essence contained in her scepter is mixed with the silk of the Queen's personal Seer (in Hatter Madigan's case the Blue Caterpillar) and energy of the Heart Crystal to create Hat and blades forever linking the appointed Hatter with his Queen, protector of no other except by her direct order and appeal. Hatter Madigan's Hat was created uniquely for him and enhanced with a conscious force to seal their union. Additionally, Hatter and Hat trained together in isolation for 12 lunar sequences to develop the ballet of movement and attack that characterizes their interface. Much like a fiercely loyal falcon, the Hat will obey no one but his master.

The Hats of the Millinery men are one of Wonderland's greatest creations. Through extravagant luck and endless research we have been able to assemble the holy trinity of elements necessary to create a Millinery Hat and at present have devoted the Institute's lab to cracking the haberdashery code to produce a limited line of martial headwear. Hopes are high that we will soon be able to test these Hats on select volunteers exhibiting the martial prowess and physicality necessary to wield such fantastical weaponry.

Can anyone find one of these puddles? What happens if I roll into one?

—S. Hawking, London

Beware of puddles where no puddles should be. They do exist. Should you step or roll into one of these portals several things could happen.

You are sucked into the Pool of Tears never to exit.

You find yourself in a Wonderland Zoo populated with creatures from other worlds who have inadvertently entered a puddle.

Or…

You are transported to a location here on earth. We trust you have heard of…the Bermuda Triangle.

"He who would travel happily must travel light."

—Antoine de St. Exupery

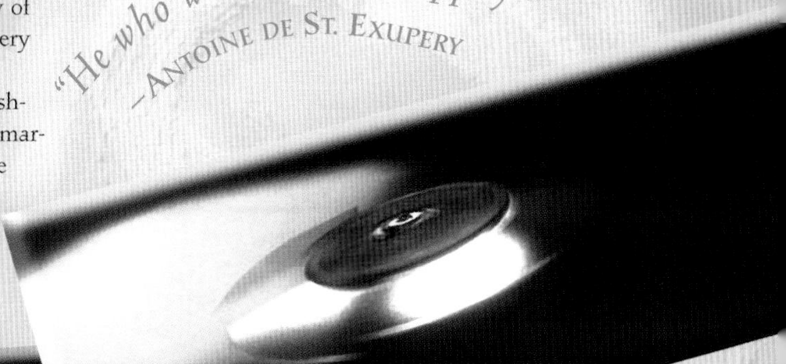

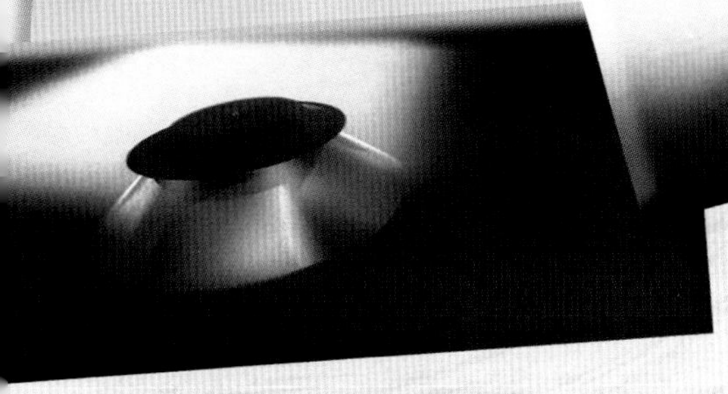

From theories based on the third- and fourth-generation retellings of eyewitness accounts, the Institute has produced this computer-generated sequence of images depicting how Hatter M's notorious hat may have unfurled.

We are fascinated by Hatter's methodology of search...more explanation please! Is it radioactive? Can anyone see the glow? What are the 'glow glasses' used by Baroness Dvonna in issue #2?

—LARRY AND SERGEY, MOUNTAIN VIEW, CA

Rest assured, the Glow of Imagination is *not* radioactive or in any other way, shape or form injurious to your health!

As readers of *The Looking Glass Wars* know, Hatter Madigan's theory regarding the 'Glow' provided him with the map that would lead him to the lost princess. Hatter was fortunate, in that all Wonderlanders are able to optically register 'the Glow of Imagination' in the manner that certain sensitives here are able to distinguish the colors of different people's auras. But most of us on Earth are far less evolved optically, so those covetous of the Glow and its potential were forced to create a mechanism to assist them in identifying and tracking it. Thus was born the cherry red lenses of Baroness Dvonna, a sophisticated set of prisms hand ground into a pattern of infinite intersecting rainbows. Discovered in a dusty curio collection dedicated to Illusion and Opera on the outskirts of Budapest, the glasses are now on loan to the Institute and kept locked in a bulletproof alchemite case to be removed only when serious matters of Imaginative investigation need to be solved.

Where do Hatter's blades come from? How are they replenished?

—GORDON FONG, LOS ANGELES

This has been a hotly debated conundrum since our investigation first began. One of the more extreme theories being proffered recently gained a startling credibility when we were contacted by the Paris Police Department following the release of Issue #1. A sharp-eyed comic fan recalled having seen a sealed off room where evidence from the 19th century was stored. Upon investigation he sent a package to us containing what he believed, based on dates and evidentiary facts, to be the blade that had pierced the French magistrate's nose in our debut issue. Few will ever experience the heady glee of discovery that enveloped the Institute with the arrival of this blade engraved with a miniature tophat and the initials HM. But all glee aside, there was work to be done and done quickly.

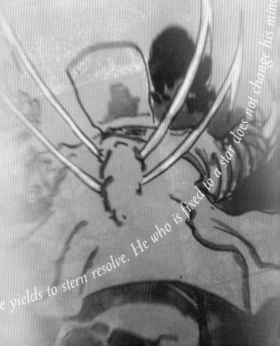

—LEONARDO DA VINCI

"He who is fixed to a star does not change his mind."

"Obstacles cannot crush me. Every obstacle yields to stern resolve."

your passport photo, you're too ill to travel." —Will Komen

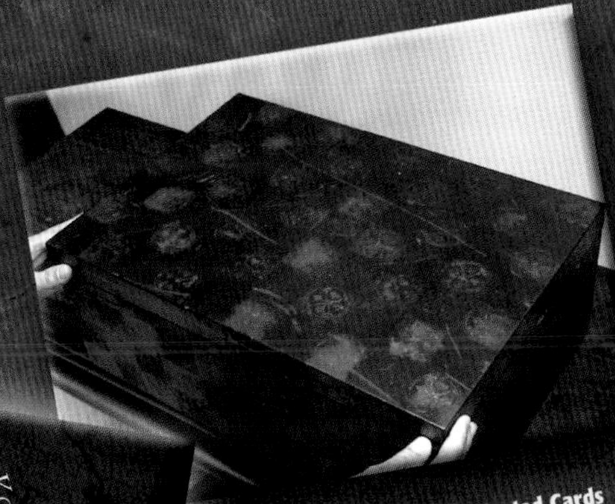

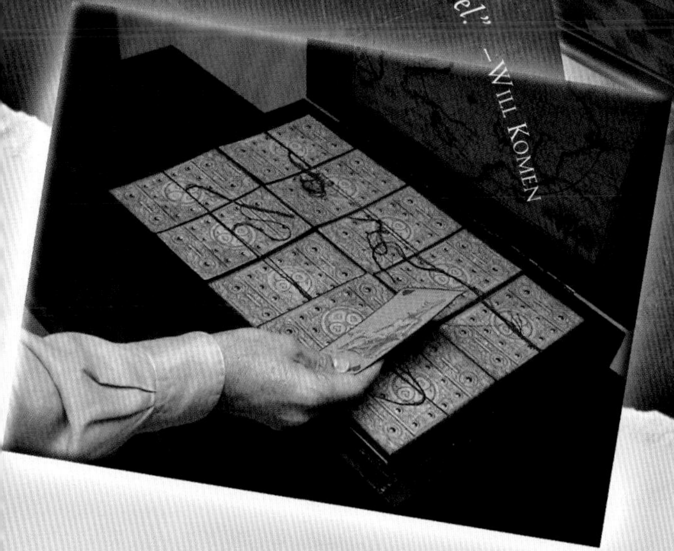

The Pandora's box of Illuminated Cards that first exposed the literary lie of Lewis Carroll's *Alice's Adventures in Wonderland.*

Crystallographic analysis found the atomic structure of the blade to be unlike any known forged metal, while spectroscopy identified a spectral element. This element, which we have dubbed "alchemite", has many of the properties of the legendary philosopher's stone. Specifically it can arrange different elements into any metal. Thus, some were led to argue that the blade is formed of crystallized metallic blood supporting the logical, albeit fantastical, theory that Hatter Madigan possessed the ability to turn his blood, a pure liquid alchemite, into blade. Once formed, the blades were forced out through the skin to be stored in the pack worn under his coat until necessity called upon their use.

However, further evidence gained from Millinery texts supports a more realistic theory that the Hatters were trained to forge their own blades. But unlike the work of a rustic country blacksmith, these blades were forged from elements only a member of the Wonderland Millinery would possess, such as the liquid alchemite that possibly flowed through their veins. All evidence and enthusiasm aside, this theory remains a theory among many intriguing theories.

How did Frank Beddor and Liz Cavalier come together to write the Hatter M series?

—Dorr Bothwell, Amsterdam

It could be said that the British Museum and an exhibit of ancient cards are what brought the writing team of Beddor and Cavalier together. A number of years ago while in London, Beddor visited the British Museum and came upon an incomplete deck of cards illuminated by an unusual glow. Intrigued by the exhibit and captivated by the images on the cards he was reminded, albeit in a vastly different way, of Wonderland. Intrigued, Beddor called an antiquities dealer he knew who specialized in collecting all sorts of ancient playing cards. The dealer refused to speak on the telephone and invited Beddor to his shop where he revealed that he in fact owned the cards missing from the museum deck. He then brought out an old, worn leather box filled with cards and told a story as he flipped one card over at a time, dramatically revealing the saga that would eventually become Book One of *The Looking Glass Wars* trilogy. →

"Trust in Allah, but tie your camel."

–Old Muslim Proverb

While Frank Beddor had uncovered a great deal of information regarding Hatter Madigan's search during his ongoing investigation of the story behind the Wonderland cards, a woman named Cavalier had even more. As an astral traveler and interstellar author Cavalier's lifelong passion of tracking the myth of a prepotent otherworldly warrior who appeared in France in 1859 to criss-cross the planet for 13 years dovetailed perfectly with Beddor's discovery regarding the truth of Wonderland. Over time, Cavalier had collected the tattered, annotated maps and coded diaries of a truly mad traveler in search of something profound. But for her, the ultimate questions remained unanswered. Who was this man and what did he search for? With the publication and revelations of *The Looking Glass Wars* the mystery was finally solved. Upon reading the book she immediately contacted Beddor and strongly suggested they meet to share their knowledge. When they finally put all of their pieces together they discovered a labyrinthine odyssey far beyond either of their wildest imagination. And that's really quite far...

How were you ever able to translate the Wonderland alphabet?

–Mr. Carl Ebbs, Ft. Worth

We must direct this question to Sir Gregory Cook, our resident radical historian and cryptolinguist. Roused from a championship computer game of GO, Cook had these insights to share regarding Wonderland's arcane and beautiful etymology. "After a dinner of welsh rarebit I had retired to my corner here at the Institute one night and proceeded to have a blinding realization that since Wonderland is the source of all the Imagination on earth it must logically follow suit that all languages found here originated in Wonderland. On that note I turned my full attention to the common roots of world language and the writing samples obtained from Hatter Madigan's journal. Several computer programs and a series of finely tuned algorithms later I was able to decipher and transcribe the Wonderland alphabet and begin to build a basic vocabulary. May I be excused now? It's my turn."

Certainly Sir Cook. Return to your world of mathematical quandaries, packaged hot chocolate and woolly cardigans.

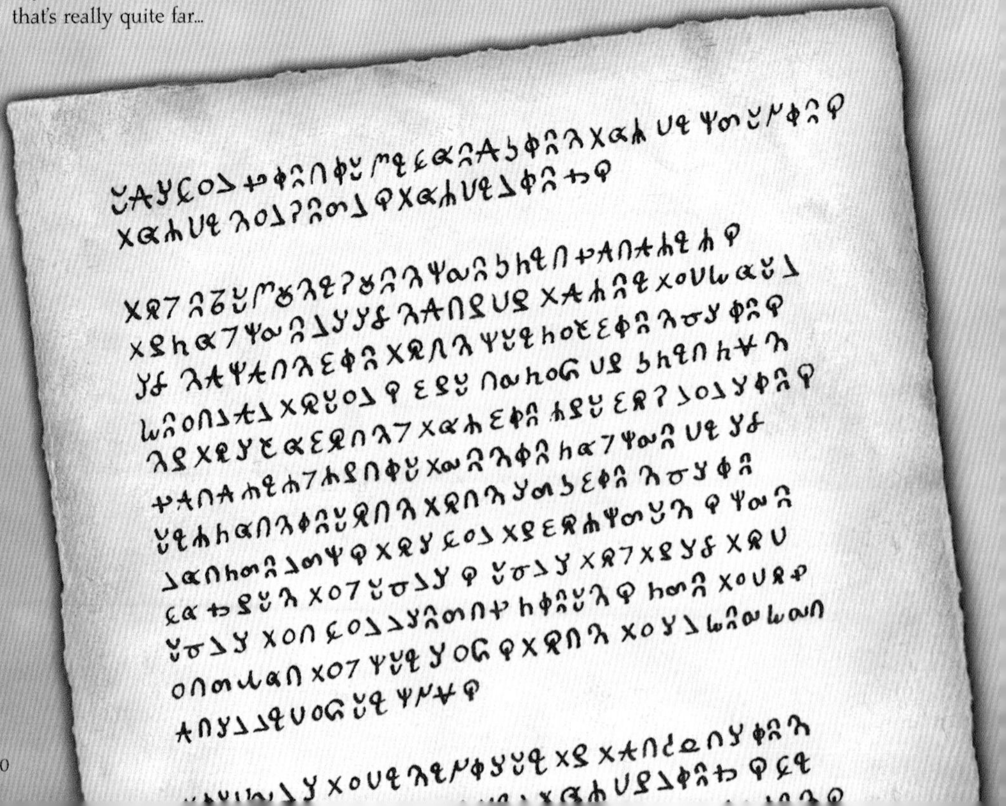

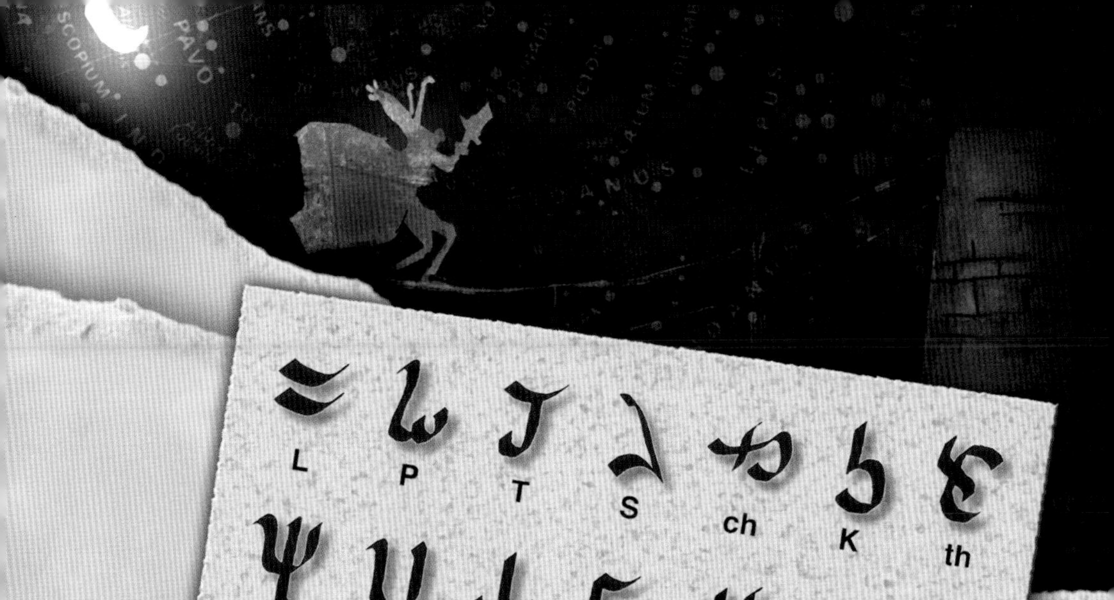
PAVO

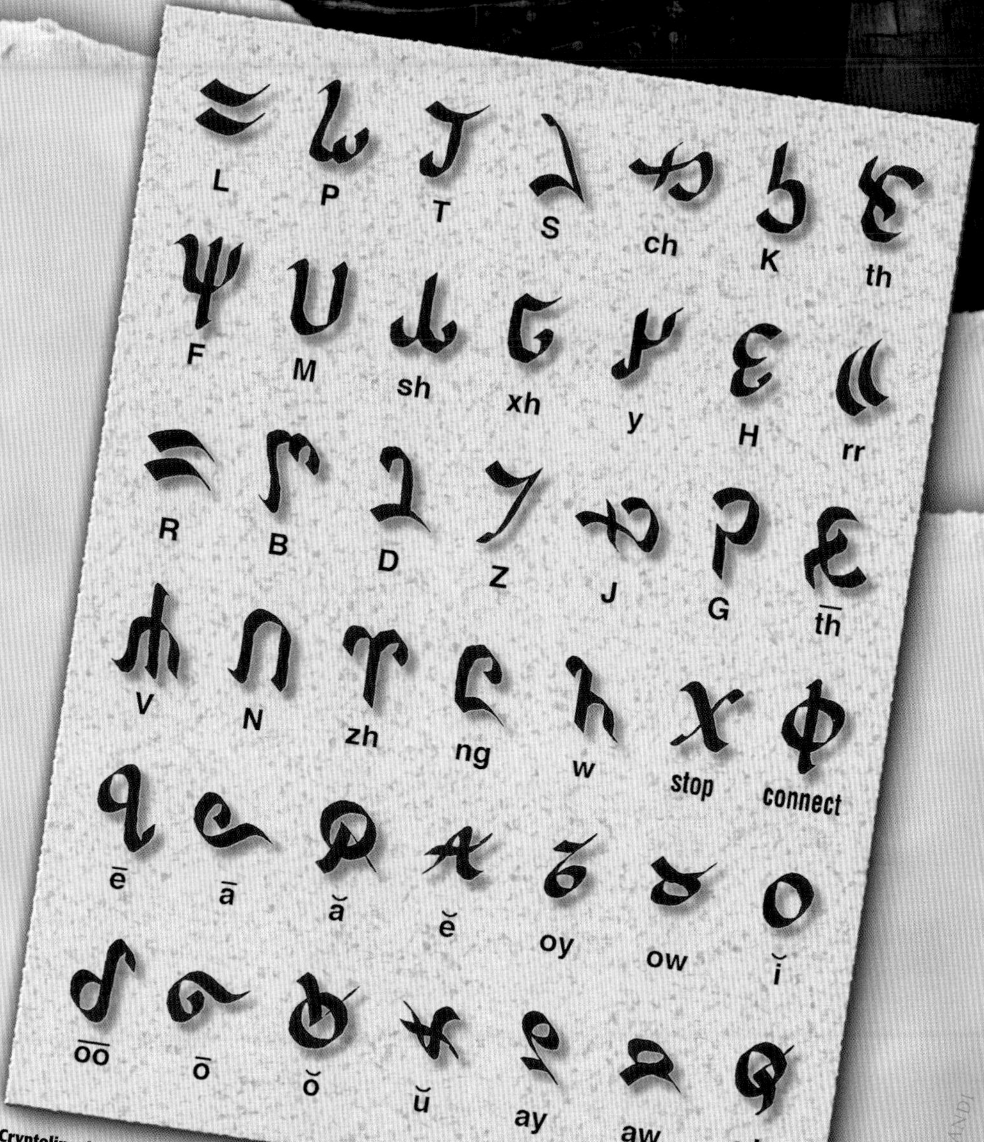
L
P
T
S
ch
K
th
F
M
sh
xh
y
H
rr
R
B
D
Z
J
G
t̅h̅
V
N
zh
ng
w
stop
connect
ē
ā
ă
ĕ
oy
ow
ĭ
o̅o̅
ō
ŏ
ŭ
ay
aw
uh

Cryptolinguist, Sir Cook, was able to decipher and transcribe Hatter's journals after realizing that since Wonderland is the source of all the Imagination on earth, it must logically follow that the Wonderland alphabet is also the source of all other alphabets. At left is one of Hatter's journal pages (see page 12 for transcription).

"You must be the change you wish to see in the world." —Mahatma Ghandi

Seeking Relics

Readers Write

Along with the great outpouring of enthusiastic questions we have also received a veritable mother lode of substantiation and support as readers send us all manner of Hatter Ephemera. Every day more packages arrive here at the Institute containing cherished 19th century family scrapbooks commemorating encounters with mysterious, tophatted travelers, yellowed letters with passages highlighted telling of a meeting in a train station or around a campfire, postcards and daguerrotypes, grainy travelogues and even the raw, outsider art of a housebound mountain in-bred who may have recorded their own sighting of Hatter Madigan in the thick, crude medium of fingerpaint.

"Every wall is a door."
—RALPH WALDO EMERSON

Ephemera Verification Alert!

Each item received by the Institute must be rigorously authenticated via carbon testing, geographical veracity and intrepid archival sleuthing. This all important and painstaking task falls to Colonel (nicknamed for his favorite fastfood) Nate Barlow, our chief of Reconnaisance and Analysis.

Col. Barlow has vetted and authenticated the following exhibits. His workload is heavy so to those of you who have sent us your keepsakes and curios, please be patient and know that every effort is being made to add your contribution to the Mapping of Hatter Madigan

From Argentina we received these two large format prints from a descendant of an amateur landscape photographer who caught these images of a man in a tophat with what appear to be blades on his back.

Curiosities

"The first condition of understanding a foreign country is to smell it." –Rudyard Kipling

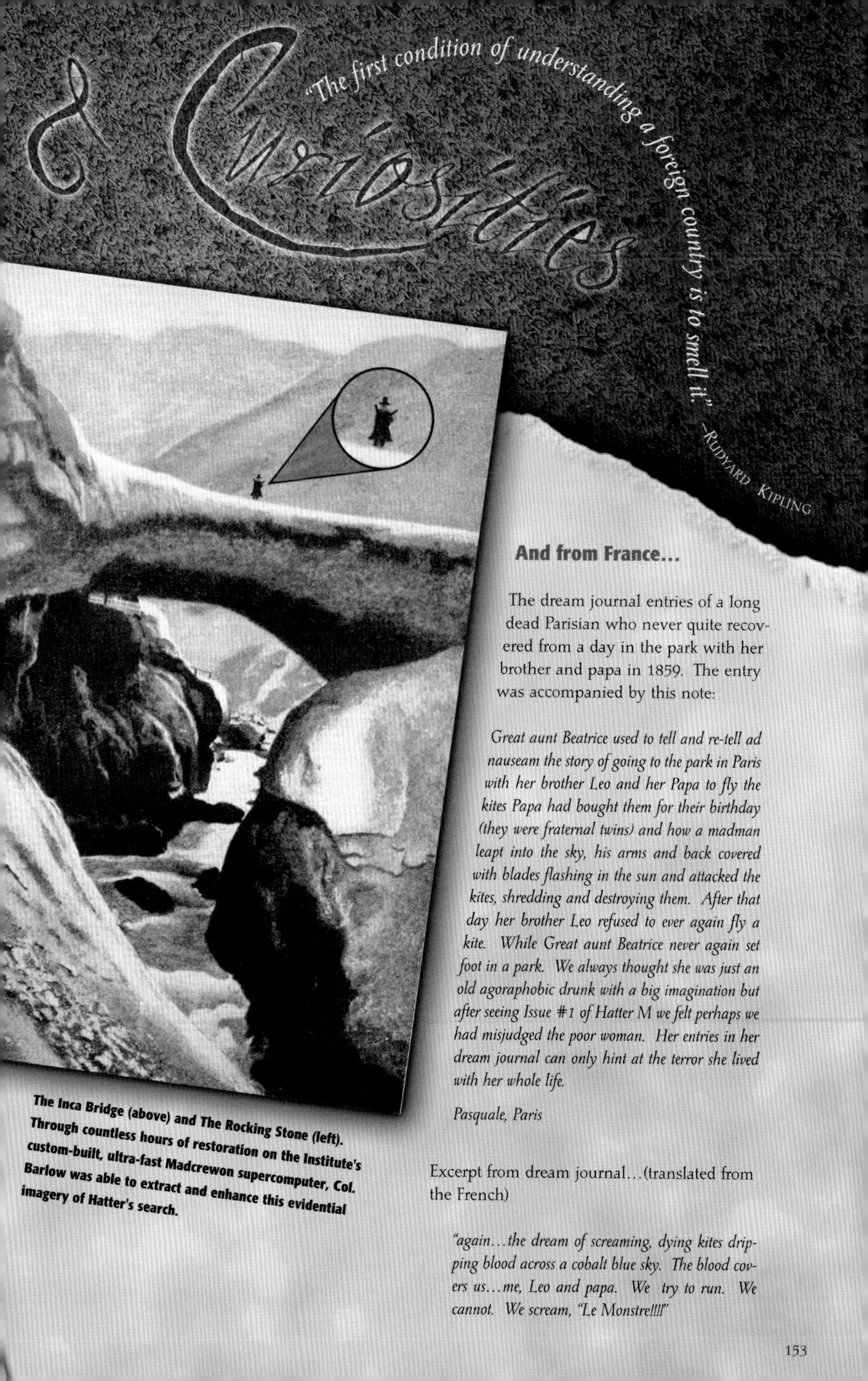

The Inca Bridge (above) and The Rocking Stone (left). Through countless hours of restoration on the Institute's custom-built, ultra-fast Madcrewon supercomputer, Col. Barlow was able to extract and enhance this evidential imagery of Hatter's search.

And from France...

The dream journal entries of a long dead Parisian who never quite recovered from a day in the park with her brother and papa in 1859. The entry was accompanied by this note:

Great aunt Beatrice used to tell and re-tell ad nauseam the story of going to the park in Paris with her brother Leo and her Papa to fly the kites Papa had bought them for their birthday (they were fraternal twins) and how a madman leapt into the sky, his arms and back covered with blades flashing in the sun and attacked the kites, shredding and destroying them. After that day her brother Leo refused to ever again fly a kite. While Great aunt Beatrice never again set foot in a park. We always thought she was just an old agoraphobic drunk with a big imagination but after seeing Issue #1 of Hatter M we felt perhaps we had misjudged the poor woman. Her entries in her dream journal can only hint at the terror she lived with her whole life.

Pasquale, Paris

Excerpt from dream journal...(translated from the French)

"again...the dream of screaming, dying kites dripping blood across a cobalt blue sky. The blood covers us...me, Leo and papa. We try to run. We cannot. We scream, "Le Monstre!!!!"

L'HOMME?
LE MONSTRE?

Un étranger de grande taille est apparu tard la nuit dernière dans les rues de Paris, portant une veste de style militaire et armé d'un arsenal de lames. Quand, attaqué par surprise par des habitants inquiets, il répondit calmement par un jet de couteaux. Coincé par un groupe de héros ne brandissant rien d'autre qu'un tapis usé, l'étranger fut soumis et enfermé dans la prison de la ville en attendant l'arrivée d'un magistrat au matin.

Dans la nuit, des rumeurs nourries par la peur et les frissons se sont répandues à travers la ville, parlant d'une trainée sanglante de cadavres échappés pendant la veillée funèbre de l'étranger.

Mais, quand la raison et la lumière de jour apparurent, les autorités françaises ne purent pas attribuer un cadavre au monstre suspect.

Ramené avant le magistrat pour la session du matin, l'étranger fut libéré de son tapis, ce qui l'amena a attaquer la cour dans un spectacle de violence maniaque, laissant le magistrat avec une narine percée et le tribunal dans une tumulte.

S'échappant par une fenÊtre du troisième étage, l'étranger bondit à travers la foule inquiète rassemblée dehors et rapidement évaporée.

Paris, Mai 1859, "Le Figaro"

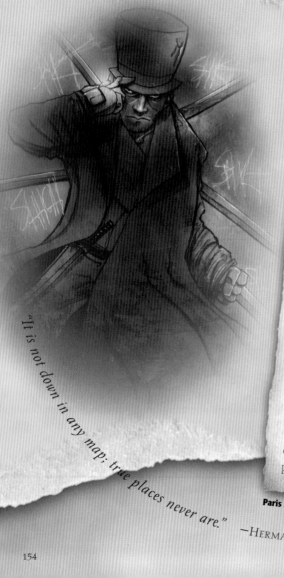

"It is not down in any map; true places never are." —HERMAN MELVILLE

MISSING ENGLISHMAN

ON EVENING OF DISAPPEARANCE, MAY HAVE BEEN IN ATTENDANCE AT PERFORMANCE OF MAGICIAN SACRÉNOIR IN CATACOMBS OF PARIS

Sir Basil Pettibone of Mayfair has been reported missing and feared dead by his grief stricken next of kin. Sir Basil was last seen on May 19 before departing on a business trip to Paris. He was due back in London within a fortnight but has yet to return. While clues to his disappearance are scant, authorities did discover one provocative lead. Found amongst his personal possessions at the Paris hotel where Pettibone had obtained lodging was an advert for a performance by the magician known as Sacrénoir that was to take place in the catacombs running beneath Paris. However promising, the clue has so far proven to be a dead end. Authorities are continuing to investigate though hope is nil. An unusually high number of reported disappearances in May has kept the Paris police undermanned and overworked.

Paris June 17, "The London Times"

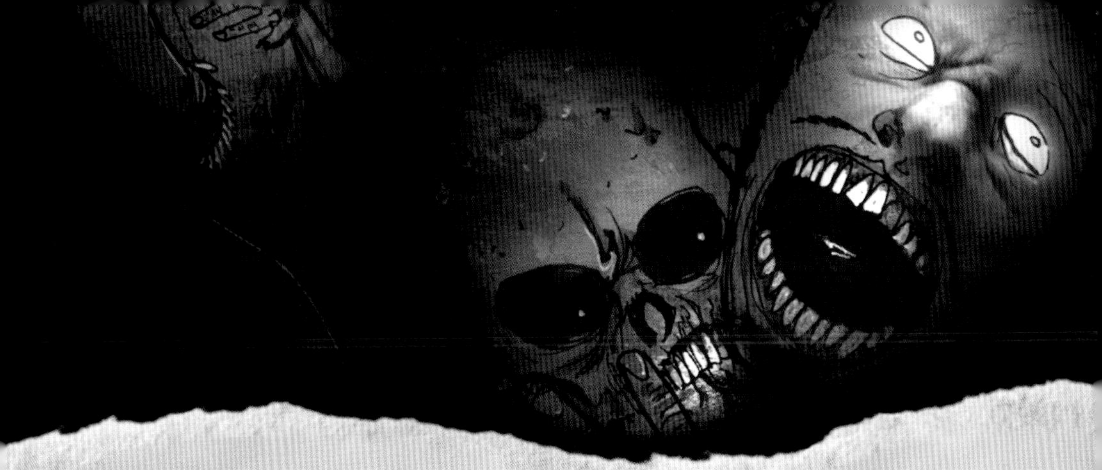

Those French...

From the Opinion Page of London Times, May 1859

A recent headline in Le Figaro shrieked L'HOMME!? LE MONSTRE!?. The article breathlessly told of an apparently foreign man in a long coat who appeared on the streets of Paris armed with an arsenal of blades. Rumors immediately circulated throughout the city of a bloody trail of dead bodies left in his wake, but when reason prevailed, French authorities could not attribute one corpse to this imagined monster. The man was locked up in the Paris jail overnight and brought before the court on nothing more than hearsay. When cornered he fought back and fled leaving the magistrate with superficial wounds (a perforated nostril). To this we respond, treat a man like an animal and he will act like an animal. Who was this man? Perhaps a soldier from another country who found himself attacked and made unwelcome by overwrought suspicions. Treat a man like a man and he will act like a man. We should all approach a stranger not as a potential enemy, but as one who may have an amazing tale to tell.

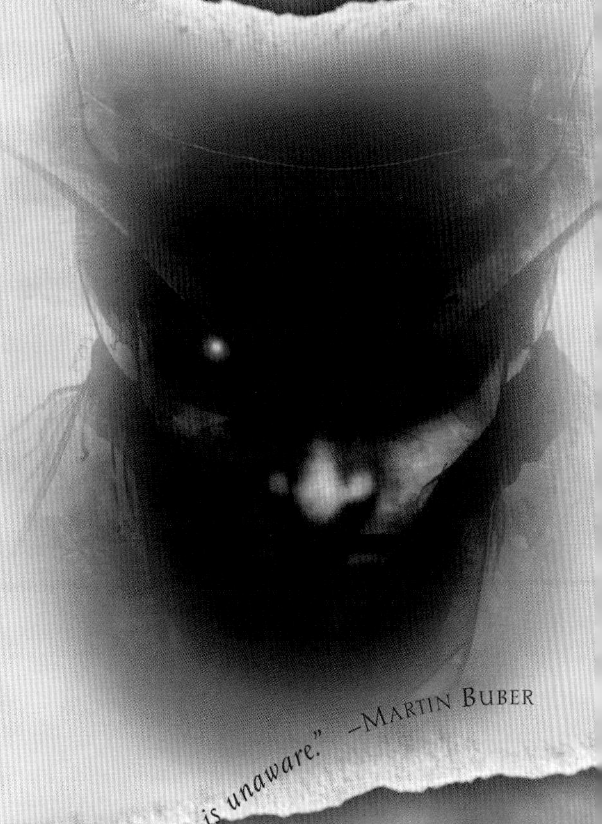

"All journeys have secret destinations of which the traveler is unaware." –Martin Buber

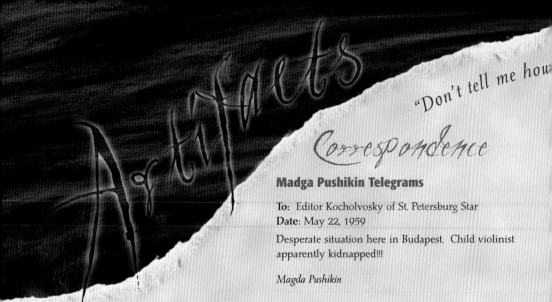

Artifacts

"Don't tell me how

Correspondence

Madga Pushikin Telegrams

To: Editor Kocholvosky of St. Petersburg Star
Date: May 22, 1959

Desperate situation here in Budapest. Child violinist apparently kidnapped!!!

Magda Pushikin

To: Editor Kocholvosky of St. Petersburg Star
Date: May 23, 1959

Perpetrators possibly connected to highest echelon of Hungarian political regime. Have several leads including man of military bearing in tophat who seems to have knowledge of the child and her history. More facts to follow.

Magda Pushikin

Please wire additional expense funds. Wardrobe emergency!

Historical sleuthing by our reconnaissance team has uncovered several long-lost documents published here.

Here is one of the two original Pushikin telegrams discovered thus far. The second is undergoing further restoration at the institute.

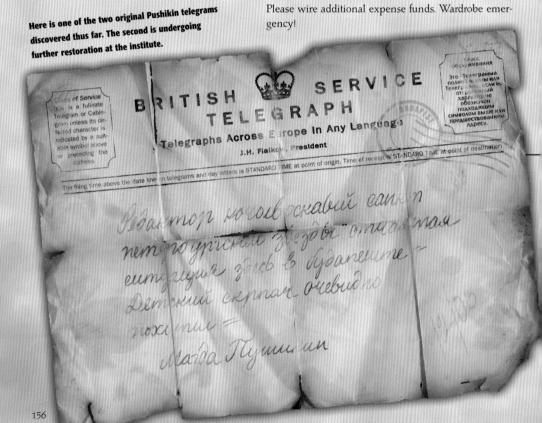

Class of Service
This is a full-rate Telegram or Cablegram unless its deferred character is indicated by a suitable symbol above or preceding the address

BRITISH 👑 SERVICE TELEGRAPH

Telegraphs Across Europe In Any Language

J.H. Fialkov, President

The filing time above the date line on telegrams and day letters is STANDARD TIME at point of origin. Time of receipt is STANDARD TIME at point of destination

Это - Телеграмма полностью или Телеграмма, если её отправлений характер не обозначен подходящим символом выше или предшествованием адресу.

Редактор кочоловоскавй санкт петроургской звезде отправная ситуация здесь в Будапеште - Детский скрипач очевидно похищени -
Магда Пушикин

156

educated you are. Tell me how much you have traveled." —Mohammad

Correspondence: Jules Verne – Victor Hugo

From Vol. VII of english translator Sir John Bales' brilliant compilation of 19th century French correspondence

---

Paris
June 1859

Dear Victor,

Life is truly a fantastic journey, particularly the life of the imagination. As you are aware from our previous conversations and correspondence, I have been at times quite hopeless and even suicidal as to the direction of my professional writing. Light librettos for mediocre operas and unprintable tales from my youth were all I had managed to pen. And yet, I knew there was a vast world within myself that I wanted to discover and explore. This world exploded before my eyes several weeks ago when I met the most extraordinary man at an exhibition of Da Vinci's drawings. Tall and forbidding in a long coat, eyes wild, hatless on a blustery day. the man did not seem to be of this world. He engaged me in a rambling conversation about a missing princess that he was bound by honor to find. Suspecting him mad, I nevertheless felt compelled to listen as there was something of the utmost sincerity to his words and expression. He told me he could see the same residue of Glow surrounding myself that he had seen on Da Vinci's work. He believed it to be an indicator of great imagination and that if he followed this Glow wherever it may lead, he would locate his Alyss of Wonderland.

For whatever reason, these words were a powerful incantation for my subconscious. Wishing him well, I presented him with my card and requested updates on his journey.

Upon returning home, I was suddenly overcome and transported by a fantastical tale that tapped into my own lifelong fascination with travel. I immediately began writing and in a matter of weeks completed the enclosed manuscript that I have titled, 5 Weeks in a Balloon. You sir, have shown such generosity of encouragement with regard to my writing that I can never thank you enough and hope that this effort will somehow justify the time spent.

Your grateful student and friend,

JV

PS: Follow the Glow!

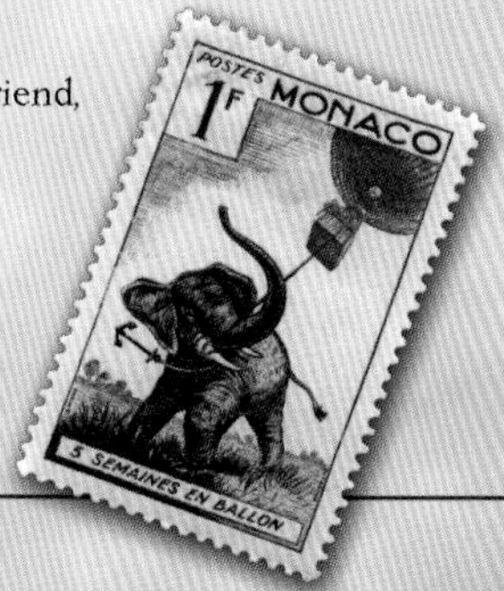
POSTES
1F
MONACO
5 SEMAINES EN BALLON

Guernsey. France
July 1859

Dear Jules,

Mon dieu! Follow the Glow indeed! I have just this moment finished your pages and hasten to send my congratulations, it seems you have finally cracked IT wide open! Your inner world is now accessible to not only you, but to all of us. I have several publishers in mind that I am certain would take this to print. But in the meantime, I am very interested in hearing more about this extraordinary man you have described. Has he been in contact with you since that providential meeting?

Your experience summons a strong sense memory from when my first poems came to me as though from another world. But I was a young man then, now I grapple with my endless tale of social misery and injustice that is (unfortunately) very, very much of this world. (ed.note: Hugo's Les Misérables was published in 1862)

Recevez, cher confrère, l'expression de mes sentiments les plus sincères

VH

[Ed. note – M. Hugo's closing has been left untranslated – it is a French expression of the highest regard coming from the heart and soul]

Geophysical Consequences

"We don't go anywhere.

Effects of Civil War in Wonderland Recorded on Earth

Following the bloody palace coup in which Redd killed her sister Queen Genevieve to take control of Imagination, astronomers and geophysicists documented a powerful energy spasm here on Earth.

The Great Red (Redd) Aurora of 1859

The night of September 1, 1859 was one of the most extraordinary of modern times. On this night a great aurora, the greatest during the past two hundred years, spread down from the polar regions to cover two thirds of the entire earth's sky. The extent to which the great red aurora of 1859 effected planetary unrest on earth is astounding. Asylums, prisons, boarding schools and barnyards erupted with aggression. Reports from astronomical observatories, newspapers, personal letters and ships at sea poured in from around the world. Explained as a solar flare, few knew the true source of the dark energy that would trigger a shift in mankind's imagination and lead to a century of world wars.

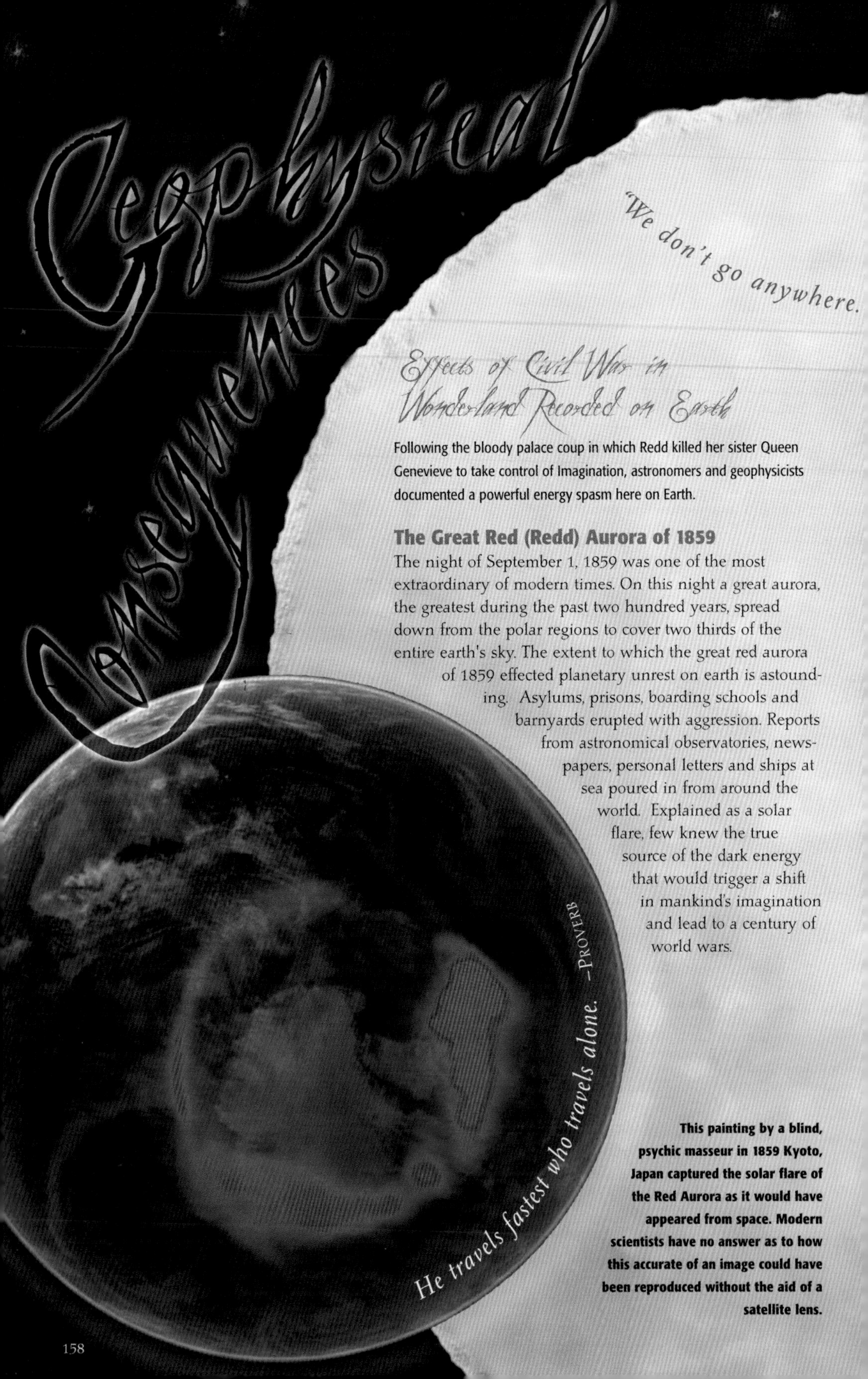

He travels fastest who travels alone. –PROVERB

This painting by a blind, psychic masseur in 1859 Kyoto, Japan captured the solar flare of the Red Aurora as it would have appeared from space. Modern scientists have no answer as to how this accurate of an image could have been reproduced without the aid of a satellite lens.

"Going somewhere is for squares. We just go!" —Marlon Brando, The Wild One (1954)

Firsthand evidence of the influx of Black Imagination...

A magnetic storm from August 28 to September 2 produced widespread effects on the world's telegraph system. Operators from almost every country on the planet filed reports of bizarre malfunctions.

An operator in France experienced the following energetic mayhem:

"At all the telegraphic stations in France the service was impeded during the whole of September 2, [1859] but especially at two periods of the day, from 4:30 A.M. to 9 A.M., and from noon to 3 P.M. These two periods were the same at all stations, and the greatest disturbances took place exactly at the same hours, at 7 A.M. and at 2 P.M. The longest wires always showed the greatest disturbances. The same day telluric currents were also observed in the greater part of the two hemispheres, in Switzerland, in Germany, in the British Isles, in North America, and throughout Australia."

Observations made at Washington, D.C., by FREDERICK W. ROYCE, Telegraph operator.

On the evening of Aug. 28th I had great difficulty in working the line to Richmond, Va. It seemed as if there was a storm at Richmond. I therefore abandoned that wire, and tried to work the northern wire, but met with the same difficulty. During the auroral display, I was calling Richmond, and had one hand on the iron plate. Happening to lean towards the sounder, which is against the wall, my forehead grazed a ground wire. Immediately I received a very severe electric shock, which stunned me for an instant. An old man who was sitting facing me, and but a few feet distant, said that he saw a spark of fire jump from my forehead to the sounder.

Effect on the telegraph Wires, from the Comptes Rendus, T. XLIX, p. 365

From the evening of Aug. 28th until the morning of the 29th the needles of the magnetic telegraph at Paris were almost constantly in motion, as if a permanent current was passing through the telegraph wires. Business was therefore entirely interrupted, and could not be resumed until 11 A.M. Aug. 29th.

For more reports from telegraph operators see those collected by Silliman and published in the American Journal of Science and Arts, 1860.

Expanding Duality

Based on the historical geophysical evidence of Wonderland's energetic impact on earth, we have developed a methodology of monitoring the symbiotic relationship between our two worlds. The powerful telescopes and infrared tracking satellites of the Hatter M Institute for Paranormal Travel have been fixed on the skies over Los Angeles, California. The results of which, though incomplete, do indicate an escalating battle of conflicting energy particles – some light and some dark. Supported by rigorous statistical evidence, it appears that Black Imagination is increasing exponentially as we move further into the new millennium. As our instrumentation is improved and refined we hope to be able to discover the source and route of these particles as they enter the earth's realm. And even more importantly, how we here on earth can assist the light particles in what could prove to be the final war for Imagination. Hearts forward, lovers of White Imagination. We have not yet begun to fight.

Process Gallery

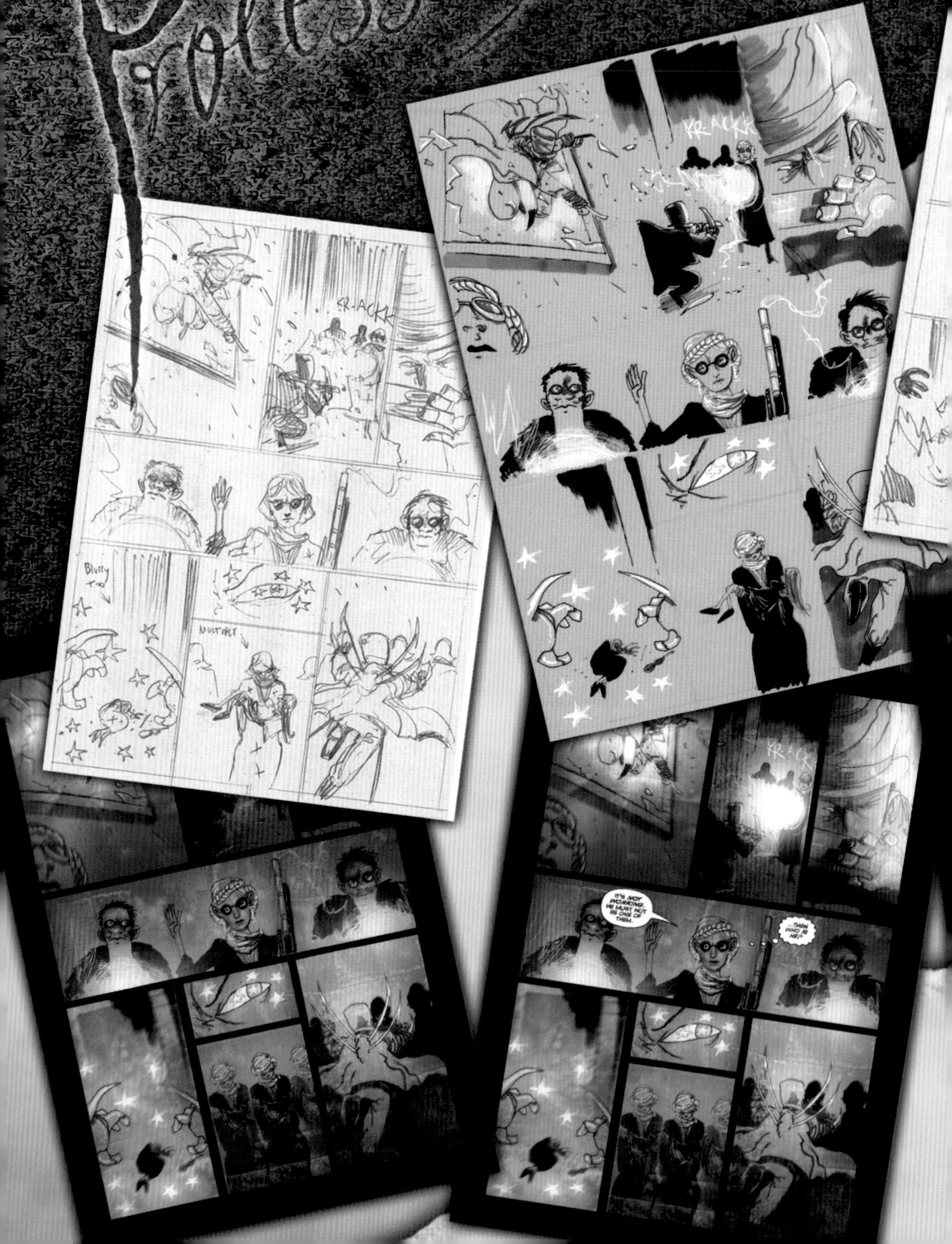
KR-ACKK
KRACKK
Blurry too
MULTIPLY
KR-ACK
IT'S NOT WORKING. HE MUST NOT BE ONE OF THEM.
...THEN WHO IS HE?

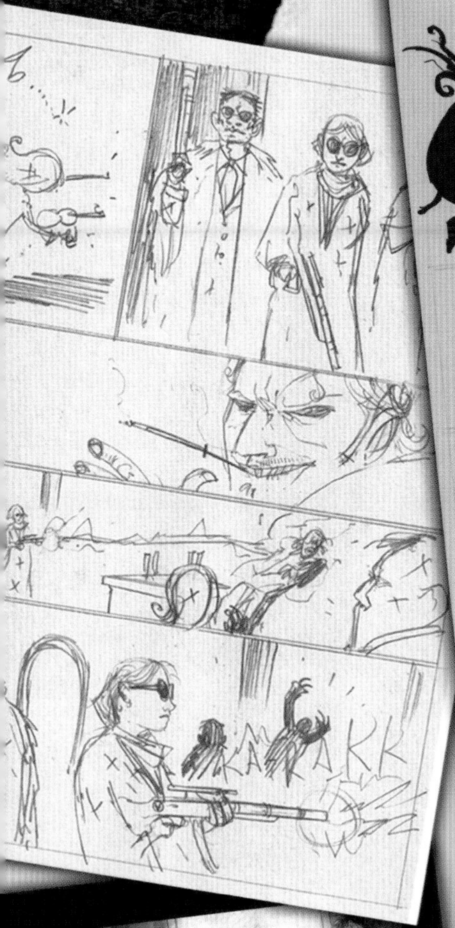

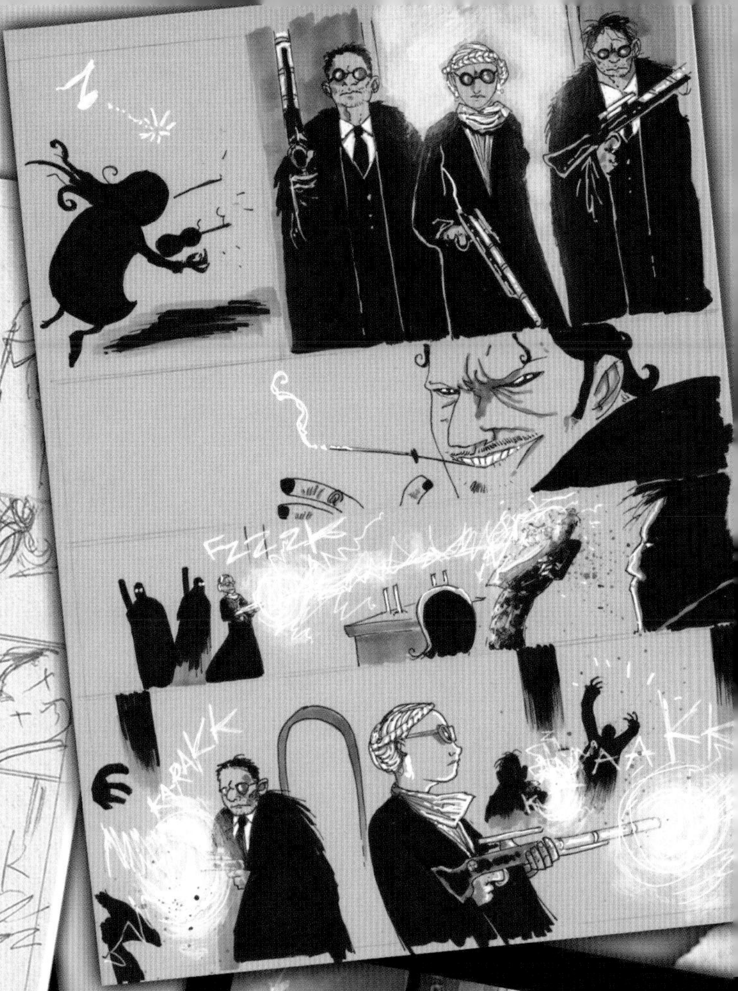

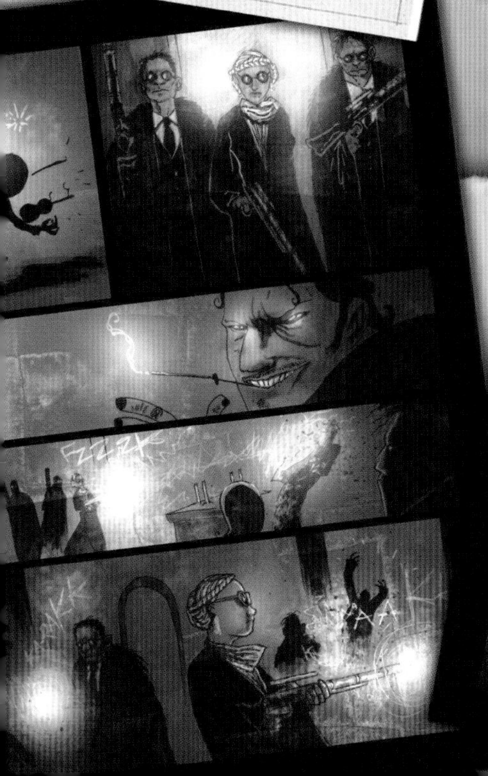

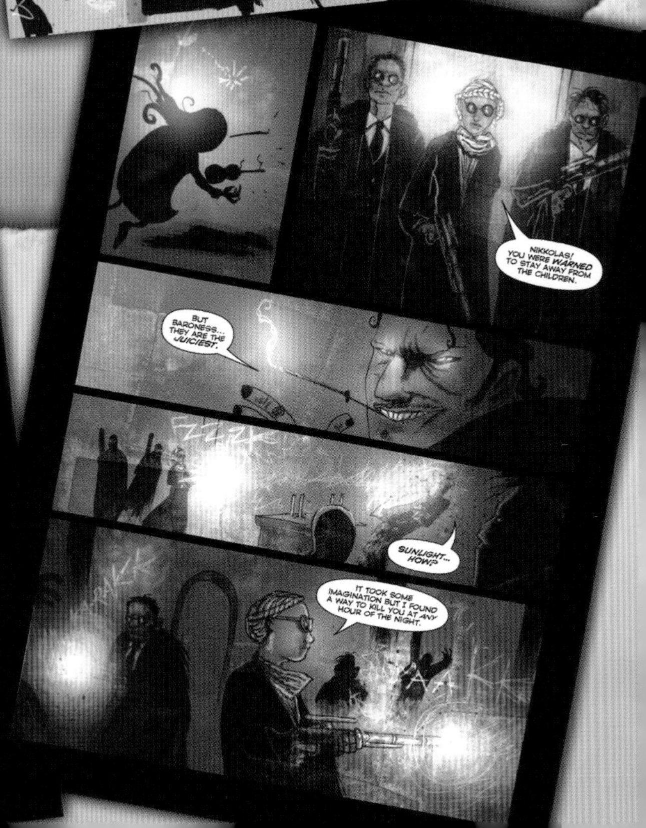
NIKKOLAS! YOU WERE *WARNED* TO STAY AWAY FROM THE CHILDREN.
BUT BARONESS... THEY ARE THE *JUICIEST*.
SUNLIGHT... HOW?
IT TOOK SOME IMAGINATION BUT I FOUND A WAY TO KILL YOU AT *ANY* HOUR OF THE NIGHT.

Concept Gallery

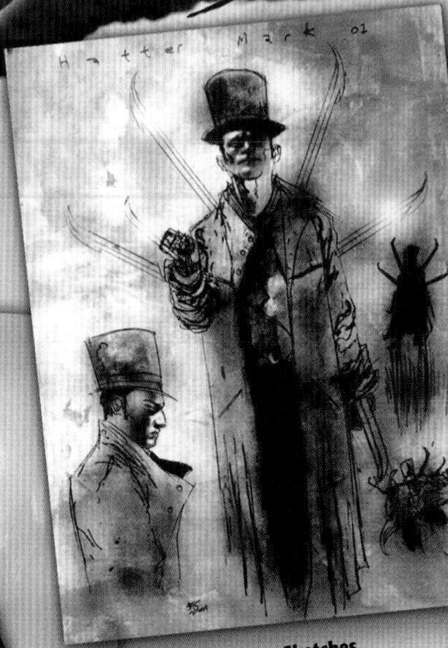
Hatter Mark 01

Hatter Sketches

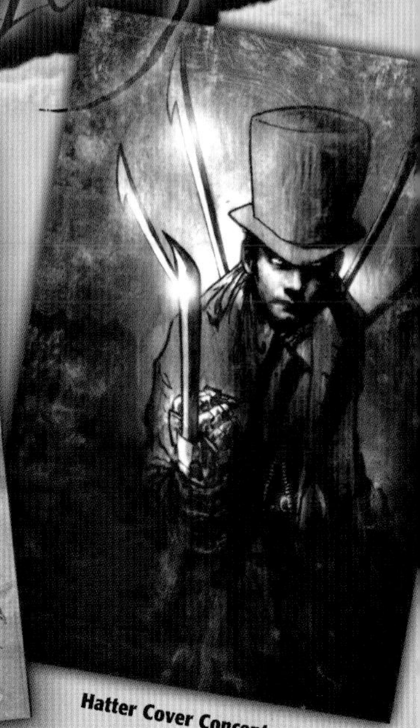

Hatter Cover Concept

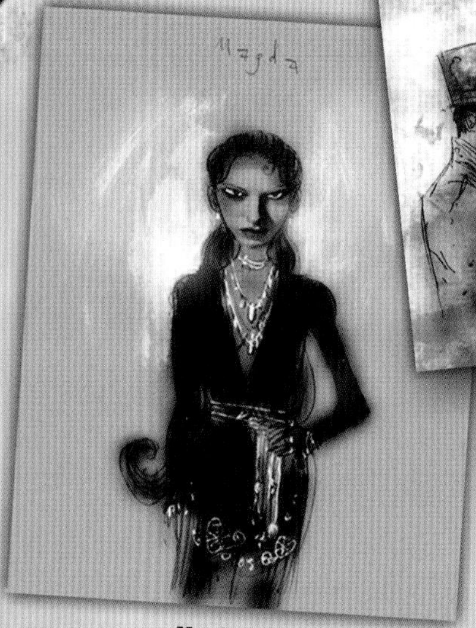
Magda

Magda Final

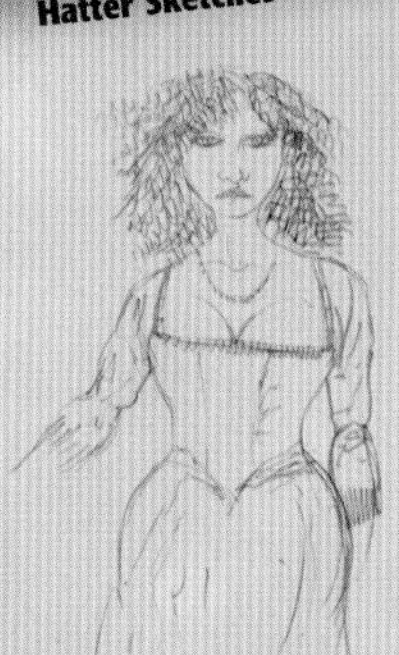

Magda Initial

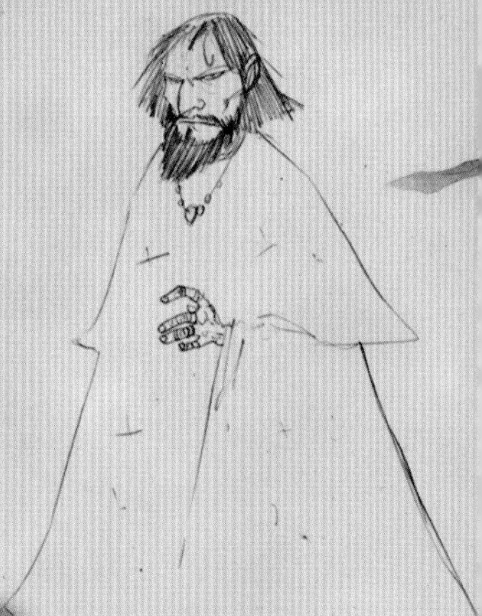

Le Mort

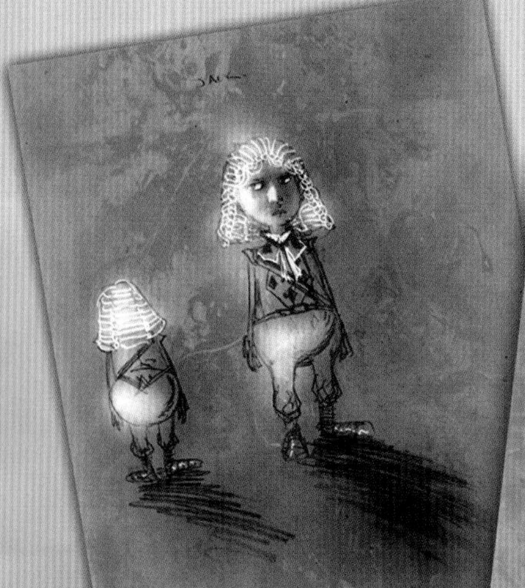

Jack of Diamonds

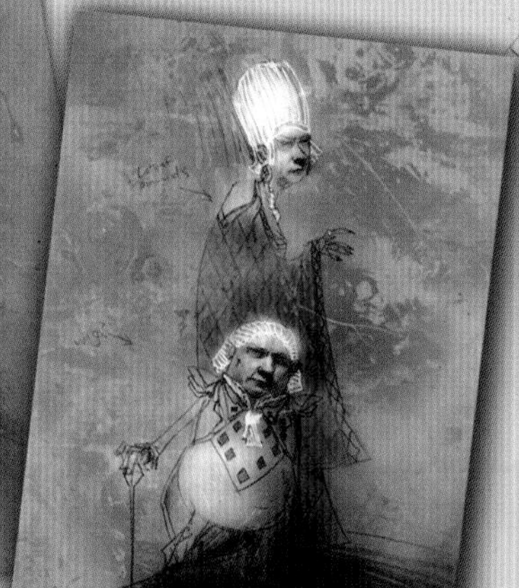

Lord and Lady Diamonds

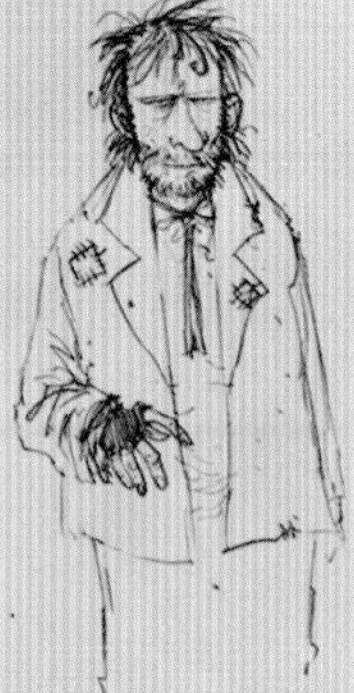

Bum Initial

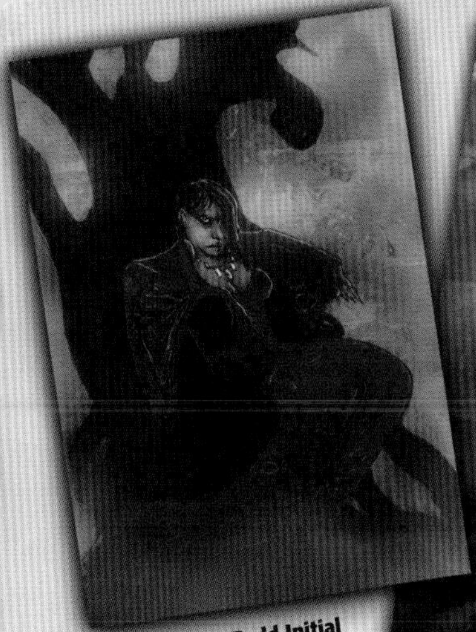

Redd Initial

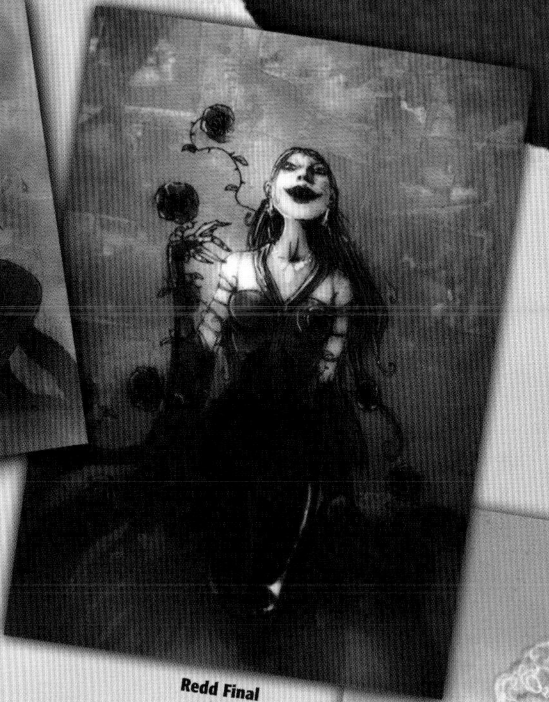

Redd Final

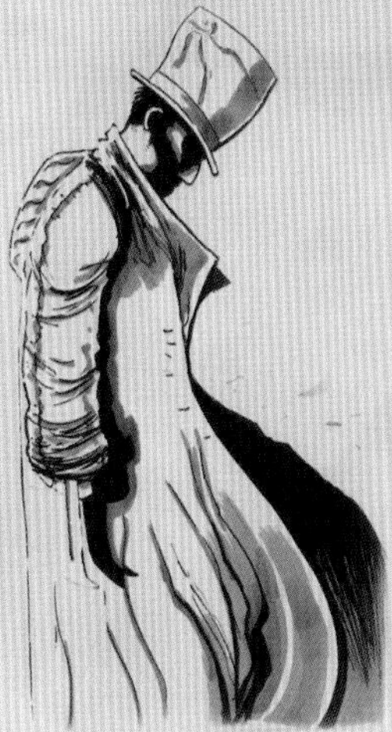

Hatter Concept

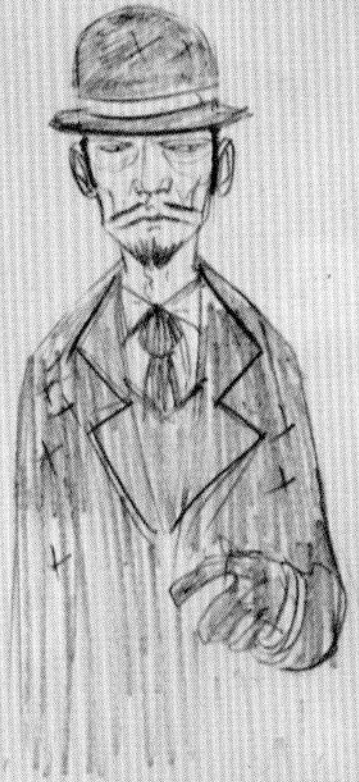

Marcel

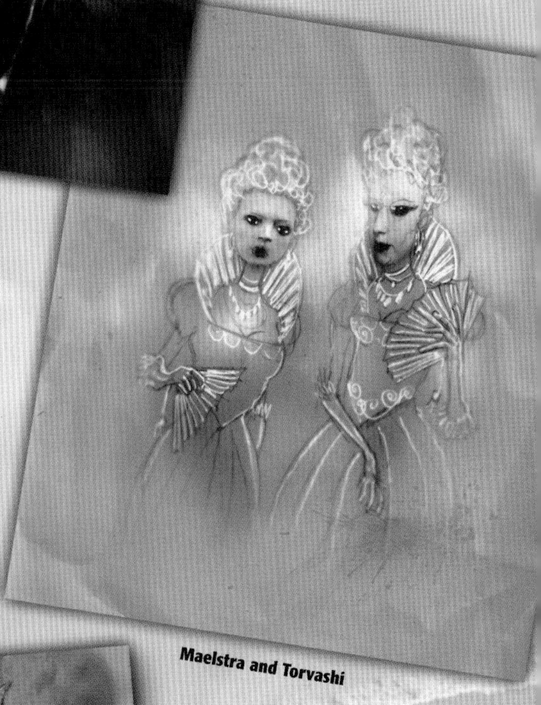

Maelstra and Torvashi

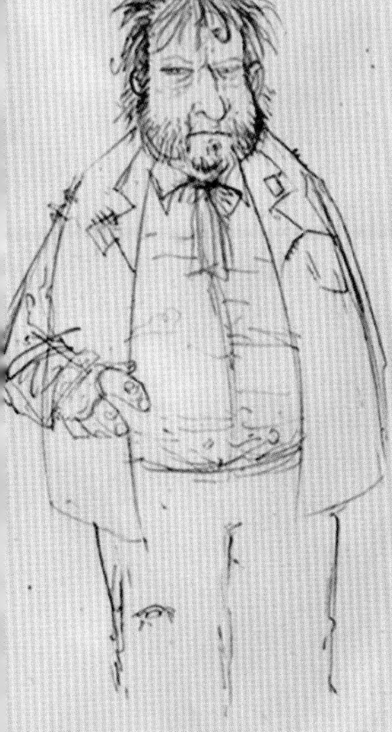

Bum Final

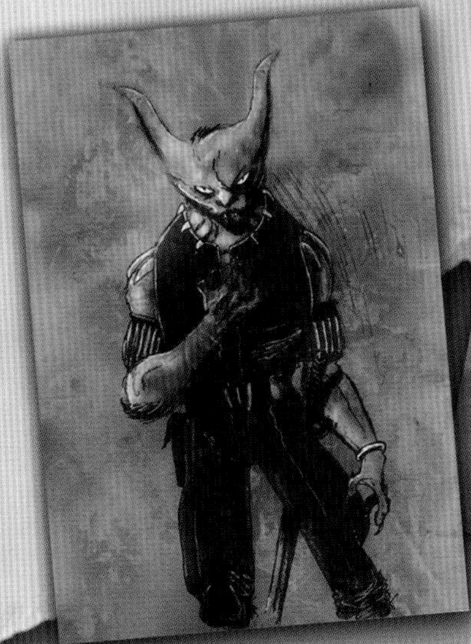

Cat Final

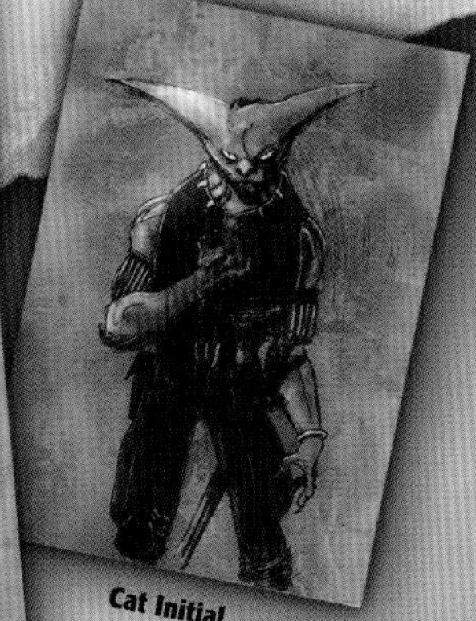

Cat Initial

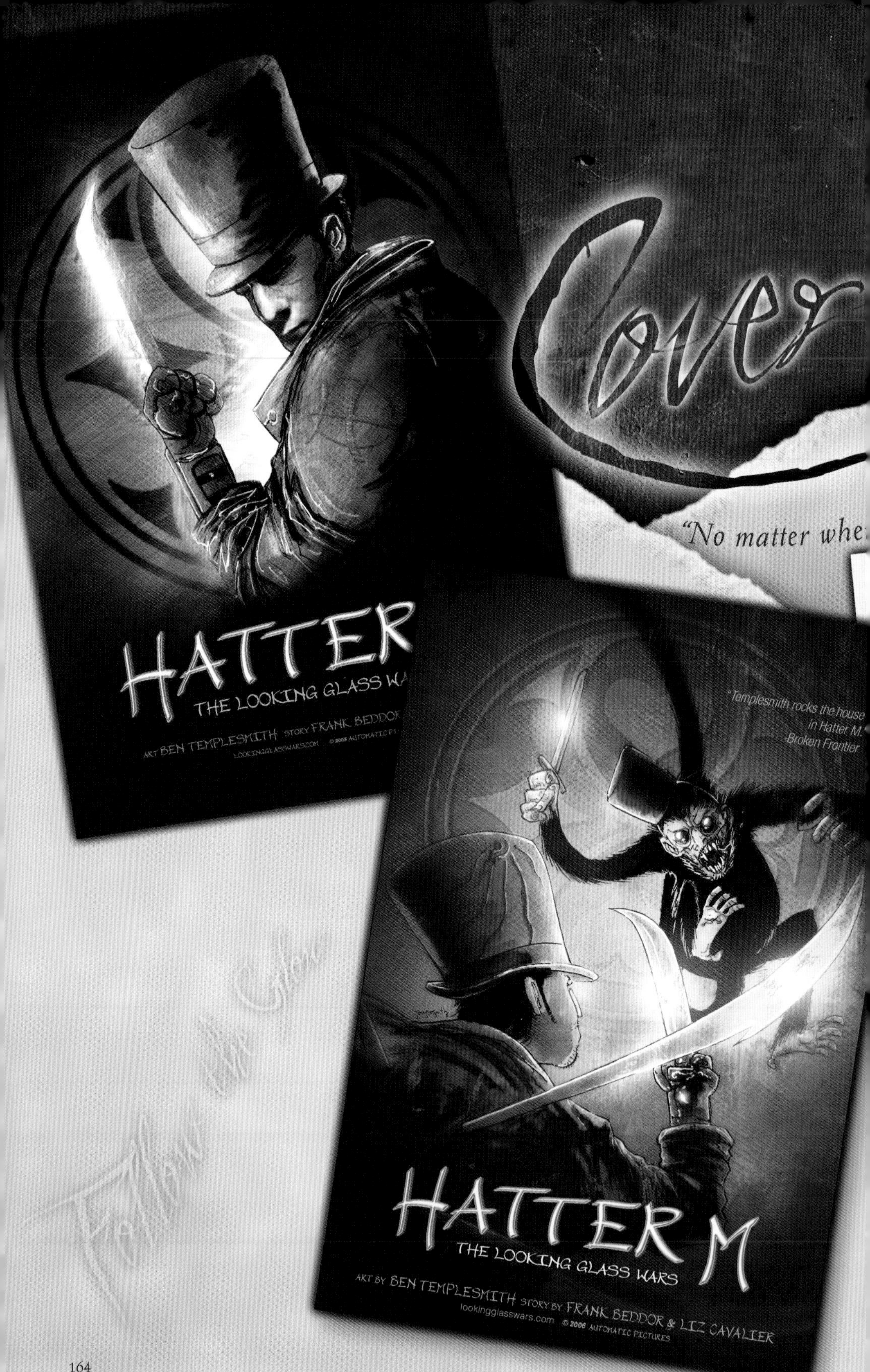
HATTER
THE LOOKING GLASS WAR
ART BEN TEMPLESMITH STORY FRANK BEDDOR
LOOKINGGLASSWARS.COM
Cover
"No matter whe
"Templesmith rocks the house in Hatter M."
-Broken Frontier
HATTER M
THE LOOKING GLASS WARS
ART BY BEN TEMPLESMITH STORY BY FRANK BEDDOR & LIZ CAVALIER
lookingglasswars.com © 2006 AUTOMATIC PICTURES
Follow the Glow

Gallery

"…ou go, there you are." —Buckaroo Banzai

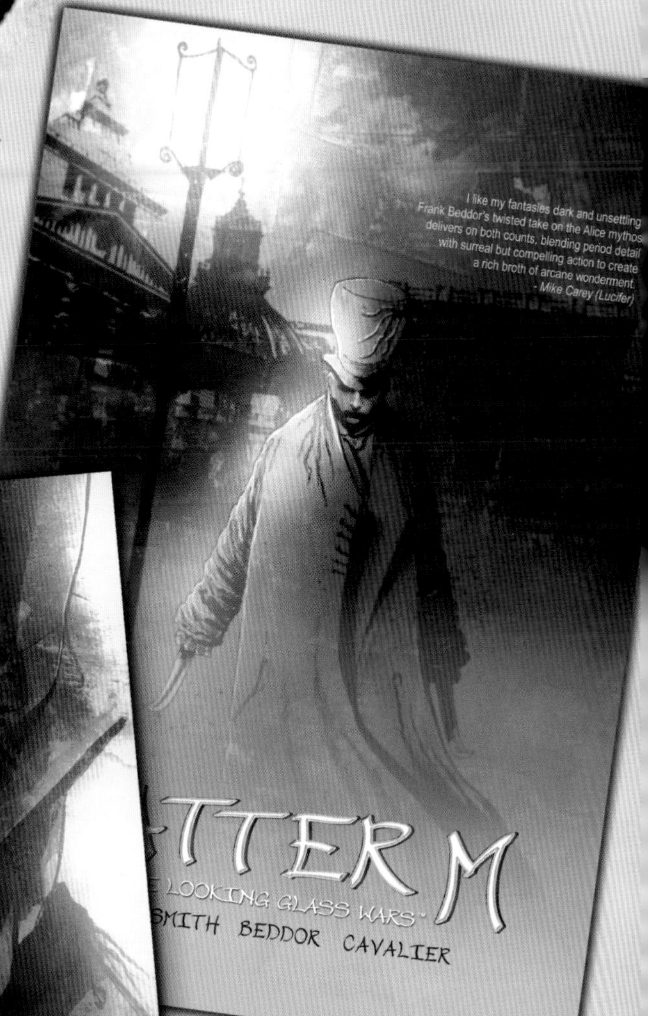
I like my fantasies dark and unsettling.
Frank Beddor's twisted take on the Alice mythos delivers on both counts, blending period detail with surreal but compelling action to create a rich broth of arcane wonderment.
- Mike Carey (Lucifer)
TTER M
LOOKING GLASS WARS™
SMITH BEDDOR CAVALIER

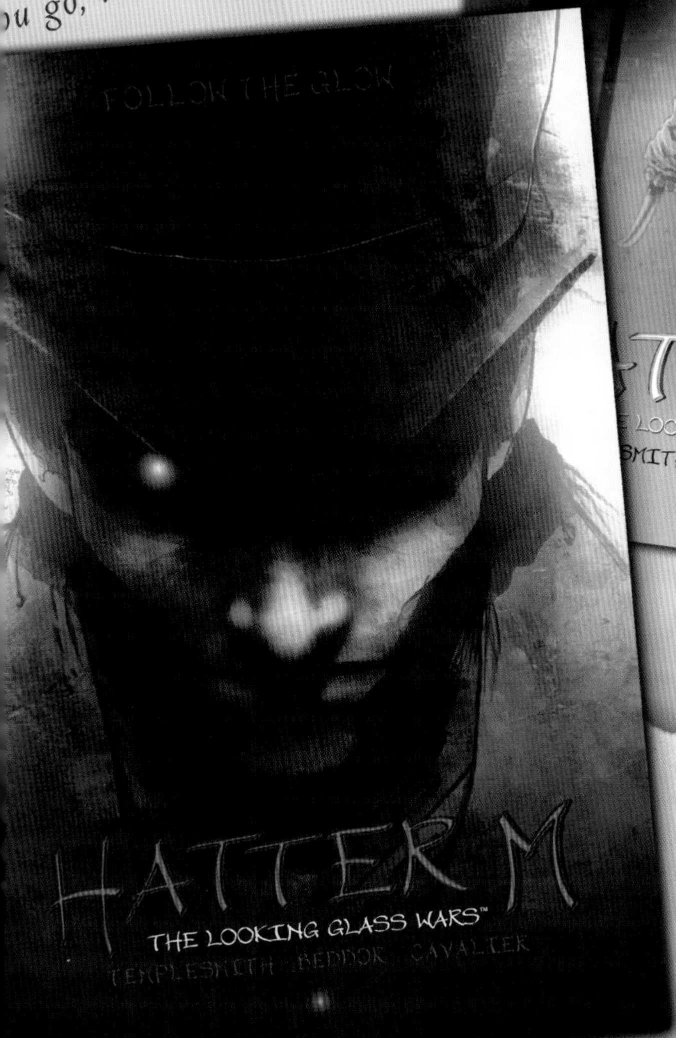
FOLLOW THE GLOW
HATTER M
THE LOOKING GLASS WARS™
TEMPLESMITH BEDDOR CAVALIER

"What am I doing here?" —Rimbaud writing home from Ethiopia

Navigate **Hatter's** terrestrial **maze** past obstacles, adversaries and allies on his **mad search** for the lost **princess** of **Wonderland**.

Good **luck** to those who **Follow** the **Glow**!

Turn the page for a special preview
of Book Three in the
Looking Glass Wars® trilogy.

P R⊙L⊙G U E

Oxford, England. 1875.

She raced up the front walk, using her imagination to unlock the door and turn the latch. Inside the house, nothing had changed. The umbrella stand and hat rack, the family pictures hanging in the hall, even the gouge in the baseboard marking where she'd thrown her ice skates one winter afternoon: everything was exactly as it had been when she'd lived there . . . so long ago, it seemed. "Please, what do you want?" the dean's voice reached her from the back of the house.

She sighted them in her imagination's eye: the dean and Mrs. Liddell, Edith and Lorina. Their clothes a good deal ripped, they huddled together on the drawing room sofa in fearful silence while Ripkins—once bodyguard for Boarderland's King Arch but now Redd Heart's assassin—stood ominously before them. Ripkins: the only Boarderlander who could flex his fingertips, pushing deadly sawteeth up out of the skin in the patterns of his fingerprints.

"Please," the dean said again.

Fingerprint blades flexed, Ripkins moved his hands fast in front of him, shredding air. Mrs. Liddell flinched. The assassin took a step towards the dean, the sisters each let out a sob and—

"Hello?" Alyss called, walking directly into the room. She had imagined herself into Alice Liddell's long skirt and blouse, her hair in a tight bun. "Excuse me, I didn't know there was company."

She tried to look startled—eyes wide, mouth half open, head tilted apologetically. Wanting to catch Ripkins off guard, she pretended to be meek, cowed, and let him grab her and push her towards the Liddells. As she thought her double would.

Where he'd touched her, there was blood.

Ripkins' hands again became a blur in front of him, churning air and moving in towards the dean's chest. Alyss had no choice but to expose her imaginative powers in front of the Liddells. With the slightest of movements, she conjured a deck of razor-cards and sent them cutting through the air.

Fiss! Fiss, fiss, fiss!

In a single swift motion, Ripkins spun clear and unholstered a crystal shooter, firing a retaliatory cannonade. Alyss gestured as if wiping condensation off a looking glass and the shrapnel-like bullets of wulfenite and barite crystal clattered to the floor.

The Liddells sat dumbfounded, their fear muted in the shock of seeing their adopted daughter engage in combat, producing otherworldly missiles out of the air—flat, blade-edged rectangles resembling playing cards, bursts of gleaming bullets. She conjured them as fast as she defended herself against them, what with the intruder making expert use of the strange guns and knives strapped to his belt, thighs, biceps, and forearms.

"Father!"

A fistful of mind-riders—ordinary-looking darts infused with poison that turned victims one upon the other in death-dealing rage—rocketed towards the family.

Alyss threw out her hand; the weapons changed trajectory, shooting towards her. She annihilated them in midair with a pinch of her fingers, becoming like gravity itself, pulling whatever Ripkins hurled at the Liddells towards her until—

The wall pushed out a score of daggers. Ripkins slammed against them and slumped to the floor.

Silence, except for the ticking of a grandfather clock.

"Oh!"

In the doorway stood Alyss's double, the woman she had, with utmost effort, imagined into being to take her place in this world: Alice Liddell who, with her gentleman friend, Reginald Hargreaves, stared at the dead assassin and Wonderland's queen. The dean, his wife and his third eldest daughter looked from Alyss Heart to Alice Liddell and back again.

"I—?" the dean started.

But that was all he managed before Alyss bolted from the room and out of the house, sprinting until she was well along St. Aldate's. Certain the Liddells weren't following her, she walked briskly in the direction of Carfax Tower, towards the portal that would return her to Wonderland: a puddle where no puddle should be, in the middle of sun-drenched pavement behind the Tower. But even from this distance she could see that something wasn't right. The portal was shrinking, its edges drying up fast. She started to run, her imagination's eye scanning the town.

"How can it be?" she breathed, because all of the portals were shrinking, the Tower puddle already half its former size when she leapt for it, closing her eyes and sucking in her breath, anticipating the swift watery descent through portal waters, the reverse pull of the Pool of Tears, the—

Knees jarring, she landed on pavement. The portal had evaporated.

Alyss Heart, the rightful Queen of Wonderland, was stranded on Earth.

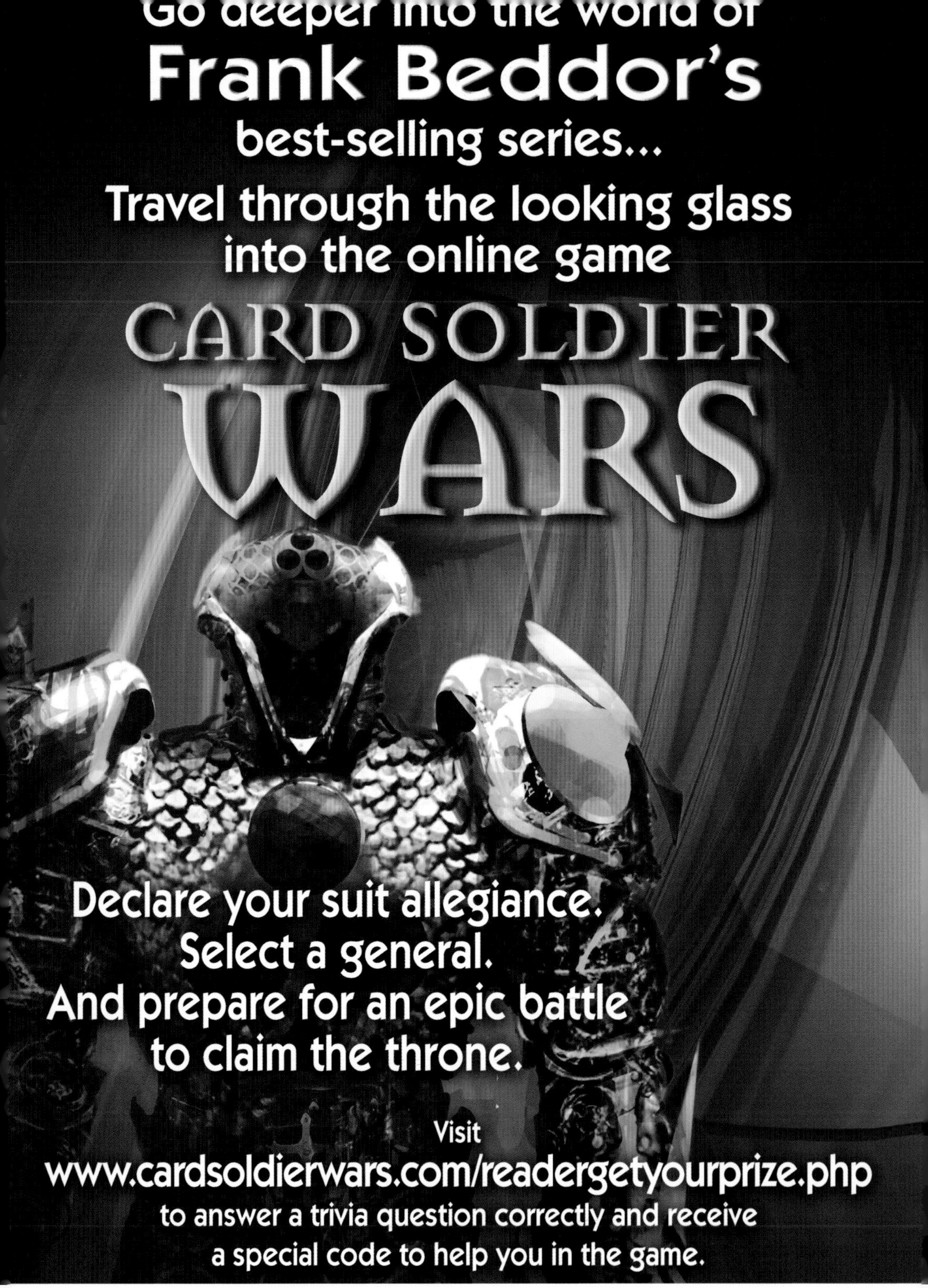
Go deeper into the world of
Frank Beddor's
best-selling series...
Travel through the looking glass
into the online game
CARD SOLDIER
WARS
Declare your suit allegiance.
Select a general.
And prepare for an epic battle
to claim the throne.
Visit
www.cardsoldierwars.com/readergetyourprize.php
to answer a trivia question correctly and receive
a special code to help you in the game.

Turn the page for a sneak peek of the game!

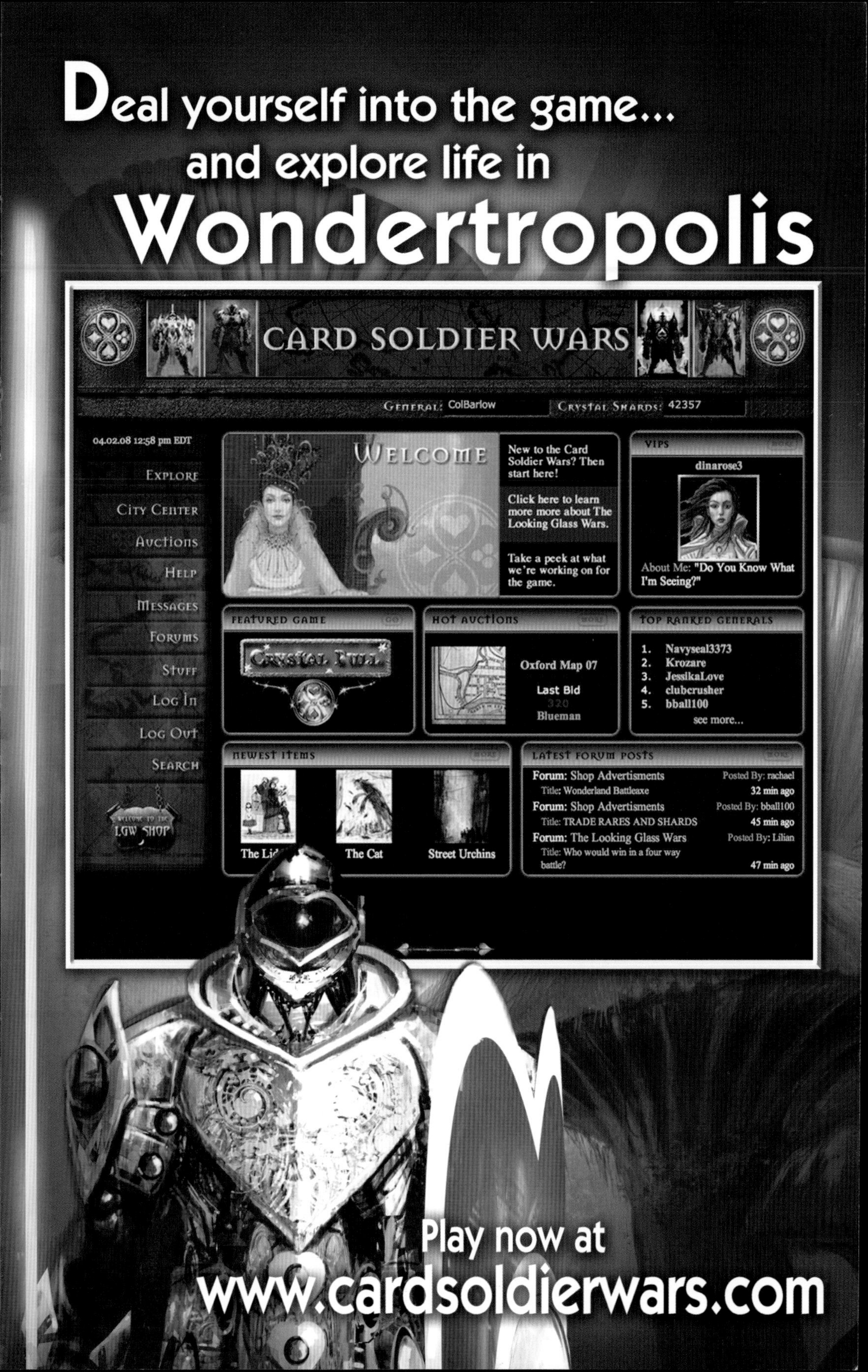
Deal yourself into the game...
and explore life in
Wondertropolis
CARD SOLDIER WARS
General: ColBarlow
Crystal Shards: 42357
04.02.08 12:58 pm EDT
Explore
City Center
Auctions
Help
Messages
Forums
Stuff
Log In
Log Out
Search
LGW Shop
Welcome
New to the Card Soldier Wars? Then start here!
Click here to learn more more about The Looking Glass Wars.
Take a peek at what we're working on for the game.
VIPs
dinarose3
About Me: "Do You Know What I'm Seeing?"
Featured Game
Crystal Pull
Hot Auctions
Oxford Map 07
Last Bid
320
Blueman
Top Ranked Generals
1. Navyseal3373
2. Krozare
3. JessikaLove
4. clubcrusher
5. bball100
see more...
Newest Items
The Cat
Street Urchins
Latest Forum Posts
Forum: Shop Advertisments
Posted By: rachael
Title: Wonderland Battleaxe
32 min ago
Forum: Shop Advertisments
Posted By: bball100
Title: TRADE RARES AND SHARDS
45 min ago
Forum: The Looking Glass Wars
Posted By: Lilian
Title: Who would win in a four way battle?
47 min ago
Play now at
www.cardsoldierwars.com

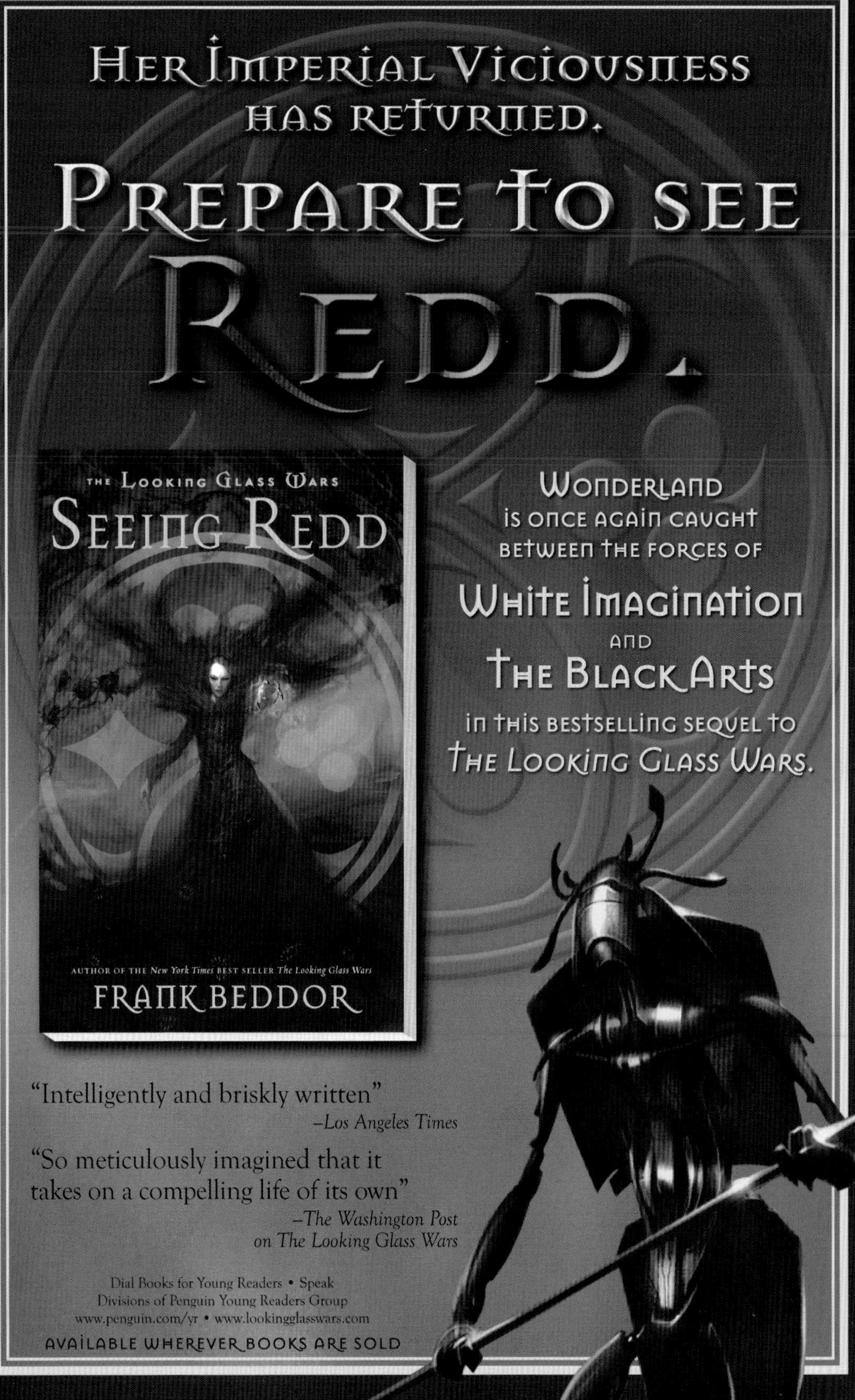

Her Imperial Viciousness has returned.
Prepare to see Redd.
The Looking Glass Wars
Seeing Redd
Author of the New York Times best seller The Looking Glass Wars
Frank Beddor
Wonderland is once again caught between the forces of
White Imagination
and
The Black Arts
in this bestselling sequel to The Looking Glass Wars.
"Intelligently and briskly written"
–Los Angeles Times
"So meticulously imagined that it takes on a compelling life of its own"
–The Washington Post on The Looking Glass Wars
Dial Books for Young Readers • Speak
Divisions of Penguin Young Readers Group
www.penguin.com/yr • www.lookingglasswars.com
Available wherever books are sold

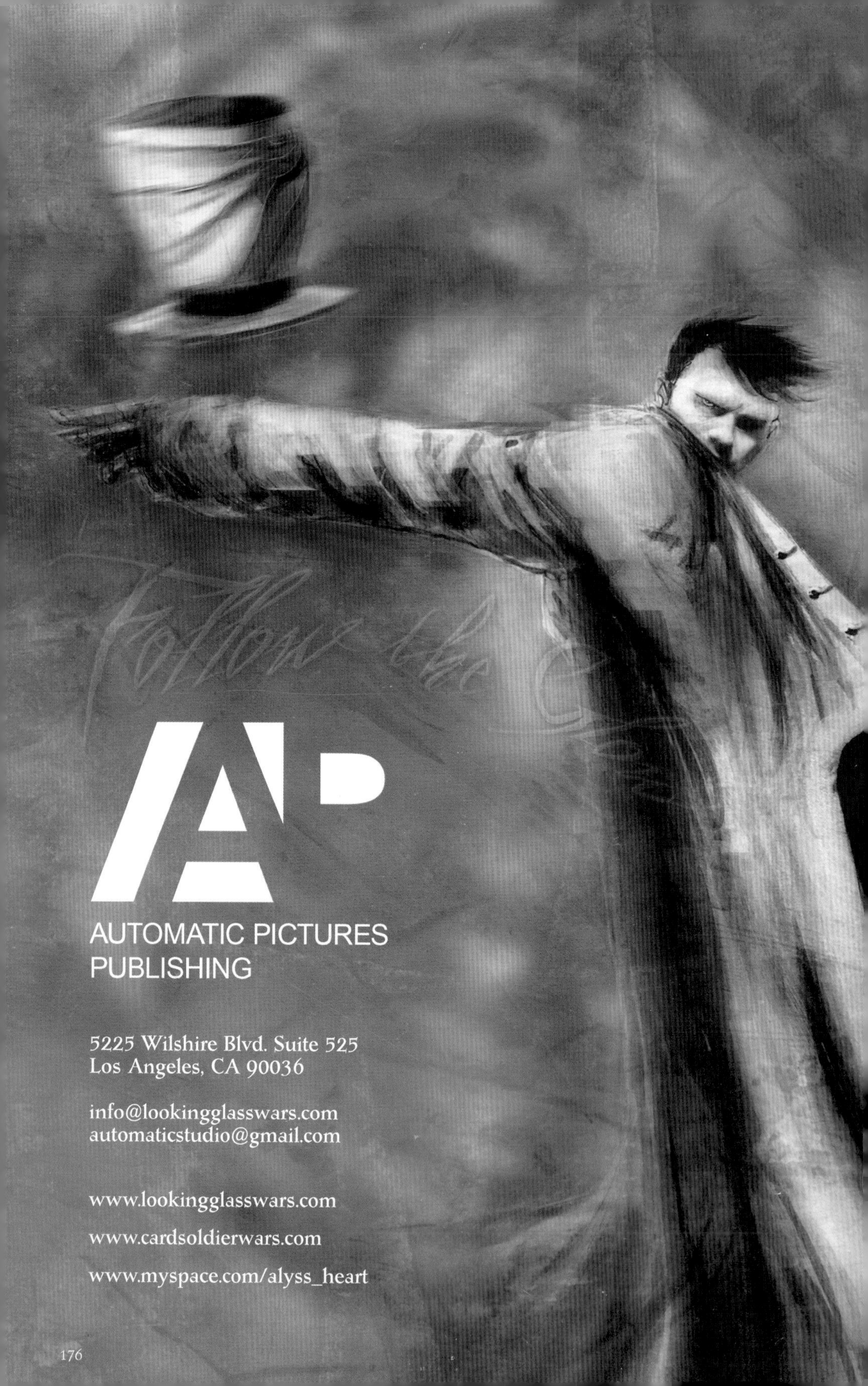
AUTOMATIC PICTURES
PUBLISHING
5225 Wilshire Blvd. Suite 525
Los Angeles, CA 90036
info@lookingglasswars.com
automaticstudio@gmail.com
www.lookingglasswars.com
www.cardsoldierwars.com
www.myspace.com/alyss_heart